J. A. d'Esterre

God-Shaped

Alan Smith is the Bishop of Shrewsbury. He was previously Diocesan Missioner in the Diocese of Lichfield and a chaplain at Lee Abbey in Devon.

J. W. Gibson

God-Shaped Mission

Theological and Practical Perspectives from the Rural Church

Alan Smith

CANTERBURY
PRESS
Norwich

© Alan Smith 2008

First published in 2008 by the Canterbury Press Norwich
(a publishing imprint of Hymns Ancient & Modern Limited,
a registered charity)
13–17 Long Lane, London EC1A 9PN

www.scm-canterburypress.co.uk

All rights reserved. No part of this publication may be reproduced,
stored in a retrieval system, or transmitted,
in any form or by any means, electronic, mechanical,
photocopying or otherwise, without the prior permission of
the publisher, Canterbury Press.

The Author has asserted his right under the Copyright,
Designs and Patents Act, 1988,
to be identified as the Author of this Work

British Library Cataloguing in Publication data

A catalogue record for this book is available
from the British Library

ISBN 978-1-85311-807-4

Typeset by Regent Typesetting, London
Printed and bound by
William Clowes Ltd, Beccles, Suffolk

This book is dedicated to the clergy and lay people of the Shrewsbury Episcopal Area of the Diocese of Lichfield, from whom I have learnt a great deal and whom I am privileged to serve as their bishop.

Contents

Acknowledgements   ix

Introduction   xi

**Part 1 Setting the Scene: The Changing Role of the
Church in the Countryside and Rural Spirituality**   1

  1 The Changing Face of the Countryside   3
  2 The Changing Face of the Rural Church   15
  3 Belief and Spirituality in Rural Britain   31
  4 God-Shaped Mission: Theological Reflections   50

**Part 2 Mission and Evangelism in Rural Areas:
Examples of Mission-Shaped Church in the Countryside**   63

  5 Innovation, Celebration and Service   65
  6 Children and Young People   74
  7 Worship   88
  8 Care and Social Action   99

**Part 3 The Wider Context: The Importance of the Family
and Apologetics**   109

  9 Passing on the Faith in the Family   111
 10 Apologetics: Is the Gospel True?   124

Part 4 Principles for Mission in the Rural Church: Listening, Learning, Acting, Refocusing

Part 4 Principles for Mission in the Rural Church:
Listening, Learning, Acting, Refocusing   141

    11 Listening   143
    12 Learning   157
    13 Acting   172
    14 Refocusing for Mission   189

Afterword   211
Bibliography   212
Index   223

Acknowledgements

I am grateful to many people for their help and support – most especially to my colleague, the Venerable John Hall, and my PA, Mrs Marion Stones, both of whom shouldered extra responsibilities during my study leave when I wrote this book. Several people helped me by discussing the material in this book, such as the Rt Revd Graham Cray, the Rt Revd Stephen Cottrell, the Revd Preb Dr Michael Sheard, the Revd Nick Read and the Revd George Lings. The Venerable Andy Piggott, Canon Robert Warren and the Revd David Runcorn read the manuscript and made a number of helpful suggestions. However, the greatest thanks goes to all the clergy and lay people who are faithfully serving Christ in the country-side, who are experimenting with 'fresh expressions of church' and whose stories are told in this book.

Introduction

The Church of England is changing. It is becoming mission-shaped – or so it is claimed. As well as *Mission-Shaped Church*,[1] we now have *Mission-Shaped and Rural*,[2] *Mission-Shaped Spirituality*[3] and *Mission-Shaped Parish*.[4] It has been joked that it will not be long before we will have mission-shaped funerals, mission-shaped Redundant Churches Uses' Committees and mission-shaped Glebe Committees. The roots of these changes can be found in a number of places, such as the 1944 report published by the Church of England entitled *Towards the Conversion of England*,[5] which was followed by initiatives such as Archbishop Donald Coggan's *Call to the North*, Mission England, and the 1988 Lambeth Conference which resulted in the Decade of Evangelism during the 1990s.

In recent years the social sciences have been enlisted in this theological enterprise. Numerous studies have been published describing how people come to faith (e.g. Finney's *Finding Faith Today,* and Booker and Ireland's *Evangelism – Which Way Now?*), how faith affects values and attitudes (e.g. Francis's and Kay's *Teenage Religion and Values Initiative*), and what makes churches grow (e.g. Gill's *A Vision for Growth*, Jackson's *Hope for the Church* and *The Road to Growth* and Warren's *The Healthy Churches' Handbook*).

The *Mission-Shaped Church* report, published in 2004, has struck a chord with many people. To date it has sold over 20,000 copies, making it the most widely read church report since *Faith in the City* was published in 1985. It has stimulated a widespread debate about the future of the Church and its mission. In the foreword to *Mission-Shaped Church*, the Archbishop of Canterbury writes:

We have begun to recognize that there are many ways in which the reality of 'church' can exist. 'Church' as a map of territorial divisions (parishes and dioceses) is one – one that still has a remarkable vigour in all sorts of contexts and which relates to a central conviction about the vocation of Anglicanism. But there are more and more others, of the kind this report describes and examines.[6]

The report focuses on two areas – starting new churches (church planting) and helping existing churches to evangelize in new ways ('fresh expressions of church'). It examines changing social trends in the UK, and in particular the way that for some people networks are becoming more significant than place. It poses a number of questions of how the Church should operate in a consumer and post-Christendom culture. It also examines church planting, and reviews progress since the publication of the report *Breaking New Ground* in 1994. In the middle section of *Mission-Shaped Church* – the longest chapter – it describes 12 categories of what it calls 'fresh expressions' or 'emerging church'. These are ways in which churches are attempting to re-engage with the communities in which they are set. Each of the categories is illustrated with examples from different parts of the country. The 12 categories listed are: alternative worship communities, base ecclesial communities, café church, cell church, churches arising out of community initiatives, multiple and midweek congregations, network-focused churches, school-based and school-linked congregations and churches, seeker church, traditional church plants, traditional forms of church inspiring new interest and youth congregations.

Mission-Shaped Church is an important and timely report, although its theology has provoked criticism in some quarters because, it is claimed, it is promoting an unbalanced view of the nature of mission.[7] It has also raised various practical questions. For example, is the Church genuinely becoming more mission-shaped or is there a degree of re-branding going on? Is there any evidence that fresh expressions of church are leading to new growth that is sustainable in the long term, or are we simply diluting our existing congregations, resigning ourselves to the individualized, consumerist approach to life endemic in contemporary society? Are fresh expressions of church sustainable without considerable resources being pumped in from elsewhere to subsidize them? Are the 'success stories' transferable or are they a result of a small group of unusually gifted and committed leaders who, if they had been leaders of more traditional churches, would have made them grow just as well? As one very gifted parish priest put it to me, 'Don't worry about fresh expressions. Give me an extra member of staff and within seven to ten years I'll give you a new all-age congregation, which is worshipping weekly and is financially self-supporting.'

One specific question has arisen that is the stimulus for this book. The vast majority of examples in the report are drawn from urban and sub-urban areas. Are fresh expressions of church essentially urban phenomena, which only really work where there is a sufficiently large population that can draw together groups of people from a shared subculture? This is a particularly pressing question for those of us who live and minister in rural communities, which are home to about one in six of the population of the UK.[8] As we shall see in the course of this book, in many rural areas the Church is extremely fragile, so much so that a number of informed commentators seriously question whether the church in the countryside has a long-term future.[9] It is noteworthy that when *Mission-Shaped Church* turns specifically to the rural Church[10] there are precisely three pages on the subject. It cites only two examples, one of which describes a church plant undertaken by a large London church (Holy Trinity Church, Brompton) based on Alpha groups run in a Hampshire manor house. This is hardly typical of most English villages, and begs the question as to what extent *Mission-Shaped Church* and fresh expressions thinking can be applied to the rural context. Archbishop Rowan Williams has argued that:

> It will not do in our mission to assume that evangelism and the routine of worship in the countryside can or should be a straight transfer from urban, let alone suburban patterns; some of the malaise and frustration that are felt in rural churches have to do with this, and the expectations brought from elsewhere, as well as expectations formed by a fantasy past.[11]

So can the principles of *Mission-Shaped Church* really be implemented in the countryside? Although the report pays lip-service to the fact that the rural context is different from the urban (it refers to the problems of multi-parish benefices and the upkeep of a large number of historic buildings in the countryside), it has little to offer in the way of positive proposals. For those of us committed to the future of the Church in the countryside it is frustrating that the report displays hardly any awareness of the issues that affect the rural Church. Fortunately, a number of people who are ministering in rural areas are now making up the deficit, in particular Gaze's book, *Mission-Shaped and Rural*,[12] which has begun the task of telling the story of what is happening in rural parishes in the 'mixed economy'[13] Church.

God-Shaped Mission builds on such work and is an attempt to contribute further to the mission-shaped debate, examining the subject from a rural perspective. Although in a few instances I draw upon examples from other places and other Christian denominations, I am writing primarily about England and the Church of England, since this is the context in which I am working as an Anglican bishop and also because it provides more than enough material for one book. Nevertheless, I hope it will be of interest to a wider audience, including Anglican churches in other provinces and those of other denominations.

Part 1, Setting the Scene (Chapters 1–4), describes some of the issues that are facing the countryside and the rural Church in the opening years of the third millennium. It concludes with theological reflection on the need for 'God-shaped mission' as the basis of a 'mission-shaped Church'.

Part 2, Mission and Evangelism in Rural Areas (Chapters 5–8), describes and discusses some of the new mission initiatives that are emerging in the countryside.

Part 3, The Wider Context (Chapters 9 and 10), broadens the discussion and places the mission-shaped agenda in a wider context. I suggest that if we are to be truly mission-shaped (whether urban or rural), there will need to be a refocusing on the family as the primary means by which faith is transmitted to the next generation. We will also need to reflect on how we can engage in public debate and find arenas in which to articulate more imaginatively the claims of the gospel.

Part 4, Principles for Mission in the Rural Church (Chapters 11–14), begins by suggesting that we need to nurture a culture of listening if the Church is going to rediscover its sense of vocation in the world. It then moves on to explore what it is to be a Church of disciples, and in Chapter 13 we look at four areas where the Church needs to act. Finally, I argue that, having captured a fresh sense of vision, we need to re-think the role of leadership and synods.

The rural Church is facing huge challenges, yet there are many exciting initiatives taking place in the countryside. This book has been written to help those involved in mission and ministry in the countryside to reflect critically on the rural context and to respond with confidence and creativity. The opportunities open to us are greater than we have had for many decades, if we are ready to grasp them.

Notes

1 Church of England's Mission and Public Affairs Council, 2004.
2 Gaze, 2006.
3 Hope, 2006.
4 Bayes and Sledge, 2006.
5 Church of England National Assembly, 1945.
6 Church of England's Mission and Public Affairs Council, 2004, p. vii.
7 Hull, 2006.
8 At the time of the 2001 census there were more than 9.5 million people living in rural England. Of these, over 600,000 lived in the areas that are officially categorized as 'sparsely populated' (Commission for Rural Communities, 2006a, p. 20).
9 For example, Francis, 1996, p. 239; or the article in *The Times*, 7 June 1985. 'The Church of England faces extinction in the countryside in the next twenty years . . . it is a picture of unmitigated hopelessness' (quoted in Russell, 1993, p. 1).
10 Church of England's Mission and Public Affairs Council, 2004, pp. 118–20.
11 Williams, 2004, p. 255.
12 Gaze, 2006.
13 This is a phrase used by Archbishop Rowan Williams in his presidential address to the General Synod of the Church of England, July 2003.

Part 1

Setting the Scene

The Changing Role of the Church in the
Countryside and Rural Spirituality

I

The Changing Face of the Countryside

Deep within the English psyche lurks an idealized notion of the village: typically, a small community of thatched cottages built around the pond and the green where cricket is played on Saturday afternoons. It has a church, a shop, a pub, a school, and a village hall. It is a community where the parson lives in a large, rambling vicarage and the local bobby cycles round the village dispensing goodwill and providing a sense of security. Nearby is the 'big house', complete with an estate inhabited by the local landed gentry. Virtually everyone works on the land or in associated roles, such as the blacksmith or the miller. It is a community where everyone knows and supports one another. We know this exists because we have seen pictures of it on the front of biscuit tins and have watched it on the television as Miss Marple solved murder mysteries.

But, of course, most of this is a fantasy, far removed from the complex reality of contemporary rural life.[1] Such idealized villages hardly ever existed. Indeed, many rural communities were not villages at all but scattered farms and cottages, where people lived miles from their nearest neighbour; others dwelt in hamlets that were nothing more than a group of houses or smallholdings with no public buildings or services. In the larger communities, people may have known everyone but they still belonged to networks within their community. Some people, for example, were 'church', while others were 'chapel'; some belonged to the Mothers' Union, others were pillars of the Women's Institute, busily making jam and singing 'Jerusalem'; and the regulars at the pub were hardly ever regulars at the chapel.

Networks of relationships existed between villages. The landed gentry, for example, would intermarry and often share a social life together. The Young Farmers would draw people from a wide area for social events based on their common involvement with the land. On the other hand, anyone who has ever lived in a village will also know that relationships are not necessarily good. There can be bitter and long-held divisions between families and neighbours, sometimes going back generations, which preclude mutual help and support.

The English rural idyll emerged with the rise of Romanticism. We see it in the literature of Wordsworth, Coleridge, Keats and Blake, the art of Constable and Turner, followed by the Pre-Raphaelite Brotherhood and William Morris. In parallel with the shift of population from the countryside to the town, there emerged a nostalgia among city dwellers for a lost Eden, complete with spinsters cycling to eight o'clock Holy Communion, cricket on the green, and warm beer.

Rural life was never like this. It was usually hard and occasionally brutal. Wages could be abysmally low. Housing was often poor and unhygienic. Many roads were impassable in winter, especially in the north of England. Transport was difficult and often dangerous. Education, except for the wealthy, was virtually unknown or, at best, rudimentary. The doctor lived in the nearest town and the hospital might be miles away. Villages were the last communities to be connected to mains water, electricity, gas, sewerage and to the telephone network.

And what of today? In recent years some aspects of rural life have changed dramatically. Better transport has meant that for many people the countryside is now easily accessible and has become a place for leisure. For others it is a place of retreat, providing a cottage for weekends away from the stress of city life. This is one view of life in the country. But in parallel with it are pockets of poverty and areas with serious social problems. Recent research has revealed the extraordinary contrasts and differences that exist in the countryside, leading to the conclusion that

> there is not a homogeneous agenda – the 'rural' blanket can conceal many important differences beneath its folds, between town and village, village and hamlet, and also between sparse and less sparse areas.[2]

To illustrate the changes that are going on in the countryside today, we are going to visit three rural families.[3]

'The Farmer'

Jim and Jane Manners are in their thirties and are the fifth generation to farm 200 acres of land on the edge of a small village.[4] Life is very different from the time when Jim's great, great grandfather first began farming in the 1840s. At that time the population of the parish was roughly twice what it is today.[5] Most of the men in those days worked on the land and the farm used to employ six full-time labourers as well as casual workers at harvest time. Nowadays Jim has to do all the work himself, although his son, Alec, lends him a hand at busy times.[6] However, Alec is quite adamant that he does not want to take on the farm. He has seen how difficult it has been for his parents to make ends meet and, like many farming families, they know of young farmers who have become so stressed that they have committed suicide.[7] Although Alec enjoys living on the farm, as a 16-year-old he wants to spend time with his friends, most of whom live in the town. There is little public transport, so Alec often feels stranded and, like any teenager, hates having to rely on his parents to give him lifts.[8]

Jim knows that if he is going to stay in farming he will have to continue to adapt; he knows from the *Farmers Weekly* that 2,125 dairy farmers have left the industry in England over the past four years.[9] Looking to the future, he is aware that rural businesses (including farming) will be part of the changes affecting all industry in the global economy. Mergers will produce large corporations, alongside which small specialist businesses will respond to niche markets.[10] Jim listened to a item on the Radio 4 programme *Farming Today* about the Countryside Agency report which argued that 'Agriculture will increasingly [have to] become a "new economy" industry – based on knowledge and networks . . . it will rely on scientific research and technology developments to provide more economically and environmentally sustainable production systems.'[11] Several farmers nearby (whom Jim and Jane have known for many years) have sold up recently, and their farms have been bought by a company that now owns 3,000 acres of land. Like many farmers from previous generations who learnt to diversify, one of Jim's neighbours has been growing soft fruit and another is producing dried flowers to make pot pourri for a major high street chain of shops.[12] Both of these neighbours rely on seasonal workers from Eastern Europe who are housed in four large caravans on one of the farms.

Jim, like other farmers, is concerned about the threat of global warming, and the pressure for a 'greener' economy is having its effect on the landscape and rural economy. He has chatted with a neighbouring farmer who has been considering the possibility of having a wind farm on his land,[13] and Jim has been looking into the financial implications of growing energy crops.[14] He has also planted trees on some of the poorer land on the edge of the farm, and is proud that there are more trees on his land than there were 40 years ago.[15]

5

Jim and Jane are acutely aware of the way that the local community is changing and that the population of rural England is growing.[16] House prices are rising, and many farmers are converting disused farm buildings into homes and selling them, usually to newcomers. Jim is one of a number of farmers who has redeveloped an old stable block into small business units, which he rents out to bring in additional income.

Whereas in the past the countryside was predominantly a place of agriculture, it is increasingly becoming a place of leisure. The Countryside and Rights of Way Act 2000 gave public access to a further three-quarters of a million hectares of land which had been inaccessible previously.[17] Jim does not mind people using the footpaths on his land, but he does complain about the urban dwellers who do not understand the countryside. He finds that some of them are a nuisance, leaving their litter and neglecting to close gates.

'The Incomer'

Along with several other newcomers in the village, George Swan and Julie Wilding, along with their young son, Henry, moved in just three years ago to escape the grind of working in London.[18] Having been burgled six times in a decade, they wanted to live in an area where there was less crime.[19] However, they have been surprised that so many people in the village are still worried about burglary and vandalism, since it seems to be so much less of a problem than when they were in London.[20] They also wanted to live in an area where people were healthier[21] and where there was a stronger sense of community, and they hoped that the countryside might provide this.[22]

George and Julie had decided to sell their house in the suburbs six years previously and had spent two years looking for suitable properties in various parts of the country. They soon discovered that there were significant variations in house prices in different regions and realized that they could not find the sort of property they wanted in the South East, the east of England, nor in the east Midlands.[23] They settled on Staffordshire, and out of the proceeds of their sale they were able to buy an old four-bedroom house with 6 acres of land on which they keep some sheep and Julie's horses.[24] As well as offering horseriding lessons, Julie runs a small business from home via the internet, selling riding equipment and clothing. She is fortunate that – like many other rural areas – wireless broadband is available in the village.[25] However, Julie was not prepared for the higher levels of power cuts, and interruptions to water supplies and the telephone system that are experienced in rural locations.[26] Her business is typical of what is happening in the countryside, in that during the past decade the number of businesses in rural areas has been growing (but at a slower rate than businesses in urban areas).[27] Rural areas also exhibit higher levels of part-time and home working, and this is increasing too.[28]

George is now retired and spends his time fishing, which is the most popular outdoor leisure activity in the UK,[29] and taking an active part in village life. He has been elected on to the parish council, the village hall committee, and the board of school governors. He thinks of himself as using his expertise from the city to help the villagers run things on a more professional footing. Because of his background he is articulate and has strong opinions, which does not always go down well with some of the people who have lived in the village for generations and think he is trying to take over. Relationships with Jim and Jane Manners are also difficult since George has suggested that the road into the village would be much prettier if they tidied up the farmyard and removed some of the farm machinery that sits on the grass verge.

Although George and Julie are involved in the village, they do not know either of their immediate neighbours, who use their homes as little more than dormitories. These neighbours commute 60 miles to the nearest city and, unlike George and Julie, do not wish to be involved in the life of the community.[30]

'The Villager'

Brian and Muriel Wallace are in their late fifties. Brian was born in the village and he met Muriel at a dance in the nearby town when they were teenagers. They have three children, aged between 26 and 18, and Brian runs the local shop and post office. Although the decline in the number of post offices has been slower in rural areas than in urban areas,[31] it has still affected many villages (only 30% of villages have a post office, the same proportion as have a shop). Having heard the government announcement that a further 2,500 post offices are going to be closed,[32] mainly in rural areas, Brian is deeply worried. Five years ago the village pub, which was run by his brother-in-law, went out of business[33] and Brian knows that the loss of the post office will probably mean that his shop will no longer be viable.[34] He thinks this is just one more example of how life can be more difficult in rural areas than in the town. Research shows that sparsely populated rural areas have proportionately fewer banks, cash-points, job centres, supermarkets and dentists than urban areas, and the proportion of surcharge-free cashpoints is lower in villages and hamlets than in urban areas.[35]

When Brian first bought the business, many more of the villagers would use the shop. Nowadays most people go to the local town for their weekly shop at the supermarket. The business has also suffered as more and more properties have been bought as holiday cottages, with the result that they are unoccupied for two-thirds of the year. A succession of people may use a property for a holiday, but they will never be part of the community. Worse still from Brian's point of view, they may well have shopped at a supermarket on the way, so that they do not even contribute to the local economy by helping to keep open the shop and post office.

Muriel works two days a week as a classroom assistant in the small primary school in the village. There are supposed to be two teachers in the school, but last year there was only one full-time member of staff, since recruitment of teachers is so much more difficult in rural areas.[36] Not surprisingly, there is a worry that the school may have to close in the next few years. The number of children at present means that it is just viable, but it will only take one or two families to move away and the situation could change quickly.[37] Muriel is proud that pupils from rural areas achieve higher educational results than their urban counterparts, both at primary level and also when the children move on to secondary school (the results from Key Stage Four show that they also have a higher level of value-added scores). There are a number of reasons for this, including fewer pupils in each class, and the phenomenon of well-to-do parents with high educational aspirations who live on the urban fringe but choose to transport their children to village schools. However, Muriel is also aware that there are several disadvantages of attending a school in a rural area, not least the fact that it will normally involve a much longer journey to school, there is often a narrower range of subjects on offer (at least at secondary level), and there are usually fewer specialist teaching staff and fewer after-school activities.[38]

Most weeks Muriel has to take her mother-in-law to the doctor's sur-gery or to the hospital in the town which is 16 miles away, a much greater distance than most urban dwellers have to travel for health care.[39] They have to use the car since there is no public transport.[40] Many of the villagers are worried that the hospital may have to close since there are regular stories in the newspaper that it is in financial deficit[41] and that there is a growing shortage of health workers in the countryside.[42] If the

8

hospital were to close, the next nearest one is over 40 miles away. Looking to the future, the increase in longevity in the UK will probably affect rural areas more than urban ones since they contain a higher proportion of older people and because the access to health provision is not as good.

Muriel is about to become a grandmother. Her daughter, Sue, was the first member of the family to go to university.[43] After Sue graduated she had hoped to return to the village, but she was not able to afford a house there and so has settled in a town about 25 miles away.[44] The family resents the fact that more and more houses in the village are being bought by affluent outsiders, while their children – who were brought up in the village – cannot possibly afford the house prices.[45] Affordable housing is one of the issues that the parish council is most concerned about, since the situation seems to be getting worse. The amount of homes being built cannot possibly solve the problem in the foreseeable future,[46] which is more acute in rural areas where there are higher levels of owner occupation and lower levels of social housing than in urban areas.[47]

Conclusion

These stories illustrate the way in which the countryside has been changing and continues to change, often rapidly. The rural idyll we painted at the beginning of this chapter is a distant memory – if, in fact, it ever did exist. For many people rural areas offer an enviable quality of life, with the result that increasing numbers now wish to live in the countryside. However, as we have seen, there is little uniformity in this picture: the countryside contains serious pockets of poverty and social deprivation, and life presents particular difficulties for the young, the ill and the housebound. With an increase in population and the number of home workers, and a decline in the number of places where people meet – such as pubs, shops and post offices – the context in which the rural Church finds itself is evolving. We need to be alert to the challenges, but also the opportunities that this presents. The Church, as in past generations, could occupy a strategically important place in supporting community life, and in so doing have a unique opportunity to engage with faith and spiritual issues.

Notes

1 One of the difficulties in writing about rural areas is the lack of agreed definitions about what constitutes a rural area. See, for example, Cloke and Edwards, 1986; Russell, 1993; Davies *et al.*, 1991, pp. 57–64; Burton, 2004; http://www.arcresources.org.uk/module1/unit1.1/text1b.01.pdf. The government has recently adopted a standardized approach to defining rurality based on settlement form, sparcity or remoteness and function (Countryside Agency, 2003b, annexes pp. 6–9; Commission for Rural Communities, 2006b). However, it is a complex method of defining rurality and is not readily understood by many on the ground.

2 Commission for Rural Communities, 2006b, p. 40.

3 These descriptions are not based on three specific families, but are typical of such families living in the countryside today. I am using them to expound many of the trends that are going on in rural areas which are set out in government reports, such as the Countryside Agency, 2003a and 2003b, and the Commission for Rural Communities, 2006a and 2006b.

4 Compared with those living in urban areas, a higher proportion of people in the countryside have lived there for longer periods, especially in the less sparsely populated areas (Commission for Rural Communities, 2006a, p. 26, Figure 11).

5 For much of the last 150 years the rural population in England has been declining (Saville, 1957; Council of Europe, 1980; Albrecht, 1993; Cawley, 1994).

6 The number of people working in agriculture continues to diminish, with the fastest decline being in full-time salaried staff. Farmers are tending to retain family members but employ fewer paid staff: 'Farmers and their families account for 62% of those working in agriculture, managers account for 4%, salaried employees 20% and casual workers the remaining 14%' (Commission for Rural Communities, 2006a, p. 112).

7 The levels of stress and suicide in the farming community are worryingly high and continue to give cause for concern (Commission for Rural Communities, 2006a, p. 112). There is also a much higher rate of male suicides among the 16- to 24-year-olds in the countryside, although a report published by the Department of Health on 13 April 2006 recorded a fall in the number of young male suicides for the first time in many years.

8 There has been a small increase in the availability of public transport in recent years in country areas, but buses and other forms of public transport still support only a small proportion of travel in rural areas. Research shows that maintaining public transport in rural areas is vital. In urban areas lack of transport can exacerbate social exclusion, but in rural areas lack of transport can be the cause of it. It often constitutes a barrier to participating in everyday activities such as employment, education, health services, shopping and leisure, as well as meeting up with family and friends. It is a particular problem for teenagers, who may have no other way of travelling apart from getting lifts from their parents. Poor transport means that people in rural areas are likely to have longer periods of unemployment, fewer choices to buy healthy food, and greater difficulty in accessing medical and dental services than urban dwellers (Commission for Rural Communities, 2006a, pp. 54–8). The countryside may be a pleasant place for the wealthy, but it is a much tougher place for the poor and those without transport.

9 These figures were obtained in response to a parliamentary question from the Shadow Agriculture Minister and reported in *Farmers Weekly* on 11 May 2007.

10 Countryside Agency, 2003a, p. 7.

11 Countryside Agency, 2003a, p. 18. Many of the changes are caused, at least in part, by relatively low agricultural prices and changes in the Common Agricultural Policy.

12 Farmers are used to the idea of diversification and having secondary occupations: 'A survey of thirty-four farmers listed in Corsley, Wiltshire, in 1905–6, including five who held over 100 acres of land, showed that twelve had taken on secondary work – running a baker, hauling coal, or a carrier's business' (Wilson, 2005, p. 42).

13 However, wind farms are only making a relatively small contribution to the country's energy needs (Commission for Rural Communities, 2006a, p. 125).

14 At the moment only relatively small areas of energy crops are under cultivation but it is predicted that this will rise tenfold between 2005 and 2009.

15 The amount of woodland has been increasing steadily since the 1970s, and nowadays more broadleaf trees are being planted than conifers. Approximately 8.5% of the country is covered in woodland, with a higher density in the southeast and the north of England (Commission for Rural Communities, 2006a, p. 120).

16 Boyle and Halfacree, 1998, and Buller and Hoggart, 1994. In the years 2003–4 alone, over 105,000 people moved into the most rural areas. The Countryside Agency has forecast that the population in rural areas will increase by four million people over a 20-year period (Countryside Agency, 2003a, p. 16). Population projections for the UK as a whole suggest that the greatest growth in population will be in rural areas. In 2006 it was predicted that by 2028 the population in the countryside is likely to rise on average by 20% (Commission for Rural Communities, 2006a, p. 25).

17 Most of this is in the north of England, which has far larger areas of land with open access than the Midlands and the South.

18 As Newby (1990) put it, 'rural Britain, which was once agricultural Britain, has now become middle-class Britain'.

19 Reported crime and the fear of crime is noticeably lower in rural areas, and between 2001 and 2006 there appears to have been a downward trend in the levels of crime in the smallest settlements. Furthermore, during the same period violent crime declined more sharply in rural areas than in towns and urban areas (Commission for Rural Communities, 2006a, pp. 62–3).

20 Despite the relatively low levels of crime in the countryside there is evidence that many people in rural areas are still worried about it (Commission for Rural Communities, 2006a, pp. 62–3).

21 There is higher life expectancy and lower rates of infant mortality in rural as compared with urban areas, which probably reflects the socioeconomic profile of an increasing large group of rural dwellers (Commission for Rural Communities, 2006a, pp. 42–3).

22 There is considerable evidence that levels of social capital are higher in rural areas than in urban areas (Commission for Rural Communities, 2006a, p. 59). For example, there is more volunteering, both informally and formally, most notably in the smallest settlements and in sparsely populated areas. Those involved in volun-

teering, however, are more likely to be aged between 55 and 64 and be in the AB socioeconomic groups. There is also a greater incidence of involvement in social and political activities in rural areas. Surveys have shown that more rural people experience their communities as being supportive. However, levels of social capital in the countryside are declining (Commission for Rural Communities, 2006a, p. 59). An important factor in maintaining social capital is the presence of the church, which has a higher profile in the life of rural communities (Commission for Rural Communities, 2006a, p. 59).

23 Rural repopulation is occurring most rapidly in the South West, the east of England, the South East and the east Midlands (Commission for Rural Communities, 2006a, p. 23).

24 It is estimated that there are between 600,000 and 1,000,000 horses, with 2.4 million people horseriding (Commission for Rural Communities, 2006a, p. 124).

25 There is almost universal provision of broadband in rural areas through normal telephone lines, but the availability of cable and wireless broadband is much lower than in urban areas. For rural settlements in the less sparsely populated areas, internet usage via broadband is at levels similar to, or in excess of, urban areas. In the sparsely populated areas, usage remains lower (Commission for Rural Communities, 2006a, p. 45).

26 Commission for Rural Communities, 2006a, p. 47.

27 However, between 2005 and 2006 there has been a decline in the number of businesses in the *most* rural areas and under-performing rural districts are not catching up with the rest of rural England (Commission for Rural Communities, 2006a, p. 100). Patterns of employment in rural and urban areas also differ. Rural areas have a lower proportion of the overall population that is of working age, higher rates of employment and self-employment, lower rates of unemployment, and lower levels of economic activity (Commission for Rural Communities, 2006a, p. 80).

28 It is estimated that 2.2 million people telework (Commission for Rural Communities, 2006a, pp. 83–5).

29 Angling is thought to be the most popular outdoor activity in the UK, with an estimated two and a half million people freshwater fishing. The economic balance in rural areas is changing such that it is possible that between them angling and horseriding may now contribute more to the British economy than farming (Commission for Rural Communities, 2006a, p. 124).

30 The Rural Affairs Committee has commented, 'The biggest social and cultural differences are now between those who live and work in the countryside and those who live there but work in towns and cities' (Rural Affairs Committee, 2005, p. 5).

31 Commission for Rural Communities, 2006a, p. 38. The number of post offices has declined from 18,400 in 1999 to 14,300 in 2007. In September 2006 Age Concern launched an initiative to try to halt closures of rural post offices. See http://ageconcern.co.uk/AgeConcern/Documents/Rural_post_offices_report.pdf.

32 The announcement was made in May 2007.

33 Two out of every five villages has a pub, although their number too is declining. The government has launched a project ('The Pub is the Hub') to enable pubs to offer a wider range of services to support their local communities and to make

them more viable (www.defra.gov.uk/rural/pdfs/services/rural-services-review-2006.pdf).

34 See www.defra.gov.uk/rural/pdfs/services/rural-services-review-2006.pdf. There are wide variations in household incomes in rural areas. They are higher in hamlets and villages compared with rural towns and urban areas, and also higher in the less sparse settlements. At the same time as this, in the sparse areas there is also a higher proportion of households in 'income poverty', with nearly a third of households living on less than 60% of the English median household income. There is a consistent gap between the level of wages paid in the most rural and the most urban areas (where it is much higher at around £130 per week) (Commission for Rural Communities, 2006a, pp. 70–9).

35 Commission for Rural Communities, 2006a, pp. 40–3.

36 Countryside Agency, 2003a, p. 12

37 The Commission for Rural Communities has compared the age profiles of rural and urban communities. The latest statistics show that rural communities tend to have a slightly lower proportion of children, particularly within the smallest settlements, and a substantially lower proportion of people between the ages of 18 and 40 than their urban counterparts.

38 Commission for Rural Communities, 2006a, p. 44.

39 On average those living in hamlets or villages make more car journeys (they travel nearly twice as far by car each year) and fewer journeys on foot than those in towns or urban areas. This is partly caused by the longer distances that rural people have to travel to work, to shop and for leisure. The exception to this are the people living in the smallest and most remote settlements where the average travelling distances are slightly lower.

40 More people living in hamlets and villages report that they have no alternative means of transport to the car (Commission for Rural Communities, 2006a, pp. 50–4). The RAC predicts that road traffic in the UK will increase by nearly 50% by 2031 and that this will have a disproportionate impact on rural areas since the road system is not designed for high volumes of traffic (Countryside Agency, 2003a, p. 22).

41 Rural Primary Care Trusts receive lower funding allocations per head of population and are more likely to be in deficit than those in urban areas (Commission for Rural Communities, 2006a, pp. 42–3).

42 Countryside Agency, 2003a, p. 12.

43 One of the unexpected contributory causes to the exodus of young people from the countryside has been the government's strategy to increase the number of people in tertiary education. This has created a small but significant population shift in which young people move out of rural areas (where there is little tertiary education apart from those institutions that were formerly agricultural colleges) to urban areas where most tertiary educational establishments are to be found. The tragedy is that most young people do not return after their graduation, with the result that rural areas currently have a higher proportion of people over the age of 40 (Commission for Rural Communities, 2006a, p. 22). The age profile of the countryside is constantly shifting. While the number of young people aged 15–24 is decreasing, the number of young people aged 0–14 is actually increasing. Stockdale (2004, p. 167) calls this 'rural out-migration'. The migration of many young people for

education or for employment is a significant factor and is partly hidden by the increased immigration to rural areas of older people. As Stockdale puts it, 'Out-migration, as a research topic, has been obfuscated by the counterurbanisation trend, which has become virtually hegemonic in the literature as an explanation of rural change.'

44 Using the criterion of affordability, it is clear that housing is less affordable in rural areas than in urban areas and that the problem is at its most acute in the South West, Northumberland, Cumbria, Derbyshire and Herefordshire (Commission for Rural Communities, 2006a, p. 35).

45 In recent years the price of property in rural areas has risen above the national average (Commission for Rural Communities, 2006a, p. 33). As the Countryside Agency report of 2003 put it, 'For some time rural England has been getting more middle class and middle aged. Wealthier households have outbid poorer people for scarce housing, and affluent incomers have replaced working class people who have moved out or died. Only about 10% of new arrivals are retired. Most are middle aged, while many young people have been leaving to find jobs and affordable housing' (Countryside Agency, 2003a, p. 12).

46 Compared with urban areas, very little research has been undertaken to examine the extent of rural homelessness and the need for more affordable housing (see Cloke *et al.*, 2001, pp. 438–53). However, the government has now become so concerned about rural housing that it has set up the Affordable Rural Housing Commission, which has concluded that a minimum of 11,000 new houses are required each year. Currently the number of new homes being built each year falls far short of this target (Commission for Rural Communities, 2006a, p. 35). The lack of affordable housing and the growth in the number of second homes has become so serious that the government is considering increasing the council tax on second homes. (Currently, councils may charge 90% of the council tax on second homes.)

47 Commission for Rural Communities, 2006a, p. 31.

2

The Changing Face of the
Rural Church

If the idealized view of the village, so beloved of novelists and television costume dramas alike, never existed, it is also the case that the idealized village church did not exist. I want to illustrate this by discussing seven views about the rural Church – or, more precisely, debunking seven myths – because these often repeated fallacies are major impediments to our engagement with the task of bringing the gospel to our contemporaries. I will then outline what I believe to be a more accurate picture of the contemporary rural Church.

Myth 1: There was a golden era when rural churches were full

Despite the folk memory of many older people who claim to remember a time when their church was full twice every Sunday, an examination of church registers shows that this was not so in the vast majority of cases. Many churches will have had a particularly gifted or popular parish priest for a period, during whose incumbency the congregations grew and became relatively large. This memory becomes rosier with the passing of the years, with the result that the vicar in question is 'canonized' and the light from his halo is still sufficiently bright to illuminate the supposed shortcomings of all his successors. Churches, of course, may have been full for special occasions, such as village funerals, harvest or Christmas, but research is unanimous in showing that few churches were packed every Sunday. The majority were only partly full – and there were times when some were almost empty.

There have also been periods when the Church was not merely unpopular, but experienced considerable grassroots opposition. Historically, it is clear that anti-clericalism was a strong contributory factor fuelling the Reformation. The enforced payment of tithes was a frequent cause of resentment in rural areas, especially when there were poor harvests. This was a significant factor in the growth of the Quakers in England in the mid-seventeenth century. Conflicts were also common when, to give a third example, Methodist preachers were setting up new congregations in villages in opposition to the established Church.

Part of the reason why the myth of full churches remains persistent is that many village churches were built or extended in the nineteenth century, and this has generated a false picture of the past in many people's minds. In Victorian England there was general disquiet at poor church attendance and it was thought that more people would come to church if additional seating were provided. Churches were re-ordered, partly in response to changing liturgical fashions, but more usually to pack pews into every available space. New churches were also built as a result of competition between denominations. All this has been meticulously documented by Gill,[1] who has demonstrated decisively that the vast majority of churches were never full. Indeed, in many communities there were more seats than there were inhabitants. For example, his study of 14 adjacent rural parishes in Northumberland shows that in 1901 there were 13,409 seats in churches and chapels for a population of 10,970 and that about 22% of those seats would have been occupied on average at the main Sunday services.[2] Ironically, the Victorian era probably had the highest levels of churchgoing since the reign of Elizabeth I when attendance at worship at the parish church was compulsory, and anyone missing church could be fined one shilling by the churchwarden.[3] This highpoint of church attendance lingers in the collective folk memory and sets a false benchmark, as it was not typical and was far above the average for the previous 500 years.

When I was made an archdeacon in 1997, one of the clergy presented me with a book, *Visitations of the Archdeaconry of Stafford, 1829–1841*. It contains the notes that Archdeacon George Hodson made in the early Victorian period as he undertook his visitations. Among other things, it records the population of parishes and also the number of communicants. Out of interest I analysed churchgoing in one of the most rural areas, the deanery of Alstonfield. I discovered that since the 1840s the population of the deanery had approximately halved and the number of communicants had also halved. Proportionately there was little difference between the present day and Archdeacon Hodson's era. What may be different (but there was no information to check it out) is that the numbers of people attending Morning and Evening Prayer has declined significantly.

The pattern of rural church attendance today varies greatly. In some of the larger villages (especially those inhabited by professional people) attendances may be quite healthy, but in many traditional village communities, congregations are often small and only just sustainable.

Myth 2: Each village had its own resident parson

The number of stipendiary clergy in the Church of England has fluctuated dramatically over the past centuries. At the beginning of the seventeenth century, during the reign of James I, there were about 10,000 Anglican clergy in England. A century later the numbers had grown, but there were many problems. For example, in 1798 it is estimated that there were about 11,194 parishes in England and, of those, 7,358 had no resident parson. Within a few years, by 1831, the number of clergy had increased to about 15,000 and in 1901 it reached a highpoint of 23,690. By 1970 this figure had nearly halved to 12,075, and numbers have declined still further, so that by 2000 there were 8,742 full-time stipendiary parochial clergy.[4] However, caution needs to be exercised in interpreting these figures. To give just one example, in the past 40 years there has been a significant increase in chaplaincy. Paul estimated that there were 480 clergy in chaplaincies in 1962,[5] but by 2004 there were about 1,100 chaplains. What is undoubtedly true is that over the past 40 years there has been a significant movement of resources from rural to urban areas. This was an inevitable change, since, as Paul pointed out in 1958, 41.7% of the clergy were ministering to 11.2% of the population.[6] This has resulted in the creation of hundreds of multi-parish benefices and rural team and group ministries.[7]

Archdeacon Hodson's notes are also revealing about the clergy and parishes in the Alstonfield deanery. In 1830 the parish of Cauldon was looked after by the vicar of Kingsley, who lived 3½ miles away and took one service on a Sunday in the afternoon. The parish of Elkstone was under the care of the vicar of Warslow, who lived 2½ miles away and the services alternated between Sunday mornings and afternoons. Neither Cauldon nor Elkstone had a resident parson.

There have been considerable periods in the past when there was no resident priest in a village, yet the ministry and mission of that church still continued. One of the significant developments in ministry over recent decades has been the rapid growth in non-stipendiary ministers, of which there are about 3,000 in the Church of England. In addition, the ranks of readers (formerly known as lay readers) have grown to about 10,000,[8] and in the past 15 years there has been a mushrooming of diocesan schemes to select and train lay people in other ministries. For example, in the Diocese of Lichfield lay people can now undertake a period of training, equivalent to that of a reader, in the areas of Preaching and Leading Worship, Outreach, Pastoral Care, Prayer Guidance, Youth and Children's Ministry, and Pioneer and Fresh Expressions Ministry. They are commissioned in the cathedral each year at the same time as the readers. Indeed, such is the growth of lay ministries that John Saxbee, the Bishop of Lincoln, believes that there is more ministry going on today in the Church of England than there has been for many decades.[9] However, in terms of the stipendiary clergy, virtually all rural parishes have to share their priest. In the more remote areas, he or she may have responsibility for up to 14 churches.

Myth 3: Rural churches are facing unprecedented change

Over the centuries our parish churches have experienced settled periods punctuated by times of profound change and upheaval. Duffy's magisterial study of the pre-Reformation church[10] paints a fascinating picture of how the ordered life of English parishes, both in towns and the countryside, was interrupted by the turmoil of the Reformation when many shrines and chantry chapels were demolished, and stained glass windows, statues and rood-screens were destroyed. Monks and nuns were ejected from their religious communities and the monastic properties and their contents plundered. It was a revolution of unbelievable proportions.

The religious turmoil continued during the decades that followed. For example, as a result of the Five Mile Act in 1665 (which attempted to enforce the Act of Uniformity of 1662) more than 1,000 clergy were driven out of the Church of England. Another period of rapid change occurred during the Victorian era, especially under the influence of the Oxford Movement. Chancels and sanctuaries were extended or raised and choir stalls were installed. Disputes about worship were so heated that the Ritual Commission was set up in 1867 to consider eucharistic vestments, incense, candles, the lectionary and liturgy. In more recent times the advent of the parish communion movement encouraged many churches to bring forward the altar to permit a westward-facing celebration of Holy Communion. The last 40 years have witnessed a further period of change and liturgical experimentation. Churches have been adapted for present needs, with meeting rooms, kitchens, toilet facilities and access for the disabled. The point is: there is nothing new in all this – rural churches and congregations have always faced change.

Profound changes in rural religion were not just confined to altering the parish church. Perhaps the greatest changes in the countryside of the past 300 years were the emergence of the Free Churches, often in reaction to Anglican pluralism and non-residency which were widespread. While Roman Catholics have never been strong in the countryside, there have been plenty of Baptists, Congregationalists (most of whom are now United Reformed Churches), Presbyterians and, in particular, Methodists. In some rural areas, such as Staffordshire and Cornwall, the majority of the population were Methodists and their rapid growth from the 1790s onwards caused a revolution in the religious life of many rural communities.

Myth 4: Most rural congregations are made up of people from the village

It is sometimes suggested that there is a contrast between urban and rural churches. The former, it is said, are often gathered or associational congregations, where worshippers are drawn from a wider area beyond the parish boundaries. This is contrasted with village churches where, it is claimed, a higher proportion of the congregation come from the immediate locality.[11] There is some truth in this, but on a number of occasions I have undertaken some informal research by asking how many of the congregation come from within, and how many from outside, a particular parish, and I have been surprised to find that there is no clear-cut divide. Some rural churches attract people from a wide area, either because individuals or their families have had a long connection with that particular church or because it provides the sort of worship that they feel happiest with.

Francis, in a study of 121 rural churches, questioned 'whether there is still a natural link between rural churches and rural society'. He concluded that it only exists 'among an ageing population who have their roots firmly fixed in the countryside',[12] but that newcomers and younger people do not feel part of the church in the same way as in the past. Rural areas, as well as urban areas, have been influenced by the prevailing consumer culture, and the congregations in village churches are becoming more eclectic than in previous generations.

Just 3 miles outside of Shrewsbury is the small village of Atcham, built around the medieval church of St Eata, which sits on the banks of the River Severn. The building incorporates stonework drawn from the nearby Roman settlement of Viroconium Cornoviorum. The weekly services are taken from the Book of Common Prayer and there is a thriving congregation with about 37 people gathering for worship each Sunday. However, of that number, just under 50% actually live in the parish. The others travel in, some from as far as Newport or Telford, a distance of between 15 to 20 miles. Part of the growth of the congregation has come about because of couples wanting to get married, many of whom live outside the parish. Despite the requirement to worship in the church regularly in order to get on the Electoral Roll, the number of weddings has increased in the past three years to between eight and ten annually. Of those who are married in the church, at least one couple each year has continued to worship regularly after their wedding.

Myth 5: Rural churches are so resilient that they will always survive

It is easy to assume that because some of our village churches are ancient, and the level of churchgoing in rural areas is higher than in urban areas, we need not worry about them too much. Such a view, however, is not justified by the evidence. The number of Methodist chapels has declined from 14,000 in 1932 to about 6,000 today. About 100 Free Church chapels are closing each year, most of which are in the countryside. Approximately 1,700 Anglican churches have closed since 1969 (although it is important to note that about 500 new churches have been opened by the Church of England over the same period). There has also been a significant decline in the number of Presbyterian, United Reform and Baptist churches. Rural faith communities are often weaker and more fragile than we care to acknowledge.

Another version of this myth argues that we need not be too concerned about rural churches since implicit religion[13] and folk religion are alive and well, and this is the natural religious expression of countryfolk. Francis has pointed out that Bailey's contention that implicit religion is firmly rooted in the nation, based on his experience of parents wanting their children to be baptized, is decidedly weak when one reflects on the decline in the number of parents bringing their children to baptism (a decline from two-thirds to one-third between 1956 and 1982).[14]

The myth of Anglican resilience in the countryside is quickly dispelled by a glance at the map of the villages around Shrewsbury. Over the past forty years the village churches at Preston Gubbals, Battlefield and Wroxeter have been made redundant.

Myth 6: The best solution is to close some rural churches, sell the buildings and unite the congregations

There are a number of aspects to this myth, which is put forward by a number of different sources.[15] For example, the idea is expressed that if you close the church and set up a trust to run it, then the villagers who do not go to church will want to take responsibility for the building. I have visited four villages where the church has been closed and I have discovered that the majority of people who are trustees of the building are former churchgoers, most of whom no longer go to church regularly. It is also clear that the amount of money that people contribute for the upkeep of a redundant church is lower than for a church that is open for worship. It also presumes that if a church closes, the congregation will transfer to another church. However, Gill argues that:

> Characteristically, membership and attendance diminish rapidly as closure nears; only half of the remaining members actually transfer to a neighbouring church after closure; and these transferred members are significantly less regular in their attendance at the new church than they were at their old one.[16]

Records of closures of Anglican churches have enabled Roberts and Francis to examine four dioceses with contrasting policies of church closures. They concluded:

> It may be mere coincidence that the two dioceses which experienced the higher rate of church closure also experienced sharper decline in usual Sunday attendances, electoral rolls, Easter day communicants, and Christmas eve/day communicants, although the common trend across all four indicators of church vitality may stretch somewhat the logic of coincidence.[17]

What evidence we have suggests that a policy of closing rural churches, at least in the short and medium term, is a very effective way of planning decline.

Another alternative put forward by some is to close the church building and for the congregation to continue to meet in a village hall or in someone's home. This sounds a wonderful idea, but there are very few places where a church has been able to maintain its worship, ministry and mission over the long term without its own building.

Prebendary David Chantrey is rector of six parishes on the Shropshire/Staffordshire border. Back in the 1970s, the last Free Church in the area, a Methodist chapel in Beckbury, closed. As far as David is aware, nowadays there is only one person in the six parishes who worships regularly in a Methodist church. There are several Methodists who worship in the Anglican churches week by week and, as a way of acknowledging this, there is a formal Ecumenical Welcome. However, looking at the situation from the point of view of the Methodist Church, it has effectively withdrawn from the area.

Myth 7: The Church of England is a rich institution because it owns so many church buildings

It is true that the insurance value of many old churches puts a high value on them, and in some cases to replace them would cost many millions of pounds. However, in most areas church buildings are a liability, not an asset. Since they are listed buildings and are often surrounded by graves, it is an expensive thing to convert a church to commercial or domestic use. There may be exceptions in some wealthy commuter villages, but in most areas to close a church and dispose of it is not only difficult, but also extremely costly.

When I was an archdeacon I was asked by the PCC of Christ Church, Newchurch, to close their Victorian church and make it redundant. Before it could be put on the market, asbestos had to be removed from the boiler room by a specialist firm. Since there were graves close to the church there had to be some exhumations and reburials, again undertaken by an outside contractor. The newest part of the graveyard was to be retained and therefore had to be fenced off. Then there was the removal and dispersal of some of the contents of the church. Finally, there were the legal costs. Not allowing for the considerable amount of time taken by the secretary

> of the Redundant Churches' Uses Committee and the archdeacon, by the time the sale was complete the modest proceeds did not cover the costs.

So far in this chapter I have commented on some of the popular views (or myths) about rural churches that are regularly propagated in order to challenge the simplistic solutions that are sometimes offered. I now want to draw on research to give an overview of what is *actually* going on in rural churches and the trends that are affecting them.

Affiliation

For the first time ever in the UK the 2001 census asked a question about religious affiliation. The categories that were offered were the major world religions (Christianity, Hinduism, Buddhism, Judaism, Islam, Sikhism) and 'any other' (see Table 2.1).[18]

Table 2.1 Religious affiliation: the 2001 UK census.

Religion	Number	%
Christian	42,079,417	71.57
Buddhist	151,816	0.26
Hindu	558,810	0.95
Jewish	266,740	0.45
Muslim	1,591,126	2.71
Sikh	336,149	0.57
Other	178,837	0.30
No religion/religion not stated	13,626,299	23.18

Source: http://www.statistics.gov.uk/census2001/profiles/uk.asp

In response, over three-quarters (78%) of the population chose to use a religious category to describe themselves. This comprised nearly 72%

of the population of the UK who indicated that they considered themselves to be Christians, and 5% who identified themselves with one of the other major world religions. The census revealed that levels of religious affiliation are even higher in rural areas than in urban areas. For example, in Shropshire 81% identified themselves by a religious category, and only 19% ticked 'no religion' or did not answer the question. Higher levels of religious affiliation in rural areas were also found by the British Social Attitudes Survey (Table 2.2) and in a study by Francis and Lankshear.[19]

Table 2.2 Church affiliation.

Religion	Percentage of respondents		
	Urban >10K (except London)	Town and fringe	Village, hamlet and isolated dwellings
Anglican	29	40	47
Roman Catholic	9	6	6
Other Christian	12	12	9
Muslim	2		
Other non-Christian	2		1
No religion	46	41	36
Refused/no answer/ don't know	0	1	2

Source: British Social Attitudes Survey, 2004.
Note: Blank cells indicate too few respondents.

The seventeenth British Social Attitudes Survey collated statistics that revealed the trends in affiliation of the major Christian denominations, as well as those of other religions and those of no religion (Table 2.3). They showed that over a 16-year period all the Christian denominations have seen a decline in affiliation. In contrast, there has been an increase in those who claim affiliation to other religions, though no details are provided. It is likely that this is due to immigration and the higher than average birth rates among those from immigrant backgrounds.

Table 2.3 Church membership in Britain, 1983–99.

	1983 %	1987 %	1991 %	1995 %	1999 %
Church of England	40	37	36	32	27
Roman Catholic	10	10	10	9	9
Church of Scotland	5	5	5	3	4
Other Protestant	7	7	6	6	6
Other religion	7	7	8	9	10
No religion	31	34	35	40	44
Base	1,761	2,847	2,918	3,633	3,143

Source: De Graaf and Need, 2000, p. 123.

Church attendance

De Graaf and Need looked at changes in church attendance (Table 2.4) and found that during the 1990s the gulf between regular attendees and those who never attend worship widened even further. There had also been a small increase in the proportion of weekly worshippers as well as an increase in the proportion of those who never worshipped.

Table 2.4 Church attendance (apart from such special occasions as weddings, funerals and baptisms) of those with current religion or brought up in a religion, 1991–9.

	1991 %	1995 %	1999 %
Once a week	12	13	13
At least every two weeks	3	3	2
At least once a month	7	6	6
At least twice a year	13	12	10
At least once a year	7	7	8
Less often	4	5	6
Never or practically never	51	55	54
Base	2,687	3,333	2,834

Source: De Graaf and Need, 2000, p. 124.

The decline of formal expressions of Christianity in rural areas is well documented.[20] Twenty years ago Francis found that only 3.8% of the population attended church in rural areas on a typical Sunday and argued that although many Anglicans would like to 'promote the community model for the rural church', we are going to have to see 'the future of the rural church in associational rather than community terms'.[21] More recent studies have pointed out another fact – namely, that only a proportion of churchgoers attend church weekly; many go on a fortnightly or monthly basis. In other words, the level of attendance on a specific Sunday is only a small proportion of those who consider themselves to be regular worshippers.[22] Furthermore, the statistics do not account for those who only worship during the week.

To put the decline in attendance into perspective, one has to remember – as we noted earlier – that there have been periods of rapid decline followed by growth in the past. For example, Schlossenberg has shown that attendance in Anglican churches dropped dramatically at one point in the eighteenth century:

Bishop Butler of Hereford compared Church attendance in his diocese in 1792 with the numbers from 1747 and found a substantial decline. In 1800 evangelical clergy from England's largest diocese, Lincoln, found that of 15,000 persons in seventy-nine parishes, fewer than 5,000 were known to attend Church, of these only 1,800 were communicants. Many of the non-attenders had gone over to Dissent, but there was still a very low level of religious participation.[23]

More recently there was a period of significant church growth in England that is often overlooked – the years between 1945 and 1958:

The later 1940s and 1950s witnessed the greatest church growth that Britain had experienced since the mid-nineteenth century.[24]

What is encouraging in these early years of the twenty-first century is that the long-term decline in rural congregations seems to have at least bottomed out, and may even have been reversed. The reason for this is that most rural churches have small congregations and it is small congregations (both rural and urban) that are holding their own or growing.[25]

Other trends

Despite the large numbers of people who claim to be Christians there has been a long and steady decline in many traditional Christian practices in the countryside, such as the number of communicants, baptisms,[26] church weddings and children who attend Sunday School.[27] The number of those being confirmed has reduced and, of those being confirmed, a higher proportion of them are female.[28] Clergy numbers have also reduced in the countryside.[29] The evidence suggests that nowadays rural ministry (where each priest has several parishes) is just as demanding as urban ministry (where clergy have, on average, more people).[30] There are now fewer church schools and a smaller proportion of pupils who attend Church of England schools than in the past.[31]

Styles of worship in rural churches

On average, the forms of worship in village churches are more likely to be traditional than in urban areas, which means that more rural churches have retained the *Book of Common Prayer*, although this is gradually changing as more and more churches adopt *Common Worship*. However, village churches are more likely to have experimented with non-liturgical All Age or Family Services.[32] Many of these types of services are now led by groups of lay people. Some dioceses have adopted a system of authorizing such groups to lead worship, and even to preach. In some cases, courses are provided to offer resources and training. In addition, many rural churches now have small groups of trained visitors to undertake pastoral work, such as preparation for baptisms and weddings and bereavement follow-up visits.

Differences between rural and urban churches

In a comparative study of the dioceses of Birmingham (one of the most urban dioceses) and Hereford (one of the most rural dioceses), Roberts found that both had declined in the numbers of full-time parochial clergy, electoral roll members, baptisms, confirmations, and Easter Day communicants:

> The Diocese of Hereford still had a greater number of its population on parish electoral rolls, a greater proportion of full-time parochial clergy

per head of population, a larger proportion of its population being baptised and confirmed in Anglican churches, and a far higher proportion of Easter Day communicants per head of population than did the diocese of Birmingham.[33]

However, one of the surprising factors was:

The Diocese of Hereford had a greater reduction, in both numerical and percentage terms, in the numbers of electoral roll members from 1980 to 2000 . . . and a greater reduction, in percentage terms, in the total number of confirmations. This suggests that the rural church cannot sustain a transfer of resources from the rural to the urban church.[34]

Although the proportion of the population attending church in rural areas is higher than in urban areas, both urban and rural areas have experienced a significant decline over recent decades.[35]

Littler and Francis, on the basis of empirical data, identified four main differences between rural and urban churches:

First, there are fewer inhabitants to support each church building in rural areas. Second, in rural areas a higher proportion of the population attends church on a regular basis. Third, there is a higher level of informal contact between local church and the local inhabitants in rural areas. Fourth, the rural clergy have responsibility for more churches and take more services on a Sunday.[36]

To summarize, the majority of services in rural Anglican churches attract relatively small congregations and often prefer more traditional styles of worship than urban churches. The decline in baptisms, church weddings and rural children's and youth work is continuing. However, the long-term decline in rural church attendance until about 2000 appears to have stopped and, on average, there is modest growth.

Notes

1 1989, 1993 and 2003.

2 Gill, 2003, p. 27. See also pp. 33–5 for other examples.

3 There are records of William Shakespeare's father being fined for missing church on 25 December 1592.

4 Roberts and Francis, 2006, p. 38.

5 Paul, 1964, p. 103.

6 Paul, 1964, p. 23. The Sheffield Report, produced by the House of Bishops of the Church of England (1974), set up the mechanism for deploying Anglican clergy more strategically.

7 It should be noted that the decline in the number of clergy also affects urban parishes. In the Shrewsbury Episcopal Area (covering the northern half of Shropshire) there are only six parish priests who have charge of one church only and this is likely to change in the next five years. Every other priest in the area looks after at least two churches. We are rapidly moving to the point in urban areas where only a tiny minority of large suburban churches will have a priest to themselves.

8 http://www.cofe.anglican.org/about/thechurchofenglandtoday.

9 The increase in the number of readers, non-stipendiary ministers and other authorized lay leaders has been documented by Francis (1985, pp. 26–7).

10 Duffy, 1992.

11 Francis (1996, p. 239) uses the terms 'associational' and 'community' to describe these two sorts of churches.

12 Francis, 1996, p. 239.

13 For a discussion about implicit religion, see Chapter 3.

14 Francis, 1989, pp. 71–4.

15 This is broadly the solution proposed by Davies et al., 1991, p. 185; Russell, 1993, pp. 174–5; and Bending, 2002, pp. 14–15.

16 Gill, 2003, p. 29.

17 Roberts and Francis, 2006, p. 54.

18 Religious self-designation is not without its problems. The 'any other' category in the census revealed the presence of 390,000 Jedi Knights in the UK. For a more detailed discussion, see Fane, 1999.

19 Francis and Lankshear, 1992b, p. 4.

20 Francis, 1985, p. 22–3.

21 Francis, 1985, p. 42, and 1989, pp. 71–4.

22 Missionary Diocese of Wakefield, 2001.

23 Schlossenberg, 2002.

24 Brown, 2001, p. 5.

25 Jackson, 2002, pp. 109–17. Attendance figures in rural parishes in north Shropshire have been increasing slightly between 2004 and 2007.

26 Francis, 1985, pp. 23–4. See also Table 6.1.

27 See, for example, Brown, 2001, pp. 164, 167, 168, 189, 191.

28 Francis, 1985, pp. 24–5.

29 Francis, 1985, pp. 25–7.

30 Francis and Lankshear, 1992b, pp. 8–9.

31 Francis, 1985, pp. 27–8.

32 Francis and Lankshear, 1992b, p. 7.

33 Roberts, 2003, pp. 34–5.

34 Roberts, 2003, pp. 34–5.

35 Francis has also charted the decline in rural church attendance (Francis, 1985, pp. 22–3).

36 Littler and Francis, 2003, p. 57. See also the article by Francis and Lankshear (1992b, p. 8), which also noted that rural clergy conduct more services than urban clergy.

3

Belief and Spirituality in Rural Britain

> When the Rector on his induction takes the key of the church, locks himself in and tolls the bell, it is his own passing bell he is ringing. He is shutting himself out from all hope of a future career on earth. He is a man transported for life, to whom there will be no reprieve ... for the day he accepts a country benefice he is a shelved man ... once a country parson, always a country parson.[1]
>
> Dr A Jessop, *Vicar of Scaring in Norfolk*, 1890

In contrast to the idealized view of rural ministry in the nineteenth century, with the supposedly full churches and happy and fulfilled clergy, Dr Jessop paints a much more melancholy picture of the country parson and his parish in 1890. Once again, his portrait alerts us to the danger of projecting on to earlier generations a pattern of life and observance that never existed. In this chapter I reflect upon the changing collage of belief and religious observance in contemporary Britain and the way it is affecting the life of the Church in rural areas. I have collated data from recent surveys about recorded levels of belief and the prevalence of religious experience, lest we construct a strategy for mission based merely on anecdotal evidence or false premises. I also want to look at alternative forms of religious practice and discuss the hypothesis that we are witnessing a profound change in the nature and style of religious observance in Britain, and the impact this is claimed to be having on the spirituality of rural Christianity.

Religious beliefs in Britain

Surveys show that although the majority of people still claim to believe in God, the number of believers has been gradually declining over the past 40 years (Table 3.1). Belief about the nature of God is also changing. For example, the proportion of those who believe in 'God as Personal' has declined from 43% in the 1940s/1950s to 31% in the 1990s.[2] Over the same period, belief in 'God as Spirit or Life Force' has increased from 38% to 40%. Gill's table shows that levels of non-traditional religious beliefs have also changed over time, with the largest growth being the number of people who believe in ghosts.

Table 3.1 Traditional religious belief in Britain.

	Percentage of British population				
	1940s/1950s	1960s	1970s	1980s	1990s
Belief					
God		79	74	72	65
God as Personal	43	39	32	32	31
God as Spirit or Life Force	38	39	38	39	40
Jesus as Son of God	68	62		49	
Life after death	49	49	37	43	46
Heaven		52	55	53	
Hell			21	26	27
Devil	24	28	20	24	27
Disbelief					
God		10	15	18	27
Jesus as just a man/story	18	22		38	
Life after death	21	23	42	40	41
Heaven		33	35	37	
Hell			68	65	64
Devil	54	52	70	64	67

Source: Gill, 2003, p. 250.

In spite of this changing profile of religious belief, at the beginning of the millennium *The European Values Study* found that the vast majority of people in Britain still felt that it was important to hold religious services after birth (58.9%), for marriage (68.6%), and after death (78.5%).[3]

Religious experience

In recent decades there have been a number of surveys of people's religious experiences. The Religious Experience Research Unit[4] found that 36% of respondents replied in the affirmative to the question, 'Do you feel that you have ever been aware of or influenced by a presence or power, whether you call it God or not, which is different from your everyday self?'[5] In another piece of research among students at Nottingham University, when asked the same question, 65% answered yes, 29% said no, and 6% were unsure.[6] Later research by Hay has shown that a significant number of people have what they consider to be religious experiences,[7] and there is no evidence that the level of such spiritual experiences is changing. Unfortunately, there has been no comparable work undertaken between urban and rural dwellers. What is clear, though, is that religious experiences are still widespread occurrences in the UK today, and that they are not necessarily related to formal religious practices or rites.

Folk religion and implicit religion

In the 1950s and 1960s it was commonplace in Anglican circles to talk up the importance of folk religion. Around the core of committed worshippers there was believed to exist a large penumbra of anonymous believers who customarily frequented the churches at Christmas and Easter and perhaps Harvest, and for occasional offices such as christenings and weddings. Never was this more the case, or so it was believed, than in rural areas where patterns of belief and churchgoing had remained largely undisturbed by the inroads of secularism. It was assumed (somewhat naively) that if only one could get the recipe right, this host of baptized but uncommitted Anglicans would flock back into the Church, boosting attendances and revealing the true strength of the Church to its critics.

Although there is some truth in this familiar story of countryfolk, the evidence of the last 40 years suggests a more complex scenario that undermines the claim that folk religion is alive and well and constitutes a hidden column in the armoury of the Church of England. For over 30 years Edward Bailey has been researching and writing on the subject of 'implicit religion' (he makes a distinction between implicit religion and 'folk religion') which is the human search for meaning, purpose and fundamental values.[8] He claims that such belief is widespread, but under-valued because it is unarticulated:

> I am convinced that what stops many people communicating their faith, explicit or implicit, is a lack of vocabulary. Religious longings are expressed in coded language, or with gestures, such as a squeeze of the hand, a smile, or a tear. The desires for God are there, but they are hard to unlock and release.[9]

He identifies three areas of implicit religion: transcendent experiences, absolute values and religious experiences.[10] He offers three definitions of implicit religion: commitments, integrated loci and 'intensive concerns with extensive effects',[11] and argues that implicit religion is far more than 'folk religion', which 'is one relatively popular expression of implicit religion'.[12]

The fundamental question about Bailey's research and writing is whether it is actually about religion, in the technical, classical sense of that word.[13] Furthermore, one of the difficulties of assessing the reality, impact and nature of implicit religion is the lack of consistent empirical research.[14] What would be interesting in the context of this book about the Church of England and rural areas is to have more information on how implicit religion specifically relates to Christian belief and practice. Here, Bailey does not provide us with much help, other than a brief discussion about 'intensive concerns with extensive effects', in which he identifies six areas of which three may be relevant:

1 Buildings are the community's sacramental language.
2 The church (building) is the major symbol of the community.
3 'Christianity' is its professed faith.[15]

Bailey suggests that the church building is a primary focus of many people's implicit beliefs. As such it constitutes one factor that is relevant for the Church's mission in rural areas, where many people in the community, including those who do not worship on a regular basis, feel that the church belongs to them.

'New Age' spirituality

Allied to Bailey's concept of 'implicit religion' is the rapid growth in the use of the term 'spirituality', which is now commonly used in schools, hospitals and places of work. Murray, writing on implicit religion from the perspective of a health-care chaplain, says:

> It is almost a commonplace of discussion in hospices to try to distinguish between the religious and the spiritual needs of patients. Religious needs include worship, prayer and sacraments. They are the overt signs and symbols of religious practice. Spirituality is not defined in the Christian sense (of the cultivation of the inner life of devotion), but in terms of the search for meaning, purpose, and ultimate values. It is a need that can be posited of every patient, and it seems to be a more comfortable concept than implicit religion.[16]

Heald, picking up on this theme, summarized the results of a BBC poll and observed:

> In summary, people cling to various general spiritual beliefs, some of which are not necessarily Christian. The survey shows that these spiritual experiences are not on the wane as many would predict, but are, if anything, increasing. Yet whilst people hold these beliefs, they do not necessarily want to be labelled 'religious' and even less do they associate themselves with a particular denomination.[17]

One of the most interesting books to be written on this subject is by Heelas and Woodhead, based on a study of Kendal, a market town in the Lake District. Their book raises acutely the question of how to define what the word 'spirituality' has come to mean. In answer to the question

> 'Which of the following is the best description of your core beliefs about spirituality?', 21 per cent of respondents to the holistic milieu questionnaire used in the Kendal Project answered 'Spirituality is being a decent and caring person'; 20 per cent 'Spirituality is love'; and 10 per cent 'Spirituality is healing oneself and others'.[18]

These responses reveal that the term 'spirituality' is now used in so many different ways that it is impossible to know what the word really means or what value to place upon people's statements.

The basic thesis of Heelas and Woodhead may be summarized in the title of their book, *The Spiritual Revolution: Why Religion is Giving Way to Spirituality*. They begin the preface with this statement:

> This book explores the spiritual revolution claim: that traditional forms of religion, particularly Christianity, are giving way to holistic spirituality, sometimes still called 'New Age'.[19]

They argue that there is a massive cultural shift underway: 'a turn away from life lived in terms of external or "objective" roles, duties and obligations, and a turn towards life lived by reference to one's own subjective experiences (relational as much as individualistic)'.[20] They suggest that this is happening in all parts of our national life, including the religious domain. Instead of living in response to external expectations, people are tending to live in response to subjective factors and according to subjective-life. They summarize these two states as 'life-as' and 'subjective-life':

> The former is bound up with the mode of life-as – indeed it sacralizes life-as. By contrast the former involves subordinating subjective life to the 'higher' authority of transcendent meaning, goodness and truth, whilst the latter invokes the sacred in the cultivation of unique subjective-life.

They think that subjective-life has become the defining cultural development of modern Western society, and argue that 'those institutions that cater for the unique subjective-lives of the "centred" are on the increase, whilst those that continue to operate in life-as mode find themselves out of step with the times'. They claim to 'have found robust evidence of a pattern: a correlation between subjective-life-as spirituality and growth on the one hand, and between life-as religion and decline on the other'. They suggest that 'the West is currently experiencing *both* secularization (with regard to life-as forms of religion) *and* sacralization (with regard to subjective-life forms of spirituality)'.[21] Heelas and Woodhead note that:

> . . . during the 1940s and 1950s 43% of the population of Britain believed in 'God as Personal' compared with 38% who believed in 'God as Spirit or Life-force'. During the 1990s, however, the respective figures become 31% and 40%.[22]

They also note that in the same poll 31% of the respondents described themselves as 'spiritual' whereas only 27% used the word 'religious'.[23]

Does Heelas's and Woodhead's thesis ('that traditional forms of religion are giving way to holistic spirituality') stand up to examination? There are several weaknesses in their argument and the jury is still out. First, is it accurate to use the phrase 'subjective-life spirituality' to describe the holistic milieux? For example, I know many people who have had acupuncture, who have practised the Alexander Technique, who have visited chiropractors and osteopaths or been for a massage, but who have not thought that there was a spiritual aspect to it. My impression is that they had a physical problem for which they were seeking relief. Heelas and Woodhead themselves point out that the practitioners of these various holistic techniques consider that they are offering something that is spiritual, while only 55% of their clients agreed with this description.[24]

Second, a closer examination of some of the statistics raises a question, which is illustrated by Table 3.1. It is correct that one survey found that there was a change in the levels of belief in 'God as Personal' and 'God as Spirit or Life Force' between the 1940s/1950s and the 1990s, but it would appear that the change took place between the 1960s/1970s and that since then (about 30 years ago) there has been no significant change.

Third, Heelas and Woodhead found that:

Seventy three per cent of all those active in the holistic milieu of Kendal and environs are aged 45 and over, with 55 per cent of all participants aged between 40 and 59 – in Kendal as a whole, only 12 per cent fall into the latter age range. Forty-five per cent of those active in the milieu are women aged between 40 and 60, with the equivalent figure for males being just 10 per cent.[25]

They found that 80% of those active in the holistic milieu of Kendal and environs were women; 78% of groups are led or facilitated by women; and 80% of one-to-one practitioners are women.[26] At the most, their research supports the claim that there is a growth in the holistic milieu among middle-aged and older women.[27]

Fourth, Heelas and Woodhead did not compare the rise of new spiritualities with other beliefs and practices from earlier times, perhaps because there is little reliable empirical evidence available. For example, in the sixteenth and seventeenth centuries there was widespread interest in and practice of witchcraft,[28] astrology and alchemy.[29] In the Victorian period there was a rise of interest in spiritualism,[30] séances, mesmerism, Swedenborgianism and druidism. Today, a number of practices have grown in popularity in the West, such as crystals, aromatherapy, numerology, feng shui and channelling which, among others, are commonly grouped together under the heading of 'New Age'. There have always been 'alternative' spiritualities that have grown and waned in popularity, and some that have disappeared altogether. How many alchemists were there in Kendal at the time of the research? What evidence we have shows that there have always been a wide variety of religious and quasi-religious beliefs and practices (see Table 3.2) and that these change over time (see Table 3.3). For example, a substantial minority of people claim to believe in ghosts and, as I noted above, this has been increasing over the past 50 years.

Table 3.2 Belief in the supernatural among teenagers (Francis and Kay).

	Agree %	Not certain %	Disagree %
I believe in the devil	19	28	53
I believe in black magic	18	31	51
I believe it is possible to contact the spirits of the dead	31	32	37
I believe in my horoscope	35	31	34
I believe that fortune-tellers can tell the future	19	30	51
I believe in ghosts	37	29	34

Source: Francis and Kay, 1995, p. 152.

Fifth, Heelas and Woodhead exhibit a strangely static view of organized religion. Religious beliefs are not held in a vacuum, and there is plenty of research to show that some regular worshippers mix superstition and other beliefs (Table 3.4) in with their Christian beliefs. What we do not know is the extent to which this mèlange of beliefs and practices has been changing over time.

In conclusion, I do not think that Heelas and Woodhead have established a strong enough case to substantiate their thesis that, 'traditional forms of religion, particularly Christianity, are giving way to holistic spirituality, sometimes still called "New Age"'. However, what they *have* demonstrated is that religious beliefs are changing and that there is a wide variety of such beliefs being practised in Kendal. The question is whether

Table 3.3 Non-traditional religious belief in Britain.

	Percentage of British population				
	1940s/1950s	1960s	1970s	1980s	1990s
Belief					
Reincarnation			24	26	25
Horoscopes			23	26	26
Foretelling future			48	54	47
Lucky charms			17	19	18
Black magic			11	13	10
Exchange messages with dead	15		11	14	14
Ghosts	15		19	28	32
Disbelief					
Reincarnation			53	57	59
Horoscopes			72	69	67
Foretelling future			41	40	46
Lucky charms			79	78	78
Black magic			82	82	86
Exchange messages with the dead	59		79	78	80
Ghosts	64		73	65	58

Source: Gill, 2003, p. 250.

or not this is a new phenomenon. History provides plenty of examples of similar claims being made that religion was experiencing a fundamental change, such as this one by a Free Church commentator writing in 1901:

> In the Church we have witnessed, to say the least, a very considerable collapse of what I may call conventional religion – that is, public opinion does much less to enforce church attendance and church communion. The change began in Scotland, perhaps thirty years ago. I remember the time when churches were full attended twice a day, when in many places non-churchgoers were quite exceptional. This is no longer the case. Many are content with occasional attendances, and, in spite of all the efforts of the churches, the number of outsiders is very great, and is constantly increasing. I question, in this respect, whether Scotland is not in a worse position than England.[31]

39

Table 3.4 Belief in the supernatural among religious teenagers in Walsall.

	Christian %	Hindu %	Muslim %	Sikh %	Non-affiliates %	χ^2	p<
I believe in the devil	30	13	41	15	25	55	.001
I believe in black magic	21	21	32	33	26	23	.001
I believe it is possible to contact the spirits of the dead	37	18	14	21	35	75	.001
I believe in my horoscope	40	45	25	42	41	25	.001
I believe that fortune-tellers can tell the future	26	21	15	33	24	21	.001
I believe in ghosts	51	35	45	41	48	14	.01
I am frightened of going into a church alone	12	10	16	12	16	10	.05
I am frightened of walking through a graveyard alone	43	49	53	42	37	30	.001

Source: Smith, 2002, p. 101.

Although I am sceptical about Heelas's and Woodhead's thesis, I think it is important to consider what we can learn from their research and from those who practise New Age thinking. It is clear that for a substantial minority of the population 'New Age' resonates with, and makes sense of, their concerns and experiences. They are part of the group of men and women who are asking fundamental questions about life and God.[32] All sorts of non-Christian beliefs are now taken for granted by people in Britain, as illustrated by the findings in Table 3.3 which show that a quarter of the population believe in reincarnation and horoscopes, and nearly half of the population believe in fortune-telling. We also know that there has been a change in some people's ideas of what God is like (from 'Personal' to 'Life-Force'). Just because people say they believe in God does not necessarily mean that they believe in the 'God and Father of our Lord Jesus Christ'.

At the same time, however, many of the people who engage in New Age practices claim to be dissatisfied with life and are seeking for meaning or for truth. We need to take both their dissatisfaction and their searching seriously because they may be more likely to explore the Christian faith than convinced materialists or atheists. To engage with them we need to listen to the questions that they are asking. They are often searching for healing or inner contentment; they may articulate a profound concern about the way that humankind has been abusing the planet, and the need to work in harmony with it; many are dissatisfied with a mechanistic view of the world and a longing to rediscover wonder. Drane, reflecting on New Age thinking, argues that:

> People feel disjointed, out of tune with their physical environment, out of touch with other people, and even unable to come to terms with themselves. There is a lot of hurt around, and there are many wounded people who are looking for personal healing. To be relevant to life in the next millennium, any religious faith will have to be capable of dealing effectively with such feelings of alienation and lostness.[33]

The Christian gospel has something to say about all of these areas, and it is significant that some of the main points of contact with such people will be found in prayer for healing, meditation and environmental action.

Despite this, there are also some significant differences between the Christian faith and New Age thinking. Indeed, one of the serious concerns about New Age perspectives is that it is ultimately about the self and self-fulfilment. This contrasts with the Christian conviction that it is when we die to self and are raised to new life through baptism that we find our deepest fulfilment not in self, but in God.

In the autumn of 2002 two rural clergy heard that a Healing and Complementary Therapy Exhibition was being planned in Oswestry. They felt it was important that the Church had a presence there and so on Sunday, 3 March 2003, the Revd John Webb and the Revd Nigel Coatsworth took a stand in the Memorial Hall in the centre of Oswestry alongside some 50 other therapists of all persuasions, offering healing. That first exhibition in town drew 2,000 people on a Sunday morning, many of whom were eager for some healing in their life: 'For Christians, so used to looking askance at "alternative therapies", it was an interesting and humbling experience. Here were some 50 or so therapists, offering a whole range of therapies, from homoeopathy and herbal remedies to Hopi Ear Candle, Reiki and Astral Photography. Some were, in our judgement, spiritually benign; some we were not sure about, while others were definitely occultic: but all wanted to make people well. They were there to serve and to heal.'

The focus was on the visitors and prayer was offered for any who wanted it. Although their stand had a large banner of the Tree of Life, they soon realized that their display was far too wordy compared with other 'touchy-feely' stalls. So the next time they took a stall they had an icon, some oil, some water, an open Bible, bread and wine, a cross and a carving of healing hands.

'We had some interesting conversations – one was with a devout Roman Catholic, fresh from attending Mass, who was studying Reiki (a school of healing with strong occultic elements). She had initially approached her parish priest, desirous of exercising healing within the Church; but being rejected, she had gone into Reiki, and was now practising this 'in the name of Jesus'. Here was a Christian, with a real heart for healing, but not welcomed by the church . . . We sensed that people in general no longer look to the Church for healing. Here is a vacuum left by the Church since the Middle Ages, which many people are seeking to fill.

'As we talked with other therapists and read their literature, what we missed was anything that would deal with broken relationships, between people or between people and God; healing appeared to be focused entirely on making people whole physically. Neither the healing of inner wounds left from the past, nor forgiveness or reconciliation, were catered for by other therapists. Some therapists who were laying on hands with 'prayer' spoke of their energy being love. They were certainly people of peace; perhaps they were, unknowingly, drawing on God's love, but there was no explicit connection with the God and Father of Jesus.'

Out of the experience of these exhibitions they have now moved into the real marketplace. Along with others, they run a stall in the outdoor market in Oswestry each Wednesday offering prayer for healing. Many people stop to talk and, on average, 12 people each week ask for prayer.

Rural church life: a distinctive spirituality?

Television and the internet ensure that there are few, if any, corners of rural Britain that are impervious to the evolving expectations and ideas current in contemporary society. A variegated pattern of beliefs and observance is reality for most of Britain today and this raises the question with some sharpness as to whether or not there is anything distinctive about the spirituality of the rural Church. Traditionally, strong claims have been made both for the quality and for the durability of rural Christianity. The rhythm of the seasons, the experience of light and dark, and the adherence to traditional rural customs that shape the lives both of individuals and communities, are all regularly cited as formative influences. Living in smaller communities where everyone is known and there is a high degree of stability in the population is another supposed factor. But are these perceptions of a distinctive spirituality justified, or is this just one more cherished fantasy that needs to be abandoned in the face of the relentless tide of secularism?

Living nearer nature

In the past, one of the stark contrasts between urban and rural Christianity was a spirituality forged by those who worked on the land and who were in closer touch with the seasons. Not many years ago every able-bodied person in the rural community would have been caught up in harvesting, to ensure that there was enough food for the coming winter. Once completed, it was followed by a harvest festival to give thanks to God and a shared celebratory harvest supper. Even today a higher proportion of rural people garden and grow vegetables than those who live in towns and cities. Flower and vegetable shows continue to be major events in the calendars of villages up and down the country. In contrast, many urban dwellers, especially in cities, have covered their front gardens in tarmac to provide additional parking spaces, and those who live in flats may have to manage with a window box.

In recent years farming has become highly mechanized, the number of people working on the land has declined significantly, and a much higher proportion of our food is now imported. Add to this the decline in the village shop and the increasing numbers of rural people who shop in supermarkets, where many products are available all year round, and one can see how the influence of the seasons is becoming marginal for many

43

people in the villages too. There is no doubt that the popularity of Plough Sunday, harvest services and suppers has declined and are no longer observed by many rural inhabitants, especially those who use the village as a dormitory. Nevertheless, these rituals are still far more common in rural than in urban areas and reflect a greater connectedness with the land.

In a similar way the reality of darkness is a feature of rural life in a way that it is not for the urban populace. For more than a century, most city dwellers have not experienced real darkness because street lighting is kept on all night. It is difficult, if not impossible, to see the night sky clearly in most towns because of light and atmospheric pollution. When I was a child being brought up in a hamlet in Wiltshire, like most rural folk we kept a torch by the back door in case we had to go outside after dark. Today street lighting has been installed even in the most remote villages. Despite this, life in the countryside is not as domesticated as it is in the town, and the clarity of the night sky is a powerful reminder of the vastness of the universe and just how small we are in comparison.

Community spirit

There are usually higher levels of mutual support in rural areas, partly because people have to rely on one another more.[34] With less public transport, and fewer shops and services, the young and the elderly are more likely to need the help of others. In more remote areas there is a presumption that neighbours will assist one another when, for example, a village is cut off after a blizzard. It may be a long wait for the snow-plough, which will prioritize the motorways and the main roads over the single-lane tracks into a village. Often it is the local farmer on his tractor who pulls cars out of the snowdrifts. This resilience means that rural folk are simply more likely to get on with things than some urban people.

Shortly after I became an archdeacon, a rural dean tipped me off that one of the small churches in a remote part of the Staffordshire Moorlands was doing some building work on the church without a faculty. A few days later I followed the winding country lane up the hills to the hamlet to find that two local farmers had replaced the

church roof. They seemed slightly surprised when I told them that
they needed permission to make repairs to the building since it was
under Faculty Jurisdiction. They saw a need and simply got on with
it. As I left they commented, 'Well, Archdeacon, next time it needs
doing, we'll be very happy to leave it to you!'

Rural traditions

Compared with urban areas, villages are much more likely to have
retained ancient traditions, some of which have religious roots. For
example, there is 'well-dressing' in Derbyshire and east Staffordshire.
Each year from May Day until mid-September, the wells in villages are
decorated with flowers to produce pictures. This practice may have had
pagan origins and for many years was opposed by the Church. It had
nearly died out by the 1950s, but has recently had a renaissance. It is
thought that it may have had its roots in sacrifices to water gods.
Nowadays the majority of wells are decorated with flowers illustrating
Christian themes. In the north of England there has been a long tradition
of dancing with swords, known as rapper dancing, and in the south of
England (and especially in Sussex) there are mummers, who perform
traditional plays. Some people claim that these too have pagan origins
that symbolize the dying and rebirth of fertility gods.

Elsewhere, the custom of morris dancing is still preserved and this
incorporates many ancient traditions with religious roots, such as the
Green Man. However, it is unclear whether any of these traditions retain
any real religious significance today (just as most of the millions of people
who turn out for Bonfire Night parties are not motivated by anti-Catholic
feelings and may even be ignorant of the event's historical origins).
Nevertheless, there is a strong sense of history about many of these
customs that speaks of a continuity with the past and fosters a sense of
community through shared celebration. Drane suggests that churches in
rural areas should consider how to engage imaginatively with practices
such as well-dressing and traditional Whitsunday marches, and build
upon them.[35]

45

A sense of place

Mission-Shaped Church points out that people are far more mobile today than in the past, but we must be careful not to exaggerate this. When I lived in Walsall and Stoke on Trent it was common to hear people talk about how parochial these urban 'villages' still are. The majority of people in Britain today are born and stay in the same area, and this is even more likely in the countryside where some families have lived for centuries.[36] Vast tracts of land still belong to the large estates, and many families have farmed the same land over generations. It is not unusual for rural people to be able to point to the graves of generations of ancestors who are buried in the churchyard. They, too, expect that one day they will be buried in the same place. This sense of rootedness is far less common in urban areas, where a much higher proportion of the population will be cremated rather than buried.

This continuity may be one of the reasons why more rural churches have a sense of history, why the communities feel that it is 'our church', and why there is a preference for traditional forms of worship. It is closely linked to a sense of 'sacred space', whether this is focused on the church building or on other ancient sacred sites in the countryside. One of the features of rural congregations is that when there is a financial crisis and choices have to be made, they would usually prefer to keep the church building and lose the services of a priest, rather than the other way round. This is also why most redundant churches held by the Churches Conservation Trust in rural areas still hold occasional services, perhaps four times a year, which draw a congregation from the local area. This is a system that allows the community the benefits of occasional acts of public worship (and rights of burial if the churchyard is still open), without the cost of maintaining a medieval building.

Small numbers

In most areas the rural Church has a quite different feel and ethos than the urban Church. One of the most obvious differences is that rural parishes have a smaller population and therefore, on average, have smaller congregations. In contrast to the town where there may be many different churches, it may be the only congregation for several miles. Most village churches have to share their priest (and possibly a reader) with several other villages, so there may only be one service each week or even one a fortnight. Several consequences flow from this. It is not possible (even if there were enough clergy or readers) to offer a wide variety of service styles. Compared with an urban church where a mixed menu of worship can be offered (a quiet, traditional service of Holy Communion without music at eight o'clock, followed by a participative all-age service mid-morning and a meditative evening service), in the village all the worshippers have no choice but to attend the same service. If someone moves into a town or suburb and does not like their local church, there will almost certainly be another down the road that will provide what they want. In a village, the worship has to strike a balance in a bid to cater for everyone's needs, which is one of the reasons why few village churches have a distinctive churchmanship. The vast majority of evangelical, charismatic or Anglo-Catholic churches are to be found in urban areas, and those Christians in the village who want that sort of worship will usually travel to the towns for it. In contrast, village worship tends to be more 'middle of the road'.

Having a smaller population also affects the way that the Church goes about its ministry and mission. A town church can afford to have strong views on controversial topics, or to offer a distinctive style of worship, or to have an up-front approach to evangelism. If someone is put off by the particular stance of a church or its style of worship, you can always find someone else to invite. This is quite different in villages where it is often possible to be in contact with every single person in the community. There is not much opportunity for a second chance if someone is put off by the Church, and it is one of the reasons why rural evangelism tends to be less overt than in the towns.

Smaller populations and smaller congregations also make it more difficult to handle differences and disagreements. In a large congregation there will be a number of activities that allow for different gifts to be used and a range of groups where people can experiment or let off steam. In a rural setting everyone is involved in everything. When someone comes to worship in a rural church for the first time there is no anonymity, such as one might find in a larger urban congregation. It is also more difficult for the casual visitor or enquirer to drop in to see what is going on without being noticed.

Summary

The proportion of those who believe in God in the UK has declined, and what people actually believe about the nature of God has also changed. Despite this, religious experiences are common and the language of 'spirituality' is widespread, if fuzzy – as seen in some of the diverse beliefs and practices that are commonly called New Age. Rural spirituality, by contrast, is less ephemeral and more traditional both in content and form. It is still influenced by its connection with nature, with a sense of history and of place. But even this is in flux as more and more urban people move into the countryside, bringing with them a different range of expectations and priorities. What is not changing is the way in which rural spirituality is still sustained by and nurtured in relatively small congregations. All of these factors are important when it comes to applying the principles outlined in *Mission-Shaped Church*.[37]

Notes

1 Quoted in *Faith in the Countryside*, 1990, p. 137.

2 Heald (2000), reporting a survey commissioned by the BBC and supported by *The Tablet* and the University of Nottingham, found that belief in a personal God had declined from just over 40% in 1968 to 26% in 2000.

3 Halman, 2001, p. 80.

4 The unit was set up in 1969 by Sir Alister Hardy and, until 2000, was based at Manchester College, Oxford. It has now moved to Lampeter as part of the University of Wales. It has undertaken empirical research on the religious experiences of thousands of people. For further information, see Hardy, 1979, and http://www.lamp.ac.uk/aht/Research/research.html.

5 Hay and Morisy, 1978, p. 258.

6 Hay, 1979, p. 166.

7 Hay, 1987, pp. 120–34.

8 See Bailey, 2000, pp. 85–8, for a discussion about the meaning of the phrase 'implicit religion'.

9 Bailey, 2002, p. 247.

10 Bailey, 1998, pp. 4–13.

11 Bailey, 1998, pp. 22–5.

12 Bailey, 1998, p. 33.

13 If one looks at the definition of religion in *Chambers Dictionary* ('belief in, recognition of or an awakened sense of a higher unseen controlling power or powers, with the emotion and morality connected with such; rites or worship; any system of such belief or worship; devoted fidelity; monastic life; a monastic order; Protestantism (*obs*)', the only sense in which Bailey might make his case is in the phrase 'devoted fidelity', but this is hardly the normal sense of the word.

14 Bailey's initial research was conducted in a pub in the 1970s.

15 Bailey, 1998, pp. 66–7.

16 Murray, 2002, p. 244.

17 Heald, 2000, p. 2.

18 Heelas and Woodhead, 2005, p. 98.

19 Heelas and Woodhead, 2005, p. x.

20 Heelas and Woodhead, 2005, p. 2.

21 Heelas and Woodhead, 2005, pp. 1–10.

22 These statistics are to be found in Table 3.1.

23 Heelas and Woodhead, 2005, p. 73. These are the statistics shown in Table 3.3. and also noted by De Graaf and Need (2000, p. 126) which were discussed in the previous chapter.

24 Heelas and Woodhead, 2005, p. 53.

25 Heelas and Woodhead, 2005, p. 107.

26 Heelas and Woodhead, 2005, p. 94.

27 Heelas and Woodhead, 2005, p. 107.

28 Roper, 1994; Barry *et al.*, 1996; and MacCulloch, 2004, pp. 563–75.

29 The presence of a wide range of alternative beliefs and practices are well documented in the literature, for example Lewis, 1975; Hole, 1980; Thomas, 1997; and Roud, 2003.

30 Spiritualism, at least in its modern form, started in 1848 in Hydesville in the USA and spread rapidly. It grew quickly in England after World War One. There are just 52,000 spiritualists in Britain today. I have been unable to find figures for previous periods, but anecdotal evidence suggests that it has declined significantly.

31 A Free Church writer from 1901 (*The British Weekly*, 24 December 1901), quoted by Gill, 2003, p. 203.

32 We should, however, be cautious about presuming that everybody is concerned about the purpose of life. *The European Values Study* asked people how often, if at all, they thought about the meaning and purpose of life. One-quarter (24.4%) replied 'often', 36.4% 'sometimes', 22.3% 'rarely', and 16.9% said that they never thought about it (Halman, 2001, p. 72).

33 Drane, 1991, p. 22.

34 See note 21 in Chapter 1.

35 Drane, 2004, p. 12.

36 See note 4 in Chapter 1.

37 Church of England's Mission and Public Affairs Council, 2004.

4

God-Shaped Mission:
Theological Reflections

We are living at a time when many people question the very credibility of the Christian faith and the worship of God is dismissed as outmoded and irrelevant. In some Christian quarters this has led to a loss of nerve. In the face of hostility it is tempting to retreat behind the theological barricades and either to justify God in terms of what he can do for us, or to turn faith and prayer into a sort of therapy. Contrary to those who see religion as the handmaid of inflexibility and intolerance, there is plenty of evidence to show that Christian belief makes a positive difference to the world. On the other hand, the worship of God is not to be reduced to the betterment of human society. In a speech in 2006 to the Royal Commonwealth Society, Charles Clarke MP spoke under the title 'Why I support religion to help British society'.[1] His notion that faith exists to bolster society is a novel one. The idea that belief is essentially utilitarian would have sounded bizarre to our grandparents, as if God exists merely in order to support the humanity enterprise.

'Man's chief end is to glorify God and to enjoy Him for ever', says the Westminster Shorter Catechism, written between 1642 and 1647. The reason God created humankind is not to bring in the kingdom of God or to make the world a better place, let alone create a mission-shaped Church. However desirable these things are, they are secondary and derivative. God created humankind for relationship; and it follows, therefore, that this can be the only theological basis of missiology. Without it there is a tendency to forget that the beginning and end of all things is God himself. In the words of St Augustine, 'On that day we shall see and we shall praise, we shall praise and we shall love in the end that has no end.'[2]

The danger with our current preoccupation to make the Church 'mission-shaped' is that we might take our eyes off God and shift our focus either to ourselves or to the Church. We are not called to worship

God *because* God makes a difference to the world. We are here first and foremost to know God and to be known by him, to love God and to be loved by him. Jesus Christ summed this up when he taught his followers that the first and greatest commandment is 'to love the Lord your God with all your heart, your mind, your soul and your strength'. The second (and corollary) commandment is to love your neighbour as yourself. Of course, the two commandments are intimately linked and elsewhere in the Gospels we see that they must not, and cannot, be separated; but it is noteworthy that he neither conflated nor confused them: the first commandment is to love God.

The being and acts of God

The main theological section of *Mission-Shaped Church* (Chapter 5) quotes a passage from an earlier Church of England Report, *Eucharistic Presidency*:

> Any theology of the church must ultimately be rooted in the being and acts of God: the church is first and foremost the people of God, brought into being by God, bound to God, for the glory of God.[3]

The quotation refers to two things: 'the being and the acts of God', but the report goes on to focus almost entirely on the second of these, 'the acts of God', the *missio Dei*, which is the guiding principle of *Mission-Shaped Church*. Two further paragraphs of *Eucharistic Presidency* are quoted with approval:

> Father, Son and Holy Spirit, who mutually indwell one another, exist in one another and for one another, in interdependent giving and receiving.[4]

and

> The communion of the persons of the Trinity is not to be understood as closed in on itself, but rather open in an outgoing movement of generosity. Creation and redemption are the overflow of God's triune life.[5]

The report develops a theology of mission by concentrating not on the 'being' of God as Trinity, but on the 'action' of God in creation and redemption. The stress on God's action in the world and the lack of any focus on the 'being of God' characterizes the approach of *Mission-Shaped Church* throughout. I am keen to support any attempt to help the Church become more mission-shaped, and have spent most of my ministry concerned with mission and evangelism, but to begin with an emphasis on action rather than on being places the focus on what the Church has to *do*, rather than on the way it needs to *be*. This, in turn, leads to an understanding of Christian life that is task-oriented and prioritizes activity: 'What I do for God', 'How I serve the Church', or 'How we work for the coming of God's kingdom'. Of course, being and doing are interlinked, and are not mutually exclusive modes. Nevertheless, being comes before doing; in other words, mission arises out of worship. Anything else tilts the focus of the Christian life and the Church in an unbalanced way towards activity. Indeed, this may be part of the reason why some sections of the Church appear to be driven (and even exhausted) by unhealthy, frenetic activism.

The book by Gaze entitled *Mission-Shaped and Rural* seems to come at the issue in the same way as *Mission-Shaped Church*:

> Practically speaking, 'We need to stop starting with the Church' and focus instead on God's mission.[6]

I would agree that we need to 'stop starting with the Church'. However, the essential starting point is not mission, but God himself. Not only do I think that the theology of *Mission-Shaped Church* needs to be rebalanced, but this is also one of the areas where I disagree with Hull's critique of the report. He believes that:

> for the church on earth . . . everything must be subordinate to mission. The church, as the report insists, is the body of Christ, the continuation of the incarnation of Christ, and worship does not represent a transcendental area immune from the concrete character of incarnation. In the life of the church militant, if worship becomes an end in itself, immune from the missionary nature of the church, it becomes a fetish. Worship is instrumental to mission.[7]

Hull is right to be critical of introspective Christian communities where certain forms of worship have been idolized or preserved in aspic to the detriment of the Church's mission. But he is wrong to suggest that worship occupies a subordinate place to mission and has merely an instrumental status. By definition, worship is focused on God, and in Christian understanding the vision of God is humanity's eternal destiny. The moment, therefore, ethics or mission predominate over doctrine and worship – or, to put it another way, the moment we allow the thought of humanity and the world to oust the thought of God from the primary place of honour – the whole missionary endeavour unravels. The basis of any theology of mission must be God himself. It is only when our lives are centred on God, when we know that we are loved and have been forgiven, that we are set free from our fears and find ourselves swept up in his divine mission of transformation and renewal. This theological perspective should inform and guide the way that we structure the Church for mission.

All Christian living and doing arises out of a sense of being caught up and transformed by the vision of God. Its wellspring is to be found in contemplation. This does not mean that Christians are content to sit all day praying in order to feel at peace with themselves. As Clement of Alexandria, writing in the third century, said, 'Most people are enclosed in their mortal bodies like a snail in its shell, curled up in their obsessions after the manner of hedgehogs. They form their notion of God's blessedness taking themselves for a model.'[8] True contemplation interrupts this cycle of self-obsession, and far from massaging our egos it can be deeply disturbing because it strips away self-delusion and confronts us with the world as God sees it, with the world therefore as it truly is. Far from fostering complacency in the face of (say) injustice or oppression, contemplation can lead us to concerted action; but it will always be activity focused and rooted in God's mission rather than something driven by our compulsions or subconscious fears.

Mission as the overflow of our encounter with God

The act of creation is God's supreme expression of love, but it is a very particular sort of creation that God is engaged in. Having created mankind he reveals just enough of himself so that those who seek him will find him, but does not reveal so much that a person is forced to follow him. This is the radical and fundamental freedom given to us by God. He invites us into relationship, into being with him. This experience of relationship in the Christian understanding precedes anything that we may do for him and is a necessary prelude to such activity because of its transformative power.

In this perspective, long before we are called to go out and participate in God's mission in the world (*missio Dei*), we are called to be immersed in the life of God himself. By participating in the dynamic of Jesus Christ's death and resurrection, we are enabled to live life fully or, to use Jesus' words as recorded in St John's Gospel, 'to live abundantly'.[9] We are summoned to life, delighting in the wonder of God and of his creation. In other words, before we can be a mission-shaped Church, we have to be God-shaped people. To find oneself being remade in the image and likeness of God is a prerequisite of reaching out to others. This is not to say that we have to be perfect before we can do or say anything. As is evident from the story of the first disciples, God is perfectly capable of using mustard seeds of faith, indifferent health, poor education, and indeed the holes in our personalities, to his glory. But unless we are constantly seeking the face of God, desiring to be re-made in his image, then we will have nothing distinctive to offer. Mission is the overflow of our encounter with God. Mission, therefore, is not our work, but God's.

Re-imagining mission in this way has profound implications. Above all, it protects us from obsessive activism and useless guilt-trips. For example, visiting a church recently I saw emblazoned across a T-shirt the words: 'Jesus is coming back soon: better get busy'. The gospel is about God's self-giving love for us as revealed in the death and resurrection of Jesus. It is no longer good news if it is an announcement of God's command for us to work for the coming of his kingdom (which sounds a very demanding and exhausting thing). Nor is it good news to be enlisted as missionaries or social activists. The good news is rather that each one of us is called into being by God, and as a consequence of this we find ourselves caught up in God's mission.

No one is left unchanged by this encounter. The love of God enfolds us and transforms us. It is, moreover, a particular sort of loving: not the so-called loving of an indulgent parent who is happy to let the child do whatever he or she wishes and lapse into selfishness; but rather that of a parent who wants the best for their children, who encourages them to explore every opportunity possible, who respects their integrity, and therefore also gives them broad parameters in which they are to live. This is the love 'so amazing, so divine, demands my soul, my life, my all'.[10] It is akin to Bonhoeffer's *costly grace*, which does not leave us unchanged but propels us outwards to others.

The generous and transformative power of the love of God that turns us outwards in the service of others is seen most clearly in the crucifixion itself. St Paul picks up on this theme when he declares that it was while we were enemies of God that Jesus Christ died for us.[11] Throughout his ministry Jesus was at pains to point out to his hearers that even pagans love their friends and families, but he was calling men and women to a more costly enterprise, a radical and extravagant loving modelled on that of God himself who 'causes his sun to shine on good and evil alike'.[12] One of the distinctive features of the Judeo-Christian tradition that Jesus enlarges upon is not only love for the stranger, the orphan and the widow, but pre-eminently love for one's enemies. To affirm that 'God is love' is to be a person concerned about the profound inequalities in the world; it is to treat each person as if he or she is uniquely created and loved by God; it is to be sent out in his name to meet 'the other'. This commitment to the poor and the outcast was one of the most striking hallmarks of the first Christians.

Extraordinary accounts of the altruism of Christians are to be found in the records of the Emperor Julian ('Julian the Apostate', AD 331–363). The empire had been Christian for barely 20 years and Julian wanted to take it back to paganism. To do this he attempted to set up charitable organizations to rival the Christians. In one of his letters he wrote to a commander on the ground as follows: 'It is disgraceful that all men should see our people lack aid from us, when no Jew has ever had to beg, and the impious Galileans [that is, the Christians] support not only their own poor, but ours as well.'[13] We find descriptions of Christian care in the works of St John Chrysostom (c. AD 347–407). In his de statuis he tells us that in the third century the church in Rome supported no less than 1,500 widows and 150 clergy. In his homilies he tells us that around AD 400 the church in Antioch supported about 3,00 virgins and widows and that the church in Constantinople financed the care of 50,000 poor people. Near Caesarea, Basil the Great (c. AD 337–379) organized a complete city of social service run by monks. The people gave it the nickname 'Basiliad'. It contained a guesthouse, a hospital, a refuge for the poor and homeless, an orphanage, a hospice for the elderly, and a school.

In examples such as these we catch the raw energy that is released within individuals and communities when we allow the grace of God to transform us. Dying and rising with Christ is not something that we can plan and implement: the only thing we can do is to offer ourselves. This prevents us from trying to build the Church in our own image and likeness so that the congregation becomes an extension of our ideas, hopes or fears. It is not unusual to hear people talk about 'my church' or 'our church' as if it is something that can be possessed. It is only when there has been a dying and a rising with Christ that we are set free to allow God to build his own Church in his own way. This way of *kenosis,* of self-emptying, is a challenge both to those who claim that the Church can never change or evolve, and to those who are so convinced that they are right, and know what God wants, that they are unmoved if those who disagree with them leave the Church.

The relationship between the Church and the kingdom

The debate about *Mission-Shaped Church* has been helped by the booklet written by Hull who offers a critique of its theology and, as he puts it, seeks to correct the theological weaknesses of the report.[14] He points out that the report does not maintain a clear distinction between the Church and the mission of God. He asks 'whether the church is the object of the mission or whether, on the other hand, the church is better regarded as a servant or instrument of the mission'.[15] He answers the question by arguing that 'the church is agent and the Kingdom is goal'[16] and develops this theme by pointing out that, 'The missiology of *Mission-Shaped Church* would have been clearer if it had consistently maintained the view that the church is an instrument or an agent of the mission of God, the outcome of which is to be the Kingdom of God':

> The empirical church is one of the principal agents of this mission; it is one of God's saving projects for the redemption of the world. The church is thus called to participate in the mission of Jesus who proclaimed the coming of the Kingdom in his life, his words, and his deeds, and who died and rose again to establish the church as an agent of that Kingdom. The church is a mission project, not the mission itself; the Kingdom of God is the object of the mission, and the life of Jesus Christ continues to be manifest through the church as it witnesses to, embodies and proclaims the Kingdom. [17]

I broadly agree with this criticism and think the report would have been helped by a more consistent use of terms. However, to say that the Church is *only* 'an instrument' or 'an agent' is to espouse a minimalist ecclesiology that represents only one strand of the more richly textured understanding of the Church to be found both in parts of the New Testament (such as Ephesians and Colossians) and, for example, in the Second Vatican Council document on the Church, *Lumen Gentium.* Here the Church is seen as 'a sacrament, sign and instrument of community with God and unity among people'.

The Church is indeed 'an outward and visible sign' of the transformative power of God at work in his world. It is one that, like John the Baptist himself, must always draw people not to itself, but to the Christ we serve. Only in this way can we be an effective instrument of his healing and reconciling love. It is why we need kingdom-oriented churches in as many communities as possible and kingdom-oriented Christians in as many work and leisure places as possible. Therefore, a significant responsibility of Christian leaders is to ensure that there are healthy churches that are working for the coming of the kingdom. At a time when the Church is facing decline, one of our tasks is to find ways of encouraging the Church to grow, not because growth is an end in itself, or because we want the kudos of running a more powerful or wealthy institution, or because we confuse the Church with the kingdom, but so that we can be more effective in bringing in the kingdom.

Some years ago I worked in a deanery where there was a dedicated priest serving in a run-down urban parish. He gave himself to the people sacrificially, to the extent that he sometimes made himself ill. He would often emphasize that he was not interested in the Church, which he saw as a sinful human institution. He claimed his inspiration was the kingdom, which he spoke about with great passion. Over his years the congregation dwindled to five or six people, and when he moved he was not replaced and the building was closed, since there was hardly any congregation left and the church was in debt. What was so sad was that he had not been able to draw others into the vision of the kingdom and build up a congregation to ensure that the work went on after he left. A fundamental part of the role of the parish priest is to lead and nurture a congregation of believers who are committed to working for the coming of the kingdom.

Hull argues, rightly, that the kingdom of God is more than the Church and that the gospel is more than an invitation to become a member of the Church. Indeed, his critique calls to mind Loisey's laconic observation, 'Jesus preached the coming of the Kingdom, and the church arrived.' The church is not a club. The New Testament is clear that God's purposes are for the whole created order.[18] Yet even a cursory reading of the New Testament reveals that what inspired and motivated the early Christians was the hope of the imminent arrival of the kingdom of God: God's rule and reign was breaking into world history. The Church was an agent or instrument of God's mission. It was not, in itself, the fullness of the good news: only a sign of it. Nevertheless, the Church as agent of the kingdom needs to be renewed and sustained in each generation. This is the concern of the *Mission-Shaped Church* report.

Transformed by love

How do we incarnate the transforming love of God among the people with whom we live and work? On the Day of Pentecost we are told that the believers were inspired by the Holy Spirit to live out the message of the kingdom, energized by the apostolic teaching, worship, breaking bread and sharing their possessions:

> They devoted themselves to the apostle's teaching and fellowship, to the breaking of bread and prayers. Awe came upon everyone, because many wonders and signs were being done by the apostles. All who believed were together and had all things in common; they would sell their possessions and goods and distribute the proceeds to all, as any had need. Day by day, as they spent time together in the temple, they broke bread at home and ate their food with glad and generous hearts, praising God and having the goodwill of all the people. And day by day the Lord added to their number those who were being saved.[19]

Later on in the missionary journeys of St Paul, we can see how this worked out in other places and contexts. In response to the guidance of the Holy Spirit,[20] Paul made his way through Asia Minor preaching a message that God had raised Jesus Christ from the dead. He too set out to form groups of believers, who were initiated through baptism. They also met regularly to worship, break bread and to share their lives and possessions. They cared for the widows and the orphans[21] and loved their enemies (which was their mission). They were passionate about inviting others to join this new way of living (which was their evangelism). Their corporate life was both a foretaste and a sign of the kingdom of God which they expected to arrive at any moment.

Hopkins,[22] reflecting on a book by Hirsch and Frost, identifies three modes or ways in which churches join in with God's missionary endeavour. He calls them attractional church, engaged church and emerging church. *Attractional church* focuses on Jesus' invitation to 'come', which stresses the importance of welcoming people into the life of the worshipping community. *Engaged church* is based on Jesus' instruction to 'go', and to get involved in service in the local community. However, as people are engaged with what is going on they are then invited to come to church.[23] The third category of *emerging church* is also based on the principle of 'go' and is about listening to and getting immersed in the community. Here people are not invited to come to an existing church, but instead are helped and supported in the process of becoming a new indigenous faith community, which is appropriate to the culture of that group or community. This is an example of 'incarnating the transforming love of God'.

This concept is also useful in countering some of the clichés that recur when writing about mission and evangelism. We are often told that we must move from maintenance to mission as if these were two mutually exclusive modes of operation. Yet the moment a group of believers gather together they have to think about how they are to care for one another and for the stranger. When the apostles appointed deacons in Acts 6 to look after the widows, this was an integral part of their mission. In other words, they had to live out the gospel principles among themselves as well as among unbelievers. The important thing about maintenance is to review it regularly to ensure that we are maintaining things for the extension and growth of the kingdom and not as ends in themselves.

The concept of 'incarnating the transforming love of God' also helps us avoid the false distinction between 'come' (sometimes used of the old model of evangelism and mission) with 'go' (which is claimed to be the biblical, mission-shaped approach). Both 'come' and 'go' are imperatives used by Jesus Christ himself. Two sets of words are used to describe the calling and mission of the first disciples: 'Come and see' and 'Go and tell'. Twice in the opening discourse of John's Gospel we hear the words 'Come and see': first from the lips of Jesus himself, and then from Philip in response to Nathaniel's cynicism. 'Can anything good come out of Nazareth?' 'Come and see,' says Philip in reply. Later we hear of John the Baptist dispatching some of his disciples to sound out Jesus. Is this man the genuine messiah or should they look for another? To their inquiry Jesus replies, 'Go and tell John what you see and hear: the blind receive their sight, the lame walk, the lepers are cleansed, the deaf hear, the dead are raised, the poor have good news brought to them. And blessed is anyone who takes no offence at me.'[24] These pairs of words correspond to the rhythm of contemplation and action we have been outlining. We need first to 'come and see', to be in Jesus' presence and be transformed by his life and love, so that we embody the kingdom in our shared life; and empowered by that encounter we can then 'go and tell' others the good news of his kingdom and invite them to discover it for themselves, in culturally appropriate ways. Lings argues that there is a similar mission dynamics to be found in the Acts of the Apostles, which he calls 'concentration and spread'. He argues that God gathers resources partly to disperse them more widely than before.[25]

This same dynamic is found in the Hopkins's category of 'emerging church'. I presume that Hopkins does not think that in an emerging church newcomers and fringe people should not be invited ('come') to the new socially involved, culturally relevant church that has been formed. Any group of believers who have been caught up in a vision of how God is working in the world will not be able to stop inviting those around them to come, and will also want to 'go and tell'.

Kingdom-focused evangelism

The sort of mission and evangelism that I have outlined above is firmly rooted in Jesus' teaching about the kingdom of God. Evangelism in the New Testament is not about creating an inward-looking, pietistic Church, serving its own interests. Authentic evangelism is always looking outwards, seeking to draw more and more people into the kingdom way of living. It does this by calling them to forsake their old way of living and values, and adopting a new life, modelled on Jesus Christ's example of self-giving love. Empowered by the Holy Spirit, the believers both model kingdom-living and work for the coming of the kingdom, and in so doing become both its sign and sacrament.

Having set out a biblical model of mission and evangelism, I turn now to look at some concrete examples of the mission and evangelism that are to be found in the countryside.

Notes

1 Reported in the *Church Times*, 24 November 2006.
2 *City of God*, XXII, 30.
3 Church of England's Mission and Public Affairs Council, 2004, p. 84.
4 Church of England's Mission and Public Affairs Council, 2004, pp. 84–5.

5 Church of England's Mission and Public Affairs Council, 2004, p. 85.

6 Gaze, 2006, p. 3. To be fair to Gaze, this section in her book is about the Church and she is not setting out to offer a comprehensive theological justification for being 'mission-shaped'.

7 Hull, 2006, p. 27.

8 *Miscellanies*, V, 11.

9 John 10.10.

10 From Wesley's hymn 'When I survey the wond'rous cross'.

11 Romans 5.8.

12 Matthew 5.45.

13 Letter 22.

14 Hull, 2006, p. x.

15 Hull, 2006, p. 1.

16 Hull, 2006, p. 3.

17 Hull, 2006, p. 5.

18 Ephesians 1.8–10.

19 Acts 2.42–47.

20 Acts 13.1–3; 16.6–10; Romans 15.19.

21 1 Corinthians 16.1–4.

22 http://www.acpi.org.uk/stories/5%20Making%20sense%20of%20emerging%20church.htm.

23 Hopkins cites Morisy's book, *Journeying Out* (2004), as a good example of engaged church.

24 Luke 7.22–23.

25 Lings, 2006, pp. 24–8.

Part 2

Mission and Evangelism in Rural Areas

Examples of Mission-Shaped Church in the Countryside

5

Innovation, Celebration and Service

There can be no doubt that *Mission-Shaped Church* is generating considerable energy across the Church of England and beyond it to engage with our culture in new and imaginative ways. It is disturbing complacency and stimulating innovation, and creating a 'can do' culture in the Church that is long overdue. All this is to be welcomed. However, there are dangers as well as challenges that we need to be alert to, in particular that the entire theological enterprise that this is sponsoring may end up inadvertently colluding with the worst parts of our individualistic consumerist culture and, in a perverse way, actually justifying the status quo rather than transforming it. *Mission-Shaped Church* could become a tool for weary church leaders, rationalizing what is going on under the banner of something new and exciting because it looks as if it has a coherent theological rationale underlying it.

Ministry among young people provides us with just such a case in point. It is not easy to involve young people in the worshipping life of the Church, particularly where congregations are predominantly middle-aged or elderly clubs for the like-minded, who have fallen into the trap of looking after their own interests. This is nothing new, and has been around for at least the past 50 years. Some of the examples of mission-shaped Church suggest that it is so difficult that we should not even attempt to integrate young people into traditional congregations. Instead we should encourage them to meet together in their own groups to worship in their own way. The risk of this approach is that such groups may get trapped into the same dynamic of the more traditional congregations, existing for the benefit of those who already attend, of the 'like minded', rather than being a congregation with a vision for the coming of the kingdom that seeks to embrace all people and is an agent for transformation in the world. Where there are congregations that cater exclusively or predominantly for young people (or indeed, the elderly), there is a need for them to be taught about the catholicity of the Church and that they are just one expression of Church among many.

What is already going on?

In the chapters that follow I want to share examples of good practice and innovative work in the rural Church in the hope that it may spark others to think 'outside the box' and have the courage to experiment and take risks. It is commonplace to caricature the countryside and its worshipping communities as uniformly dull and sterile. In reality, there is considerable energy and imagination in many rural church communities that deserves to be affirmed and celebrated by a wider public. Despite the decline in rural church life, it would be wrong to give the impression that rural churches have not been concerned with mission and evangelism. During the 1990s the magazine *Country Way* featured numerous examples of rural mission, such as lunch clubs for the elderly, and chaplaincy to the agricultural community. It also featured many instances of rural evangelism, as part of the Decade of Evangelism, such as pub breakfasts (both for men and for women), the JIM (Jesus in Me) Project, 'From Minus to Plus' (delivering a booklet to every house around Easter) and 'On Fire' (organizing Pentecost parties).

Alongside these initiatives, rural churches, like urban churches, have used process evangelism courses, such as Alpha, Emmaus, Start and Credo. The anecdotal evidence is that these work better in commuter villages where there are professional people, rather than in the more remote rural areas still inhabited by villagers who have lived in the same place for many decades.

In order to write this book I have collated material from four sources: the Fresh Expressions website, the responses of diocesan rural officers and missioners, the responses to a request for information about fresh expressions in the *Church Times*, and the Mission Action Plans from the Shrewsbury Episcopal Area for which I am responsible.

The Fresh Expressions website has provided the most extensive list.[1] Of the 535 examples of fresh expressions registered in October 2006, 88 identified themselves as 'rural' (15%). Fifty-six of the rural fresh expressions were Anglican (64%), 22 were Methodist (25%), one was United Reformed Church (1%) and nine were 'ecumenical' or 'not affiliated' (10%). Since there are more Anglican and Methodist churches in rural areas than other denominations, and since this website is sponsored by the Anglican and Methodist Churches, it is not surprising that there are fewer examples from other Christian denominations.

The second largest source of material came as a result of placing a notice in the *Church Times* (which was also circulated on the Missioners' Mailing and the Rural Officers' mailing). This attracted 56 responses in letters and emails, mainly from practitioners in parishes around the country.

Those who registered their fresh expression of church on the website or who contacted me were a self-selecting group. It is clear from their responses that there exists a wide diversity in what people consider to be a fresh expression of church. The website did not offer any definitions, but provided a number of categories, some of which were overlapping. It was left to each person who wished to add an entry to decide if they qualified and also to choose which categories best described what they were doing. I encountered the same problem with some of the correspondents who contacted me personally. Some of the examples that I collected from both sources could clearly be described as fresh expressions of church, whereas others described activities that my training incumbent was doing when I was a curate 25 years ago, such as a midweek Parents and Toddlers Group with informal worship, and far from being innovative was simply considered to be part of the normal life of a church. Clearly, for that particular church what they were describing was a fresh expression of church for them.

Other entries detailed new initiatives, but it is not clear to me that they were 'church', except in the loosest definition (such as holding discussion groups for enquirers or running a residential centre that offered counselling). What this illustrates is that there are not two clear-cut groups, 'traditional' and 'fresh expressions/emerging church'. Rather, it is more helpful to view the rural Church as a wide spectrum with 'traditional' at one end and 'fresh expressions' at the other. In the middle there is a large swathe of churches who are experimenting with all sorts of groups, services, venues, styles and networks. For the sake of this book (and in order to offer a full as possible description of what is going on in rural communities), I have erred on the side of generosity of definition.

Third, I examined the Mission Action Plans[2] produced by the Anglican churches in the Shrewsbury Episcopal Area. Having launched Mission Action Plans in 2003, I have now seen in the region of 150, of which 103 were from rural churches, many in their second or third annual revisions. A number of the plans give examples of alternative worship and innovative youth and children's work that would fall within the definition of fresh expressions. I identified eight examples of what could be broadly described as rural fresh expressions of church in north Shropshire. Only two of these featured were on the Fresh Expressions website, which indicates that there are probably large numbers of new initiatives that are not formally recorded anywhere in the public domain.

As part of my research I phoned a number of people who were running fresh expressions of church in rural areas. One evening I spoke to a woman who told me: 'After six years, next Sunday will our last monthly meeting.' She described how she and her husband had become Christians in a small village. They lived near the Anglican church, which was part of a multi-parish benefice of 11 churches, staffed by a stipendiary parish priest and a non-stipendiary priest. They were aware of the gap between what went on in the worship of the church and many of the non-churchgoing people in the area and wondered how they could make Christianity more accessible. The clergy encouraged them to try something and they were helped by four other Christians who belonged to a large evangelical church in the nearby town. Using their own home, they ran study groups, two Alpha courses and 'Hot Potatoes' – an evening of food with discussion about topical issues. 'Hot Potatoes' eventually came to an end, but out of the experience came the idea of regular meetings in a public venue. They started to meet in the dining room of a local pub, chosen because it was central to all the villages. From this arose a monthly evening of music, discussion, food and praise. They found that most of those who came were Christians who were struggling with the worship in their home congregations, some of whom travelled long distances in order to attend. Many of them valued these meetings, since they offered an important time of personal reflection. Some people even started holding similar events in their home churches. However, hardly anyone from the existing congregations in the 11 village churches supported the meetings and some of them actually felt threatened by them. After much prayer it was decided that after six years it was time for the meetings to cease. Engaging in mission-shaped Church is not always about success stories, in the sense that an initiative will continue for ever. Sometimes it is about setting out in faith and seeking to discern what God is saying as we travel. Mission-shaped Church is sometimes part of a much longer process as we learn by doing, and then moving on.

'Fresh expressions' in rural areas

The national Fresh Expressions website invites people to describe what they are doing. The respondents are offered 14 different categories[3] to describe their activities and they are allowed to tick as many categories as they wish. The 88 rural entries between them ticked 150 boxes and gave some indication of how the leaders described what they were doing:

1	Alternative worship community	18
2	Base ecclesial community	2
3	Café church	15
4	Cell church	7
5	Children's fresh expression	21
6	Church arising out of community initiatives	12
7	Fresh expressions for under-5s	11
8	Multiple and midweek congregations	20
9	Network-focused church	7
10	School-based and school-linked congregations and churches	6
11	Seeker church	5
12	Traditional church plants	2
13	Traditional forms of church inspiring new interest	7
14	Youth congregations	18

What does this tell us? The responses can be grouped together in a variety of ways, some of which overlap. However, two areas emerge as the most significant. First, there is a cluster of initiatives that are specifically focused on children and young people. Adding together children's fresh expressions, fresh expressions for the under-5s, school-based and school-linked congregations and churches, and youth congregations, we have 56 ticks (37%), indicating that this is the area that is generating the greatest level of activity. Second, there is a concentration on new styles of worship, such as alternative worship communities and café church (33 ticks or 22%). These two areas were also the most commonly featured by my correspondents and from the Mission Action Plans that I examined.

What is significant are the areas that have been developed least. Only five rural churches indicated that they have started seeker services. Such services require a high level of organization and input, as well as the need to be able to attract a group of people who want to explore the Christian faith, and it may be more difficult in rural areas where the population is smaller, transport is more difficult, and there are fewer facilities. Only two churches have undertaken traditional church plants, perhaps because there are already so many church buildings and congregations in rural areas. It is not surprising, therefore, to discover that more energy has been put into developing new congregations in existing church buildings (20 fresh expressions ticked the multiple and midweek congregations box). Just seven churches indicated that they were developing network churches, which may reflect the difficulty of developing such churches when the networks are much smaller due to lower population density in rural areas.

Two rural churches have developed base ecclesial communities. This is a very specific sort of initiative, inspired by the liberation theology movement of South America, which works among poor and marginalized urban communities. *Mission-Shaped Church* cites the example of the church in Davenport and the principle of 'learning by doing' which resulted in the provision of a yacht for disadvantaged young people. Clearly this has been a worthwhile project, although it is questionable whether it is really an example of a base ecclesial community in the sense that it is commonly used in South America. While base ecclesial communities may be appropriate and possible in some poor urban settings, this has not taken off in rural England in any significant way.

Analysis of the data reveals a striking difference between rural and urban areas. In urban areas there were a number of examples where pioneer missioners (sometimes accompanied by a group of other Christians) had moved into an area. They were not given charge of an existing congregation or chaplaincy and may not have even been given the use of a church building. With the minimum of guidance they have begun to listen to, and relate to, an unchurched group of people in a variety of ways and to allow a new style of worshipping community to emerge.[4] In most cases a full-time church planter has been financed by either the Anglican or Methodist Church. Examples include Sanctus 1 in Manchester,[5] Church without Walls in Stoke-on-Trent,[6] Safe Space in Telford,[7] and Eden in Steyning.[8]

There are not many similar initiatives in rural areas, which partly reflects the different social context of the Church. First, in urban areas there may be several generations of people who are almost totally unchurched. They may not have even been into a church for a funeral because in urban areas the vast majority of these take place at the crematorium. By contrast, in rural areas many churches still have considerable contact with most of the population through the occasional offices and the Christian festivals. It is not unusual for a church in a small village to have seen 30–40% of the villagers in church over the Christmas period. Many rural areas are not starting with a 'blank sheet', since most people have a closer connection with the church. Warren, writing of the tension between parish-church versus gathered-church, makes an interesting point when he suggests that on the rural/urban axis 'it is soon evident that rural churches find it easier to be engaged and more difficult to be distinctive, whilst urban churches often find it easier to be distinctive yet more difficult to be engaged'.[9] When a church in a rural area takes a stance on a controversial issue, it risks alienating people of goodwill who live in the village and support the church, even if they do not attend very often.

Second, and allied to this first point, research shows that levels of social capital are higher in the countryside than in urban areas.[10] In recent years most Western governments, not least our own here in Britain, have been concerned about the apparent decline in social capital, a concept that is not easy to define,[11] but that basically relates to levels of mutual trust and support in society. Research shows that Christians are major contributors to social capital. For example, Gill has questioned the way that some sociologists have interpreted the data about the difference that churchgoing makes to people's attitudes and behaviour. Based on the data from the British Household Panel Surveys and the British Social Attitudes Surveys, he concluded that:

> The mass of new data shows that churchgoers are indeed distinctive in their attitudes and behaviour. Some of their attitudes do change over time, especially on issues such as sexuality, and there are obvious moral disagreements between different groups of churchgoers in a number of areas. Nevertheless, there are broad patterns of Christian beliefs, teleology and altruism which distinguish churchgoers as a whole from nonchurchgoers. It has been seen that churchgoers have, in addition to their distinctive theistic and christocentric beliefs, a strong sense of moral order and concern for other people. They are, for example, more likely than others to be involved in voluntary service and to see overseas charitable giving as important. They are more hesitant about euthanasia and capital punishment and more concerned about the family and civic order than other people. None of these differences is absolute. The values, virtues, moral attitudes and behaviour of churchgoers are shared by other people as well. The distinctiveness of churchgoers is real but relative.[12]

A recent study, sponsored by the Department for Environment, Food and Rural Affairs (DEFRA), illustrates the wide variety of ways in which rural churches contribute to their local community.[13] The social dynamics in rural areas are quite different from those in most urban areas. Therefore, at a time when many facilities and social services are being withdrawn from the countryside, it is clear that there is an increasingly important role for the churches to play.

Third, in an urban area there may be numerous subcultures and networks among which it is possible to plant a church. In contrast, rural areas with much smaller populations will not have sufficient people with the same interests or concerns to start a group: typically there may be only one or two people who have problems with addiction, mental health or who wish to attend a parenting class. In the countryside, where public transport is minimal and roads are not as good, the only way this might be done is by working across a benefice, a team ministry or even a whole deanery, but this may make it unviable.

The Fresh Expressions website reveals that most examples of new ways of 'being church' in the countryside are much more modest in their aims and operate on a mixed-economy approach. The majority of them, to use Hopkins's categories again, are of the 'attractional' and 'engaging' type of mission. Many of them are running worship in alternative venues, or at more convenient times, or using contemporary styles of music and worship. In the following three chapters we look at some specific examples of rural fresh expressions of church and reflect on them.

Notes

1 www.freshexpressions.org.uk/index.asp?id=1. Fresh Expressions is an initiative sponsored by the Church of England and the Methodist Church.

2 Mission Action Plans are described more fully in Chapter 13.

3 These were the 12 categories used in *Mission-Shaped Church* (Church of England's Mission and Public Affairs Council, 2004, pp. 43–83), along with two new ones: children's fresh expressions and fresh expressions for the under-5s.

4 As described by Hopkins (not dated) in Chapter 4.

5 www.sanctus1.co.uk.

6 www.churchwow.co.uk.

7 www.wayoutwest.co.uk.

8 www.edenzone.com.

9 Warren, 1995, p. 29.

10 See note 22 in Chapter 1.

11 Bourdieu (1985, p. 248) suggested the definition: 'the aggregate of the actual or potential resources which are linked to possession of a durable network of more or less institutionalized relationships of mutual acquaintance or recognition'. Hall

(1993, p. 167) defined it as 'the propensity of individuals to associate together on a regular basis, to trust one another, and to engage in community affairs', while Putnam has offered several different definitions, such as 'features of social organization, such as trust, norms, and networks, that can improve the efficiency of society by facilitating coordinated actions' (1996, p. 34), 'features of social life – networks, norms, and trust – that enable participants to act more effectively to pursue shared objectives' (1999, p. 417) and 'connections among individuals – social networks and the norms of reciprocity and trustworthiness that arise from them' (2000, p. 19).

12 Gill, 1999, p. 197. Gill has pointed out that a number of polls (e.g. BBC, 1955, and ABC, 1965) showed a clear correlation between churchgoing and attitudes (Gill, 1999, pp. 38–40). This has been backed up by a European Values Systems Study Group Survey, Abrams *et al.*, 1985, pp. 50–92, Francis, 1982, and Francis and Kay, 1995.

13 Farnell *et al.*, 2006. See also Smith, 2004, pp. 193–213, and Falk and Kilpatrick, 2000, pp. 87–110.

6

Children and Young People

Over the past century the Church of England has seen a massive decline in the number of children and young people with whom it has contact. Table 6.1 shows that the number of babies being brought for baptism has fallen from 65% of live births in 1900 to 21% in 2000. Over the same period the number of children who attend Sunday Schools has dropped from 55% of the population to 4%,[1] and the number of young people being confirmed, singing in church choirs, bell ringing or attending church youth groups has also declined. The reasons for this are complex and there is no consensus over the causes. However, it is clear that young people ('Generation Y') today see themselves and the world very differently from older people ('Generation X' and the 'Baby Boomer Generation')[2] and that a major part of the task of fresh expressions is to listen intently to them and to discover how to communicate and share the gospel in culturally appropriate ways.[3]

Table 6.1 Church of England baptisms, 1900–2000.

	Live births in England	Church of England infant baptisms	Percentage
1900	865,135	564,364	65.2
1920	887,490	603,947	67.8
1940	567,710	365,075	64.3
1960	740,858	411,650	55.6
1980	618,371	226,450	36.6
2000	572,826	122,000	21.3

Source: Voas, 2003.

The fall in the number of children and young people in the Church will have long-term consequences. Francis, in a study of 4,948 11-year-olds, found that even when children have a nominal connection with a denomination (such as those who were baptized as children but have not habitually attended church), they had a more positive attitude towards Christianity than those children who have had no denominational connections.[4] Conversely, those who have had little or no contact with the Church are less likely to become believers and churchgoers in their adult years.

When we try to envisage the future of Christianity in rural areas, it is relevant to recall the statistics quoted in Chapter 1 – namely, that the number of young people in the countryside, from birth to 14, is increasing, while the number of 15- to 24-year-olds is decreasing. This trend is likely to continue and has implications for work with young people and for church schools. It is encouraging therefore to know that it is in this area of children's and youth work where most fresh expressions appear to be taking place in both the Anglican and the Methodist churches.

Listening to parents and children

Most of those churches that are working successfully with young people have spent time listening to them and to their parents. The average churchgoer does not have young children (especially in rural areas where he or she is more likely to be in the sixties age group and older), so it is easy to lose touch with the expectations of the younger generation. It is no good congregations presuming that children will behave in church in the same way that their grandparents did 50 years ago. Parents and children today have far higher expectations about quality of the welcome, the worship and the after-service care.

> I heard of one church that wanted to develop its work with young families and children. It decided that the best place to start was by listening to as many parents and children as possible. The church members soon realized that there was a great many different concerns, although these fell broadly into two groups. Some of the parents (and particularly the mothers) wanted to discuss issues of

parenting, including such things as potty training and discipline. As a result they brought in experts to run discussion groups. The second group was comprised of those who quite liked the idea of coming to church, but found it impossible to keep their children quiet. It was difficult to arrive in a large, strange building and expect their youngsters to settle down immediately to worship. At the suggestion of one of the parents, they put on drinks and refreshments before church and created a play area. This gave the children time to run around and use up some of their spare energy. They could meet the other children, ask questions about the building, and not be told to keep quiet. Once they felt relaxed and at home, two teachers, who were members of the congregation, gathered the children together and helped them to calm down and be still, so that the worship could begin. This proved to be a much better arrangement for both the parents and the children and was successful at helping families become part of the worshipping community.

Toddlers

Many churches have run groups for toddlers and their parents. Some of these are simply social groups, meeting on church premises, that offer support for parents and their toddlers, and as such they are an important expression of care, fulfilling a valuable role. However, some churches have tried to develop these groups, drawing on insights from fresh expressions, so that they 'become church' in their own right, with worship, teaching and outreach as an integral part of the programme.

Woodstock, situated just to the north of Oxford, is, as someone put it, 'a small town with a rural mentality'. Some years previously the Parish Church of St Mary Magdalene had organized Pram Services, but they had ceased and for some time the church was not running any activities for young children during the week. An opportunity presented itself when new church rooms were opened. Celia Humphreys gathered together a group of eight young mums to discuss what they would like to do. They decided they wanted to meet weekly on Friday mornings during term time for one and a half hours and call it the Buggy Club. Some older people were recruited to help with refreshments and to be a listening ear. Contacts were made via friends and also through the ante-natal clinic at the local GP practice.

Nowadays, dad, mums, grandparents and carers bring their under-3s to the sessions which include Christian stories, craft and songs, and on average 27 families attend each week. There is even a Buggy Club prayer which most people know by heart. The group is not just for the benefit of those who attend. For example, they have encouraged people to prepare shoeboxes to be distributed via Operation Christmas Child.

Some of the parents see the Buggy Club as their church. However, it also acts as a bridge to the church's main Sunday worship and in particular to the monthly family service, at which between eight and ten new couples have started to attend regularly. It also provides a way into the Alpha course. Several of those who come to Buggy Club have been on courses and some are also helping to run them. There is a constant stream of requests for baptisms and three couples have been married in the church.

The Fresh Expressions website lists a number of groups for pre-school children, similar to the Buggy Club. One of the features of a fresh expression of church is that it should not be seen simply as a stepping stone into the main Sunday morning worship, but should be an authentic church in its own right, meeting at a different time and in a different place. The Buggy Club has moved part way along this path. However, this raises an important question. What happens when the children go to school and no longer attend the pre-school group? Will the parents and children continue to worship in some way and be shaped by the gospel or will they stop 'being church'? This question, of course, is not a criticism of the Buggy Club *per se*, since it is a dynamic that affects many groups.

When I was a curate in Yorkshire we had four women's groups in the parish. Members of the Townsend Women's Fellowship were all aged in their late seventies and eighties. The group had been formed 60 years earlier and members had grown old together. There was the daytime Mothers' Union whose members were aged in their fifties and sixties, and the evening Mothers' Union group for working mothers in their thirties and forties. During my curacy there was concern that the young women in the parish were not joining the evening Mothers' Union group, since they felt that they did not have much in common, so they decided to form a young wives' group. Essentially each of the four groups comprised women of similar ages and interests who, on the rare occasion they recruited new members, attracted like-minded people. The three groups for older women lamented the lack of willingness of younger women to join them, since their main concern was the interests and concerns of the existing members.

Returning to the question of work with young people, one of the most difficult challenges for church leaders is to reflect on how the parents and children will be helped and supported to enter into another, culturally appropriate, fresh expression of church when their children are too old for the group. In discussions with church leaders, I found that a number of them are acutely aware of this issue, although no one appears to have developed a strategy to address it.

Children

Ministry with children in the countryside is demanding. In a typical rural congregation it is not easy to find volunteers to lead it and the situation has been made more difficult by the legislation on child protection which requires at least two adults to be present. For many village churches, finding even *one* suitable and willing volunteer to work with the two or three children is challenging enough.

Since there are only a tiny number of children in each age range, it is often difficult to form groups that have enough children to make them viable. One experienced country vicar commented that work with young people goes in cycles. You have to watch out for groups of toddlers, children or youngsters of a particular age and attempt to build the work around them. Once they grow older the group may close and it is important not to feel a failure if there is a period with no youth work. Another alternative for rural churches is to think in terms of running children's or youth work across a united benefice, or even a whole deanery, in order to have a large enough pool of young people to work with.

The Wrockwardine Deanery sits between Shrewsbury and Telford and is a team ministry, led by a team rector and served by two team vicars, a curate, four readers (one of whom is also a prayer guide) and two retired clergy. There are 13 Anglican churches in the deanery, one of which is a Local Ecumenical Project with the Methodist Church. Following a period of extensive consultation, it was decided that the priority was to develop work among families and young people. The objective for the first year was 'to improve the outreach amongst primary age children', in the second year the objective was 'to encourage whole family worship' and in the third year 'to encourage the integration of secondary school age children in our churches' life'. In order to achieve this, three things were set up: *Pathway People* is a parent and toddlers group that meets alternate Monday afternoons in Longdon on Tern village hall. This builds on the work of the groups for even younger children called 'Pushchair People'. At each meeting different themes are explored using Powerpoint presentations, songs, crafts and Bible stories. Sometimes some form of action is taken – for example, on one occasion each individual was involved in writing letters to people in different parts of the world. The emphasis is on getting everyone involved and participating. *The King's Club* has two parts. The Tuesday group meets immediately after school and is for children aged five to eight. It attracts about 24 children. The Wednesday group involves about 18 young people aged nine to eleven. Both groups have a relaxed atmosphere and are highly participative, using puppets, DVDs and practical activities including games, crafts, prayer, singing and dancing. The team also runs an annual summer children's club for five- to eleven-year-olds over three mornings, culminating in a celebration on the final Sunday in

Rodington Church, in co-operation with the Methodists. Themes in past years have included Fun and Fair (2004 and 2005), Narnia Day (2006) and Xpedition Force (2006). Among other things, the programme incorporated puppets, story telling, singing, and visiting attractions. Fundamental to the week is the follow-up programme, linking with parents and carers. A team of about 20 helpers have been trained to lead it and it is hoped that they will eventually take over the leadership from the clergy, and even expand the programme further.

The Wrockwardine Deanery is one of many places that has found that clubs and workshops often work well during the school holidays and that it is possible to draw together children from a whole deanery. Years ago, there were fewer midweek activities for children, so the church found it relatively easy to run regular meetings during term time. Now, especially in some of the commuter villages, the children are rushing round from music lessons to football to dance classes, and the church finds itself in a highly competitive market. In many families both parents are working and it is often easier to engage with children during the holidays. Activity days, for example, on Good Friday, have growing in popularity since there may be nothing else organized for the children on that day. Indeed, I have heard of one church that has stopped running children's work during the school term and now concentrates on activities and worship during the Christmas, Easter and summer school holidays.

Young people

For many years we have known that, as young people grow older, fewer of them maintain regular contact with the Church. In his book *Rural Anglicanism*, Francis concluded that 'the rural Anglican church is still able to recruit young people after the age of five, [but] it tends to lose them again by the age of thirteen'.[5] He went on to summarize the problems facing Anglican churches working with young people:

. . . the problems of attracting young people to take Christianity seriously in the first place; the extent of other attractions that are competing for the young person's attention; the churches may be operating with out-of-date education theory and old-fashioned curriculum materials compared with schools; the lack of people with the professional skills and the time to work with the children; the lack of financial resources, most of which are directed in maintaining the historic church building; and the lack of appropriate plant from which to operate.[6]

The Church of England report *Faith in the Countryside* also observed the problems of youth work in rural churches and found that many felt that they were failing because they could not run the sort of youth work that is common in urban areas. They were often

overlooking the very different possibilities available to rural churches to work with their young people in creating small groups tailored to local needs – groups more likely to be fluid in format and membership and therefore able to respond to peaks and troughs of numbers in particular age-bands, and the changing interests of their members.

The report also noted that 'many young people talked of the lack of relevance of worship and church life to their own lives, though they appeared to retain a keen interest in the spiritual dimension'.[7] However, some recent research has questioned the extent to which young people have an explicit God-shaped hole that they are seeking to fill, if only the Church can get the formula right:

The young people we interviewed were not dissatisfied with their lives. We found no evidence of them looking for a transcendent 'something more'. Yet inherent within much Christian youth ministry is the assumption that young people do have an innate need to look for some greater purpose and meaning beyond day-to-day life.[8]

And:

We argue that the allegedly widespread phenomenon of a growth in eclectic seeking among young people, burgeoning on the back of a decline in religion, is illusory.[9]

Despite the considerable number of challenges in running children's and youth work in rural areas there are many examples of good practice, both of traditional and of new styles of youth work, and it is not unusual for churches to use contemporary teaching materials and state-of-the-art equipment, even in the smaller villages.

In 2002 Michael Whittock, the Rector of Hanwood, Longden and Annscroft with Pulverbatch in Shropshire, and his wife Carol, along with fellow leader Graham Lewis, began a post-confirmation nurture group for young people. Since then the group has developed into two groups that meet fortnightly on Thursday evenings: *Ignite* for 11- to 13-year-olds, and *Encounter* for 14- to 16-year-olds. There are now 36 young people involved. The programme normally begins with some sort of activity or game after which there is worship, comprising songs, prayers, Bible reading and often some symbolic action. The songs are usually accompanied by CDs, but two of the lads play guitars and they are now beginning to lead worship. A time of teaching follows the worship, which usually includes a talk, a sketch, a DVD presentation, discussion, or Bible study. They then split up into smaller groups for prayer which the young people lead themselves. Once a term they have Holy Communion. They also offer an annual Youth Alpha course for new people which can lead to confirmation if they wish. They have their own Youth Church Council. Some of the young people have been involved in 'Soul Purpose', when they joined with other young people clearing up an estate in Shrewsbury. In 2006 they decided to do something similar in Hanwood under the title of GoServe. In March 2007 they also had a GoServe in Longden, Annscoft and Pulverbatch. Michael Whittock observed: 'We rarely see them on a Sunday for all the usual reasons. For instance we have some 14-year-old boys who play football for local teams on Sunday morning. But they never miss Thursday night. For them, as with the majority of our members, Thursday night is their Sunday. I believe we can call this group a "fresh expression of church". We gather in the name of Christ, we worship the Trinity and we attend to the word of God and prayer. We celebrate the Eucharist and we reach out to others. There is apostolic oversight, and there are links with the wider Church through that oversight, confirmation, and reporting to the Parochial Church Council.'

What is so interesting about Michael Whittock's ministry is the way that the young people have been given permission and encouragement to 'be church' in their own context. But, as with the Buggy Club, there is a question about how this will be sustained over their lifetimes. There is also a danger that it will eventually fold as the young people leave to go to university or move away for work or family reasons, unless new youngsters are recruited on a regular basis. Alternatively, are there ways that this young church can transcend barriers of age and culture to be a group of 'kingdom-shaped' believers who can go on growing and serving?

Regional youth work

In some parts of Britain youth work is being supported and resourced from nearby towns or cities by larger churches that have additional resources, or even full-time youth workers. Since many village churches have just one or two young people and are not able to form a viable youth group or youth church, they draw in the young people from the surrounding rural churches to a central venue. This is not always easy and can cause resentment from some of the hard-working country clergy who would love to be able to run their own groups. However, in some areas it may be a better solution than having no youth work at all.

'Soulexer is a monthly Celebration for young people with worship, teaching and ministry with Soul Survivor values and an online community for discussion and friendship. The young people, mainly between fourteen and nineteen years old, come from all over Devon and keep in touch with each other via the website message boards. The website also contains prayers and teaching, and photographs of recent events. Around two hundred regularly attend the monthly worship.'[10]

Perhaps the most important challenge for church leaders in rural areas is to foster a spirit of co-operation and try to broker the best solution in situations where there is little other provision for young people.

Church schools

In 1985 one in four primary schools in England was a Church of England voluntary controlled school. Many of these are situated in rural areas and therefore they have a smaller number of pupils than the national average: they provide education for about 17% of the primary-age pupils.[11] Over a number of years there has been a gradual decline in the number of Church of England schools in rural areas as a result of closures and amalgamations.[12]

Francis found that having a church school (either controlled or aided) did not, on average, make any difference to the number of six- to nine-year children involved in the church on a Sunday,[13] but a church-aided school did make it more likely that the church would have contact with more young people during the week.[14] Five years later, in another study, Francis and Lankshear found that the presence of a church school was associated with more signs of church vitality than in comparable parishes without a church school.[15]

Much of the impact of a church school is to do with the ethos and spirituality of the school community. In some circles during the 1970s and 1980s there was a trend to emphasize the similarities between church schools and community schools. They were seen as the caring arm of the Church and a way for it to serve the local community, but there was little that was distinctive and the Christian dimension was often played down. In recent years there has been a significant shift in parental expectations, which is itself re-shaping church schools. It has become clear that many parents choose to send their children to a church school in part because of their high educational standards, but also because they want something different and distinctive from that which is offered by community schools. In reaction to the growing secularism of British society there has been in some quarters a hope that their children will learn something of the Christian faith and morality. Hand-in-hand with this cultural shift has been a growing emphasis on 'spirituality' (which is admittedly an ambiguous term). Many teachers have come to realize that children are often more open to the spiritual realm than adults, that they may be less daunted by periods of silence, and in particular they find it easier to use their imaginations. A number of teachers have discovered that with appropriate support children can quite easily settle into extended periods of stillness and meditation. Not only does this make children more spiritually aware, but it can also affect the ethos and quality of relationships in the school.

Ali Jenkins, the head teacher at Great Wishford Primary School, with 100 pupils, talks about a sense of awe and wonder needing to be part of a school's atmosphere. Assemblies were relaxed, enjoyable and challenging: 'There must be time to listen and be silent, to talk and to question, to sing, pray and reflect'. On Shrove Tuesday there were 'forgiveness pancakes'. The children met in class and talked together about things in their lives they were not proud of. Then they drew pictures showing those things. Each picture was placed within a pancake shape and placed in a book of forgiveness.

On Ash Wednesday each class discussed a pledge they might make, for example, helping someone with work or looking out for someone who was sad in the playground. The four classes in the school each chose ten pledges, marking the 40 days of Lent. On Good Friday, the pledges were arranged around a large cross.

During Lent, small stones were placed in a corridor along with a bowl of water. The stones could represent a worry: children – and staff – could hold a stone, think about the worry, and then drop it into the water, and move on. The previous Advent the school had joined parishioners in the local church, led the service and done the same thing, with the stones representing something they were not proud of. 'The adults saw the genuineness of the children and felt humbled. One man said if a child took one stone, he'd need a handful. Every adult in the church took part.' It is important to recognise the transforming potential and witness of children's spirituality and find imaginative ways of allowing it to change the church.[16]

The challenge for those rural parishes that are fortunate enough to have a church school is how the two institutions can work in partnership and maximize links with the local community. A church school presents opportunities not only to serve the local community, but to engage with a wide range of people about faith and the spiritual dimension of life. The obvious (and easiest) points of contact are at the festivals, since most schools have carol services and special events at Easter. Indeed, in some places such celebrations have become a focal point for the whole village community.

There are some instances where schools have been willing to co-operate with the local priest in holding confirmation classes during the lunch break or at an after-school club. In at least one place this has been developed by holding a confirmation service in the school itself to which members of the church congregation have been invited. However, this probably only makes sense in a church school where there is a regular celebration of the Eucharist.

All Saint's Church, in Belton in Lincolnshire, was struggling with its children's work. The traditional Sunday School did not seem to be working very well, with few children attending each week. After a period of prayerful consultation and listening, they came up with a number of initiatives aimed at families. CHATS stands for CHurch At The School. There is a Church of England (voluntary controlled) primary school in the village which holds its act of collective worship in the hall. It was decided that once a term the all-age Sunday worship would move from the church into the school. The Methodists from the neighbouring chapel were also invited to share in the service. They have found that at least 55 people attend the services, including a number of children who are not regular members of the congregation. On one occasion the new head teacher was commissioned in the school service, when all the governors were also invited. Twice a term the church runs CAM in the school: Children's Activity Mornings. Using videos, games, singing, prayer and craft work to explore Bible stories, the 15 adult helpers and six teenage helpers work with an average of 30 children each time.

The key to developing fresh expression of church in co-operation with church schools is the quality of relationships and the depth of involvement with the staff and children. Derek Spencer, who has been instrumental in initiating and growing Eden,[17] a congregation for young people that meets in a school in West Sussex, is clear that it is his day-to-day involvement with young people in Rydon Community College and in Steyning Grammar School that provided the essential foundations for the success of the church. He is in the schools most days of the week and helps by leading assemblies, working as a classroom assistant, and by being around with the young people during the breaks. This is a good example of the kingdom-focused evangelism that was described in Chapter 4.

Despite the decline in the number of children and young people who are closely involved in the Christian faith, there are plenty of instances of good practice of working with youngsters to illustrate how rural churches are engaging – and can engage – with the younger generation today.

Notes

1 Brierley, quoted in *Mission-Shaped Church* (Church of England's Mission and Public Affairs Council, 2004, p. 41).

2 For a discussion about generations ('a group of people who experience and respond to specific socio-historical conditions in common ways, depending in part upon age'), see Savage *et al.*, 2006, pp. 4–8.

3 Savage *et al.*, 2006, Chapters 8 and 9.

4 Francis, 1990.

5 Francis, 1985, pp. 43 and 46–7.

6 Francis, 1985, pp. 47–9.

7 *Faith in the Countryside*, 1990, p. 229.

8 Savage *et al.*, 2006, p. 123.

9 Savage *et al.*, 2006, p. 136.

10 http://www.freshexpressions.org.uk/directory_searchresult.asp?id=134& rts=2051. See also www.soulexeter.co.uk.

11 Francis, 1986, p. 10.

12 Francis, 1985, pp. 27–8.

13 One of the reasons why the Church of England's Partners in Mission Consultation *To a Rebellious House?* (1981) was critical of church schools was because so much effort had been put into them with little apparent results in terms of the Church's mission.

14 Francis, 1985, p. 100.

15 Francis and Lankshear, 1990.

16 Quoted in *Seeds in Holy Ground* (Rural Affairs Committee of General Synod, 2005, p. 25).

17 The project is described more fully in Gaze, 2006, pp. 69–70.

7

Worship

For some people a village church, with its stillness and sense of holiness, is a powerful pull towards God and worship. They are attracted by its history, its ancient roots where worship has been offered for centuries, and its ambience as a sacred place. Despite his ambivalence about religion, Philip Larkin still recognized the church as 'a serious house on serious earth'. For some, however, an ancient church building can have the opposite effect and be alienating. For those who were educated in modern, warm schools and who shop in brightly lit supermarkets, an old church can appear creepy and scary. Some years ago I was struck by the comment of a 14-year-old boy who, having been told that there were graves under the floor of a particular church, refused to go in because, he said, 'it's full of dead bodies'. He found the building offputting and did not want to go near it. On another occasion a neighbour commented that when her husband had taken some overseas visitors to visit Lichfield Cathedral, she had preferred to sit outside in the car because she thought it was 'sinister' and was fearful to go inside. For those of us who are familiar with church buildings it is easy to forget how they might appear to a newcomer. In some cases the building itself, which may be badly lit and with a musty smell, can be an obstacle that prevents some people engaging with the Christian faith.

For others, it is not the age or the strangeness of the church that is the problem, but its temperature or lack of facilities. There are many older people who dare not risk sitting in a cold church in the winter, or who for medical reasons need to be near toilets. Likewise, parents nowadays expect to have a place where babies' nappies can be changed. Of course, many rural churches have responded to the challenge by re-ordering the church and installing facilities. However, this is not always possible and in some cases conservation concerns have prevented a PCC making significant improvements to the building. In other ancient churches it has proved difficult, if not impossible, to heat the building to a reasonable temperature. For most villages there are not many choices, since there may not be other venues available. However, some congregations have opted to worship in an alternative venue for at least some of their services.

The Revd Jim Mynors recorded his experience of developing church life in a rural area:

'When I arrived in Fowlmere (population 1,100) in 1988 I was told that I would bury half the congregation before I left. So it was. Some of the elderly congregation I inherited made small children so unwelcome that most young families simply gave up. The Sunday School and youth work had folded. And the "fellowship group" that met for prayer and Bible study had very little to do with the life of the parish church, but included members of other churches who travelled elsewhere to worship but lived in the village. With the arrival of a musical couple with a free evangelical, Bible College background, the stage was set for creating an alternative church to serve the young (who lived in 50% of the housing just built), saving them the trouble of relating to the old and traditional. From time to time I worshipped with this Fresh Expression, not least for my own benefit. I even encouraged them to start their own children's work which met everywhere in the village except the parish church.

Yet they were like the People of God in Exile. My commitment to the Heterogeneous Unit Principle, and this rather unusual lesson I drew from Holy Trinity Brompton, led me to work for a different outcome. To cut a long story short . . . when I left in 2001 one churchwarden representing the traditionalists and one from the fellowship group were working happily together. The children's work had been given a proper home in the newly screened off South Transept of the parish church (thanks to the vision of a 90-year-old!). The same space is used for informal worship and the growing youth club, led by the free evangelical musicians who also learnt about Anglican chanting and were asked to run the traditional choir as well as a "music group". The leader of the fellowship group had become a lay reader, prepared even to take Book of Common Prayer Matins if required, though more at home with today's youth culture. Now, in 2005, the church is a real mix of ages and traditions and a catalyst for healing a divided community rather than a rallying point for the disaffected. And the Millennium Book of the Village has recorded this for posterity.'

All-age services

One of the important insights that became mainstream in the 1980s and 1990s is that children are not part of tomorrow's Church, but of today's Church. Experience has shown that when congregations encourage people of all ages to take an active role in their ministry and mission, they are more likely to grow, both in their discipleship and numerically. This is not always easy, especially for those congregations with a more formal style of worship that does not cater for young children who wish to run around and enjoy the effect of shouting in an echoing building. Some churches have responded by building a soundproof narthex to which parents can retreat if necessary, and in which the service can be heard through the sound system. Elsewhere churches have worked hard to find ways to involve children of all ages in the main Sunday service, such as St John the Baptist, Maesbury.

Maesbury is a village in Shropshire, just to the south of Oswestry. The parish has a population of just over 640 inhabitants. There is a community school that draws children from the surrounding area. The small mission church is interesting because it originally came in kit form and was assembled in four days in 1906. The worship at St John the Baptist Church is a good example of how a rural congregation can relate to all ages. The non-stipendiary priest in charge, the Revd Robin Martin, and his wife Brenda, took over responsibility in 1999 and immediately began to engage with the young people of the parish. Children of five years and above are invited to play a part in the Sunday Holy Communion service. The youngest start by carrying the cross and, as they get older, progress to reading out a brief descriptive introduction before each of the readings. Others act as cantors to lead the singing, and others are servers at services of Holy Communion. Most years three or four

> young people from the parish are confirmed. As the oldest member of the congregation (who is a mere 97 years old) said 'We love having the children as part of the service – it's their church as well as ours.'

One of the important questions facing churches that are offering all-age worship is how to nurture Christians in their faith when they come from very different backgrounds and have different needs. The danger is that everything is reduced to the lowest common denominator, so that there is a minimalist liturgy, hymnody is routinely replaced by children's choruses, and preaching is made simplistic. This is unlikely to sustain those who have been Christians for a longer time or who wish to have their minds stretched and imaginations enriched. All-age worship does not mean that everyone has to participate in every part of the service in the same way. Some churches have found ways of designing services that combine periods of corporate worship with opportunities for different levels and styles of learning.

In recent years there has also been a growing appreciation of the way that different personality types affect the fact that people worship and learn. In a series of books, Francis and Atkins[1] have reflected what can be learnt from applying the insights of Myers-Briggs to preaching. Personality types can also affect the way that some prefer to worship, and it is one of the reasons why exploring alternative styles and forms of worship is important if we are to relate to the wide range of personality types found in our communities. While large urban churches may have sufficient resources to do this, rural churches will need to work strategically with one another to be able to offer a range of worship styles and learning opportunities.

Café-style church

The style and ethos of worship in churches varies greatly. Some buildings and services highlight the transcendent nature of God and of worship. Perhaps the best examples of this are our cathedrals and abbeys. Typically the focus of worship takes place far away from the congregation at the east end, which is usually raised above the level of the nave and sometimes behind a rood screen. The worship tends to be more formal, with a stress on ritual, vestments, anthems and liturgy, all of which speak of the 'otherness' of God.

In other churches the emphasis is on the immanence or 'nearness' of God. Here the architecture of the building tends to be of less importance. The worship may be led from among the congregation, who may even be sitting in a circle facing one another, or in an arc. The style tends to be less formal – indeed, the minister may not wear robes. There is more likely to be extemporare prayer, which will have an informal feel, invoking Jesus or the Holy Spirit, rather than formal language addressed to 'Almighty God'. Some churches have taken this relaxed style further and have begun to experiment with café-style worship, where participants sit around tables for worship, discussion and prayer. It is argued that some find this more informal approach to worship less threatening and are able to engage with those sitting around the table with their questions. The Anglican church in Groombridge has a wide variety of worship on offer, but has also decided to introduce a café Eucharist on an occasional basis as part of their outreach.

The Church of St Thomas the Apostle, Groombridge, is in the Diocese of Chichester. The village (described as 'a dormitory village four miles south west of Tunbridge Wells') has a population of about 15,000 inhabitants and the weekly Sunday congregations vary between 80 and 100, with a further ten to twelve attending midweek worship. There is a voluntary-aided church school in the village, where places are much sought after. The priest in charge, the Revd Tony Fiddian-Green, works halftime in the parish, which he combines with other responsibilities in the diocese. Over the past few years they have developed a number of different styles of worship: the Café Eucharist takes place every three months in the school hall at 9.30 a.m. The regular congregation is encouraged to invite their friends and neighbours and there have been up to 130 in attendance. People sit around tables, which are decorated with cloths and flowers, in groups of about eight. The children are always included in every part of the service. There are just two lively hymns and one short Gospel reading followed by a two-minute explanation. After prayer and silence, there is a short eucharistic prayer, after which the bread and wine is passed around from person to person. It concludes with a simple breakfast of rolls, croissants and drinks, followed by prayer and blessing. The church holds a Youth Service four times a year, which is organized and led by the young people. Between 80 and 100 attend, which mainly comprises teenagers but also some of the older congregation. It was decided that a rock band (who come from neighbouring churches) should play, which was an exciting innovation in a traditional rural church. The speaker is a young person and the evening ends with refreshments. About four times a year (and held between each Café Eucharist) is Brunch at 11.30 a.m. on a Sunday which runs for about 35 to 40 minutes. Tony Fiddian-Green attends the planning meetings and the events, but does not take the lead. It is designed by and run specifically for young families, especially those who do not want to get up early enough for the Parish Mass, or who just do not come to church. The families provide the music and musicians, they lead the worship, and instead of a sermon there is a forum of questions and answers. They also cook the food. School Eucharists are held once a term. There is careful preparation beforehand, with lessons in school years four to six. The liturgy is shortened and sometimes experimental. For example, they recently held a 'picnic Eucharist' based round the 'Feeding of the 5,000' as they all sat on a hillside. Blessed Bread after the Orthodox tradition is used for those not confirmed. There are plans to re-order parts of the church to provide a self-contained, warm, carpeted area for a variety of initiatives, such as pensioners' lunches, a pre-school breakfast club and an after-school Crafty Church for the children.

Café-style worship can be a good way for seekers or enquirers to worship in a low-key way. There will be little worry about whether to stand or sit at the right point or what to do when it comes to communion. The weakness, however, is that it can be almost entirely built around discussions, film clips, contemporary music and sermons *about* God, and gives little opportunity for participants to focus the mind and the imagination on God himself. At some point in worship there is a need to be time for quiet and to centre down on God, and this needs careful introduction and encouragement if the café-style approach is to help the participants enter into worship.

Cell church

One of the worrying features of contemporary British church life is that larger churches are more likely to be declining than smaller churches. The reasons for this are complex but part of the explanation appears to be that, in our increasingly impersonal society, when people choose to attend church they may also be looking for a sense of belonging. The larger the congregation, the more difficult this is to achieve. It is also harder to support and motivate large groups of people to engage in outreach. In a big congregation it is also more difficult to spot when regular members of the congregation are not present or are slowly drifting away.

Some churches have responded to these dynamics of human relating by learning from overseas churches that have been rethinking the nature of Church and making the basic unit not a congregation, but a cell. Many people presume that a cell church is simply a congregation that has mid-week groups that meet together as an extra activity for the enthusiasts. However, cell church is quite different.[2] The fundamental ecclesial unit to which people belong is the cell, which is basically a mini church in its own right. The cell encourages every member to exercise a ministry. They worship and learn together, and care for one another. It is a place where people can get to know each other and build up strong relationships. One of the fundamental insights about cells is that just as in the natural world when a cell grows it will reach the point where it divides into two and both start to grow again, so with cells in churches. One of their fundamental aims is to increase in numbers and then multiply. Cells join together on a regular basis to worship, which may or may not take place in a dedicated church building or on a Sunday. There are several advantages of cell church. There are many more opportunities for leadership, since each cell needs leaders. Members are more likely to feel valued in a small group. Some people have also found that it is easier to invite a seeker or enquirer into the relaxed surroundings of someone's home, rather than to a service in a church building.

The Revd Stuart Darlison is vicar of three villages in Lincolnshire: Welton (population about 3,500), Dunholme (population about 1,800) and Scothern (population about 800). These villages, which lie 5 miles to the north east of Lincoln, have been expanding as new people (many of whom are commuters) have moved into the area over recent years. In 2004 it was decided to restructure the churches along the principles of cell church. Some of the parishioners had already been members of Bible study groups, but it was a major change to help them explore what it was to be cell church. Initially eight cells were set up, but it proved to be too big a change for many existing members of the Sunday congregations, and now only four of these are still operating. Unfortunately, no cell has survived in Scothern, the smallest of the three villages, which has the oldest congregation and the most traditional forms of worship. People join cells through various means, but one of the main avenues is drawing on those who were members of an Alpha group. As the cells have developed they have begun to exercise ministry in the areas in which they are based and Stuart is hoping that some of the neighbouring parishes will follow their example and also set up cell groups.

Alternative times for worship

The vast majority of Christians have always worshipped on a Sunday, the first day of the week, the day of Christ's resurrection. In the past, it was set aside as a special day for worship and few other events or activities would have been organized. That consensus has now broken down. With shopping centres open and car boot sales abounding, churches have begun to see that they have to respond to an individualistic, consumerist culture that expects choice. More flexible working practices, longer holidays, combined with greater prosperity, has also had its effect in permitting committed members of congregations to go away for weekends, sometimes on a regular basis. Most churches have offered midweek worship for many years, including the observance of major saints' days, although this usually attracted either the very committed or the elderly. Today, many churches have found that by having worship on a variety of days and at different times, they are more likely to attract worshippers. Some church planters who are working with emerging church have also discovered that midweek meetings and services are more popular than those on Sundays. Indeed, there are some new congregations that only meet midweek.

Saturday@6

Spurred on by the publication of *Mission-Shaped Church* and encouraged by his area bishop, Stephen Cottrell, the Revd John Cooper, Rector of Wootton, drew together a small group of people from the congregation to think about the times and the different styles of worship that St Peter's Church offered. They observed that some people found that Sunday was not always a good time to get to church and that even regular churchgoers were sometimes missing due to other activities. Consequently, they felt it was important to offer a greater variety of worship opportunities each weekend for the regulars, and also to build up a new congregation of people who had been worshippers in the past and of people who were seeking. With limited resources, they thought that it was essential to plan something that was achievable and sustainable. They set up a fortnightly service called Saturday@6. It has a structured but informal feel to it (the congregations sit in a semicircle in the nave) and runs from 6.00–6.45 p.m., which keeps the evening free for those who have other engagements to go on to.

Two years on there is a core congregation of about 20 people of all ages, including children and babies. It has increased the numbers of weekly worshippers in the church although it has not been so successful in attracting seekers. A confirmation class has emerged from the new congregation and the success of Saturday@6 has encouraged the church to think about what else can be done to engage with the people in the parish.

Music and worship

One of the difficulties for rural ministry is that few churches have sufficient resources to work with young people or to develop a distinctive, culturally specific style of worship. It is all that they can do to run one service a week or a fortnight, and there is little choice about the style of worship. One deanery has set up a music project to address this problem through an initiative that brings a few young people together from each parish to create acts of worship that they both plan and lead.

The Wem and Whitchurch Deanery is in north Shropshire, on the Cheshire border, and is made up of villages grouped around two small rural towns. The lay chairman of the deanery, Christopher Corbet, has worked with the laity and clergy of the deanery to set up a project to enable young people over the age of ten to create and lead acts of worship in a more informal style than is usually to be found in the churches in the area. In phase one, the deanery has employed Paul Savill to prepare, direct and produce the acts of worship. There is a steering committee made up of lay and clergy from the deanery which retains ultimate control. Paul has recently set up, with some Christian friends, a worship music consultancy and already works with a number of schools in the area. He himself leads worship at, and is a member of, Market Drayton Methodist Church.

Each year three or four acts of worship are planned for churches in the deanery, based around the major festivals. Prior to each event there are two Sunday afternoon workshops where young people are formed together into a worship band and practise some of the songs that will be played in the act of worship. Where there are gaps in the array of talent, Paul Savill and his friends add in their own musical skills. They also supply almost all of the hardware for sound production. Each workshop begins and ends with prayer.

The acts of worship are held after a further practice session on Sunday afternoons. The instrumentalists and singers lead most of the worship. Paul has also looked for and brought in young and committed preachers from elsewhere. For those who are not musical there is an opportunity to be involved in running other parts of the service. Not surprisingly, it attracts people of all ages. There are plans to develop the project and to employ other musicians to ensure that there is a wide range of musical and worship styles on offer.

One of the important features of the project is that it is creating a context with gifted, professional leadership, where the young people themselves can take responsibility for worship. They are learning skills of planning, leading prayers and worship, and public speaking, which is developing a new generation of young leaders.

We can see from the examples that I have quoted in this chapter that some rural churches are experimenting with different styles and times of worship, and are using alternative venues. Generally these have seen some growth in the numbers of worshippers and sometimes attract younger people. However, they often require a high level of input from the leadership of the church, which may not be sustainable if they rely on stipendiary clergy who may have several other churches in their care.

Notes

1 For example, Francis and Atkins, 2005.
2 Potter's *The Challenge of the Cell Church* (2001) is one of the few books that reflect on cell church from the perspective of the Church of England.

8

Care and Social Action

The face of the countryside is changing. New housing is being built and many of those who are moving in come from towns and cities. The rapid rise in house prices means that many people who were brought up in the rural areas can now only afford to live in the nearby town. In attractive villages, more and more properties are being purchased to be used as holiday homes. One Cornish MP recently referred to a village where 80% of the houses are now second homes. Fewer people are working on the land and many more are working in tourism, the service sector and tele-cottaging.[1]

At the same time, as I described in Chapter 1, the numbers of pubs, shops and post offices are declining, which means that there are fewer communal places where residents can meet one another. This is having a detrimental effect on the quality of village life and exacerbates feelings of isolation. The population in rural areas has a higher than average number of elderly people. In some parts of the countryside, which otherwise appear affluent, there are small pockets of poverty that can leave inhabitants isolated and unsupported. Social capital may be at a higher level in the countryside than in urban areas, but it is declining – as elsewhere throughout the UK.

In summary, although many rural areas are highly sought after places to live, especially for those who enjoy good health and have money, the picture is not as uniform or as rosy as one might assume. Beneath the veneer of stability and rural tranquillity lurk considerable social problems that need to be addressed, and which present the Church with new opportunities for service.

Rural isolation

Not only is the number of elderly growing as a proportion of the general population, but they are increasingly moving into rural areas. This is changing the make-up of many village communities. This demographic change is usually portrayed in a negative light or as a problem, but it needs to be viewed in a more imaginative way. Many older people, particularly the newly retired, are an untapped resource. They have more free time and good health, and often bring energy and experience to a community which can be harnessed for the common good. By the same token they need to be encouraged to become actively involved in the life of their local church. Inevitably a more elderly population will in time also become a pastoral challenge since there will be more sick and housebound residents living in the countryside. Their isolation can be compounded by the fact that because many young people cannot afford to live in villages they are rarely on hand to care for dependent family members and support them in their old age as would have happened in the past. The care of the elderly is something we will explore later in greater depth.

If communities are going to survive and be healthy then it is important that time and energy is invested in creating good networks, where relationships can be built and sustained, and support offered in time of need. Often the church is ideally placed to help in this process of building and maintaining social capital. This can be through organized events, as in the following illustration from Witney, or may be a simple initiative made by a member of a congregation, as at Newtown.

The tiny village of Newtown lies just to the north west of Wem in Shropshire. It has a population of just over 300 inhabitants and still maintains a Church of England (voluntary controlled) school, which draws children from the surrounding villages and from Wem. The Victorian church, dedicated to King Charles the Martyr, is home to a small but dedicated congregation. One of them, Margaret Fox, has trained on the diocesan scheme and has been commissioned as a Pastoral Care Minister in the parish. It is now widely known in the village that every Wednesday afternoon she goes to sit in the church, so that it is open for anyone who wishes to pray or who wants a listening ear over a cup of tea and biscuits. Most weeks at least one person has come into the church to talk with her. Some of those who drop in are not even regular churchgoers. When it feels appropriate, Margaret offers to pray with people or they light a candle. It is a small but highly valued piece of ministry that builds community and contributes to social capital in a rural area.

Discovery Days in Witney

When plans were being made for the building of a new community called Madley Park estate near Witney, the Oxford Diocese decided to appoint a priest to begin church planting. The estate is in the parish of St Mary's Cogges so the vicar, the Revd Andrew Sweeney, was involved in the negotiations, and in 2003 the Revd Penny Joyce was licensed as associate minister. She moved in to live on the estate. At that stage there were just 264 houses. Within three years the estate has increased to more than 1,000 homes. There is no community centre on the estate, but the head teacher of the local community school was so supportive that she made a classroom available for Penny to use. As a result, she is now involved in the school and takes assemblies on a regular basis.

Penny realized that there was a window of opportunity as the estate was being built. As people moved into new houses they are looking for friends and activities, so it was good that she was living there as the community developed. Her first task was to get to know as many new residents as possible and to immerse herself in the community. She organized Discovery Days, a community-building venture, which aims to help those who have recently moved in to discover their neighbours, discover what real community is and, later, discover God. A wide variety of activities were set up: toddler groups, café gatherings, clubs, singles groups, network lunches, social events and walks. Some of the initiatives were quite imaginative, such as 'Pamper Evenings' for women who get together for a massage, a manicure or some other activity, accompanied by a glass of wine. One of the ways that Penny has built up these activities is by having invitations ready to hand out for the next event.

A newly formed Residents' Association, of which Penny is the chair, has been pivotal in the development of the estate and for forging good relationships. It meets four times a year and provides an opportunity for residents to meet with town planners and local councillors.

Christian worship is expressed through Jigsaw, an interactive family gathering on Sunday afternoons from 4–5 p.m. Between 20 and 30 children and their parents attend, of whom 90% are non-churched. Four groups meet on the estate, two are for Christians and the other two are Seekers' groups. In the early part of 2007 there were two Alpha groups. Penny hopes that these groups will soon start to meet together for celebrations, although this is more likely to be on a midweek evening, rather than on Sunday morning. Surprisingly for a new estate, there is a residential home for 60 elderly people, Madley Park Care Home. Penny leads services there every Sunday evening for about 20 residents and once a month there is a service of Holy Communion.

Penny has found that many of those who are moving on to the estate have a negative view of the Church. Consequently, she has approached mission from the perspective of the incarnation and has concentrated on building relationships. She is convinced that for many people belonging comes before believing. Therefore clusters or cells are important places for people to meet and where teams can emerge. One of the unexpected pressures that she has faced has come from Christians, even other clergy, asking her to justify what she is doing.

Young people

Many rural churches find it hard to engage with young people today, and there is often a cultural gulf between a predominantly older congregation and the teenagers. Despite this, many villages are undertaking good work among the younger generation. Unlike urban areas where it may be possible to start a totally new expression of church, it is more likely to take a mixed economy approach, such as the work developed by the Revd Roger Anders.

The United Benefice of Adderley, Ash, Calverhall, Ightfield and Moreton Say, under the leadership of their priest in charge, the Revd Roger Anders, has been developing and expanding a varied programme of work with young people in rural north Shropshire for several years. The villages are small, with the population ranging from 174 to 684. Most of the churches, except for Moreton Say, are fairly traditional in their worship and have not catered for children for a number of years. Currently there are three initiatives:

'*Benefice Praise and Play*' is for 3- to 8-year-olds and meets on Sunday mornings in Calverhall Village Hall from 9.30 until 10.15 a.m. One of the difficulties of running children's work in a sparsely populated area is that no village has enough young people to form a viable group. It was decided to run it as a Benefice group. There are currently about 24 families on the books, who travel to the central venue from the surrounding villages. There is play followed by worship, which follows the themes of the lectionary and uses music, stories and craft. This is seen as church in its own right, not just as a bridge into the church building for the more formal services.

'*Ash to Adderley*' is the name of the caring arm of the church. For many young people who live in the countryside there is little to do and there are few facilities. Not surprisingly, there are occasionally problems with vandalism. This project is led by a full-time paid youth worker, who is assisted by volunteers, most of whom are church members. They run youth groups in the four different village halls and the Benefice Centre once a week. At the moment the groups cater for two age groups. The 8- to 11-year-olds meet in after-school clubs. The 12- to 18-year-olds have evening youth clubs. It is hoped that the older age group will be split into two shortly to cater for the 16- to 18-year-olds and, in particular, to help them into employment. During the summer there is work with the young people during the day and other activities are organized, and it is hoped to introduce endeavour programmes for outward-bound activities. The older group also have a varied programme, such as making films, producing a magazine for the local area, and even gaining experience towards a qualification in youth work. This is helping with their social and educational needs and is a good example of the church working to strengthen the local community.

Third, there is '*The Max*', an annual weekend camp run in the area for young people, some of whom belong to the churches and others who have no connection with them. The aim is to bring the young people and their leaders together for a programme of activities. Various rock bands play over the weekend as well as a worship band. There are sports, such as archery, as well as Bible studies, music, craft, theatre, dance (all of which can be taken back to their home churches at the end of the weekend). There is a Sacred Place for quiet with candles and images, as well as a prayer tree on which prayer requests are hung and which are used in the Sunday morning worship. Last year prayers were texted into a Max mobile as well, the theme of the weekend being 'Pray as you go'.

All of this children's and youth work is supported by the Benefice Centre which is based in one of the vicarages and rented from the diocese. It provides an office space for the incumbent, the youth leader and the deanery youth worker, and space for equipment and resources for the young people, as well as providing a church office and centre for the community.

What is so significant about this work with young people is that it takes a multi-faceted approach, offering practical help for the teenagers to develop new skills and to move into employment, as well as exploring the spiritual dimension of faith in culturally appropriate ways. A wide range of people from the villages are drawn in to help with the activities and the worship, which also produces an important interface between the church and the community.

The elderly

We are living in an ageing (and sometimes an ageist) society. In 1948 the legal definition of an old person was a person over the age of 48. By 2003 there were 20 million people aged 50 or over in the UK. This was a 45% increase from 13.8 million in 1951. It is estimated that the proportion of the population aged 50 and over will grow by 36% in 2031 when they will number 27.2 million. As one article in the *Guardian* put it, 'By the time you finish reading this, your expectation of life will have increased by six minutes.'

It is often asserted that as people grow older they become more religious. This is sometimes cited as a reason why the Church of England should not be overly concerned about the lack of young people involved in the Church. Voas and Crockett suggest that an examination of religious trends based on the British Household Panel Surveys does not support this view. The preponderance of older people in church, they suggest, simply reflects the fact that they were brought up in an age when a higher proportion were practising Christians. As the young generations age, fewer of them are attending church.[2] If this is correct, then it is a worrying trend for those churches that have relied on a regular supply of older people to support the Church and its ministry. It is also a challenge about how we can engage with the elderly, especially those who have had no significant contact with the Christian faith.

Along with an increase in the numbers of older people has also been the growth in residential and nursing care. One such place is the Mount House Nursing and Residential Home in Shrewsbury, which is owned by the Revd Robert Parker, which has taken the needs of the residents seriously and experimented with new ways of being church, in the context of a residential home.

In 2001 an experiment was started by the Very Revd John Petty, the former Dean of Coventry Cathedral. Like all residential homes, there had been a tradition of a local priest visiting it on a regular basis to bring Holy Communion to those who wanted it. However, after consultation it was decided to develop the spiritual dimension of the care and to offer regular daily services that would be easily accessible to those residents who wished to participate. Instead of importing a style of Church into the Mount House, it was an attempt to grow an authentic, culturally relevant form of Church which would be part of the normal programme. There are now two daily services, which are open to people of all denominations. Many of the residents need help to get up in the morning and it has therefore been decided that the best time for the first service of the day is at 11.30 a.m., which allows an hour before lunch. There is no chapel, so the armchairs are arranged in a circle and there is also space for wheelchairs. The liturgy has been specially designed by John Petty and it includes a Taizé-style service of chant and psalm, Bible readings, a hymn and prayer. The evening service is Compline, using the traditional language of the Book of Common Prayer. Some of the residents do not have good eyesight, so it was important to use language that was either easy to learn or familiar, so that no one is excluded.

On Sundays there is a fuller service in the afternoon which lasts for about 45 minutes. It includes hymns and is accompanied by the piano. The families of residents are invited and a number attend regularly. Active participation is encouraged and there may be a solo verse or two sung by a resident. Services are produced in large print for those whose sight is failing. Every other Sunday morning, there is Holy Communion upstairs in a Lounge Chapel. The sacrament is then taken downstairs to be administered to those in wheelchairs, before going on to those who cannot leave their rooms. There is no compulsion for any resident to take part in the spiritual life of the home. However, at one point, 54 out of the 57 residents were communicants.

In addition to the regular pattern of worship, John Petty has found a way to celebrate key events and anniversaries for the residents. In the context of a service there is a 'This Is Your Life' presentation to which family, friends and staff are invited. There is laughter and sometimes tears of joy, as messages are read out and memories and photographs are shared. At other times there have been services of blessing for a Diamond Wedding Anniversary and a Platinum Wedding Anniversary. On a number of occasions there have been parties for residents on significant birthdays. At a hundredth birthday party of one resident, the card from the Queen was read out by the Deputy Lord-Lieutenant. All this work is undergirded and supported by the Simeon Trust[3] who share these and other ideas by running conferences to support the elderly.

Looking outward to the world

There is a natural tendency for congregations to look inwards and to serve the needs of those who attend. After all, it is these people who are giving sacrificially to keep the church running and one might presume that they have the first call on the vicar's time. Faced with the maintenance of an ancient building, much time and effort is spent on fund raising and maintenance. A congregation that is focused on self-preservation and survival does not appear very attractive to those on the outside.

However, in many communities there are those of goodwill who are eager to make the world a better place and who are willing to join in (even if they are not believers) if they can see that the Church is making a difference to the community or wider afield. For example, many churches have found filling shoe boxes with toys each Christmas to be sent abroad for needy children attracts many who are happy to contribute. More fundamentally, a congregation with a 'can-do' attitude and that looks outwards to the world, is more likely to be welcoming.

The Revd Jeremy Stagg, Team Rector of Cheswardine, Childs Ercall, Hales, Hinstock, Sambrook and Stoke on Tern writes:

'It started as the re-ordering of St Peter's Church at Stoke on Tern was drawing to a close: we had been so fortunate in having money from a bequest to re-equip the building for the twenty-first century that we decided to make a substantial thank-offering. From that spark ignited a passion to build a church in an impoverished township in South Africa. Personal friendships between England and South Africa meant that the desperate need of people in Greenfields, a township above affluent Knysna on the famed Garden Route, was felt as keenly as if it were in Shropshire. The building should house not just a worship centre but community, medical, feeding and training facilities too and would be part of the Anglican Church in that country.

'Turning the vision into reality has been a huge blessing to the people at St Peter's, but not without the occasional hurdle as serious debate got underway. Some £40,000 sterling was needed. Some residents in the village asked some difficult questions: "Surely funds given to St Peter's should be for the benefit of the local community?", "Aren't many foreign countries corrupt – will the money yield the hoped-for result?", "Since Greenfields is so close to Knysna, shouldn't they look there for financial support?", "What about the local projects close to home that need our support?" These, and many other worries, were genuinely believed and strongly felt.' Jeremy was clear that if they were to enable the building of a church in South Africa, it should not have to be at the expense of a schism in their own church. 'The debate was completely open – questionnaires, open meetings, emails to and from South Africa, articles in the parish magazine. In the end, the PCC made a donation of half the required sum and held a Gift Day to raise the balance. Over £11,000 was pledged on the day; the remainder, and more, came in within six weeks.

'Four representatives of St Peter's flew to South Africa in the autumn, building started in Greenfields township, and on 28 October 2006, just 13 months after the Gift Day at Stoke on Tern, the new building was consecrated. Its dedication? St Peter!

'The initiative has gained widespread support from within the church, the parish, the benefice, and further afield. Schools and community groups are still raising funds. And St Peter's at Stoke on Tern is growing in spiritual maturity and – dare we say it – numbers.'

Initiatives such as the building of a new church in Greenfields not only benefit needy people elsewhere, but they also transform the morale of the congregation, who feel they have made a real difference, and raise the level of faith in the church. The ongoing links with an overseas church open the wallets and purses of a congregation and bring alive the intercessions in church Sunday by Sunday.

Notes

1 Commission for Rural Communities, 2006a, pp. 83–5; The Countryside Agency estimated that 2.2 million people telework (Countryside Agency, 2003a, p. 15).

2 Voas and Crockett, 2005, p. 5.

3 www.simeontrust.co.uk.

Part 3

The Wider Context

The Importance of the Family and Apologetics

9

Passing on the Faith in the Family

I began my curacy in a parish in Yorkshire 26 years ago. It had a large parish church and three separate Sunday School buildings in different parts of the town. I regularly heard stories from the older people in the parish who would talk about the Sunday Schools in the 1940s and 1950s when hundreds of children had attended each week. There was a sizeable team of adult leaders allocated to each Sunday School. They described the annual highpoint of the year, the May Day procession, when scores of children would parade from each of the three Sunday Schools through the town to the parish church for a special service. By the time I arrived in 1981, one of the Sunday Schools' buildings had been turned into the church hall. Then in my first year the newest Sunday School building (built in the 1940s) was sold off for alternative use. Some years later the third Sunday School building was disposed of, simply because there were too few children to justify the cost of keeping the building going. The Sunday School movement, which has been such a powerful tool for evangelism in previous generations, was no longer as effective as a form of outreach.

Some months ago I was asked to give a talk entitled 'Passing the faith on to the next generation'. In preparation I made a list of the ways that we seek to share the faith with young people: church schools with their daily act of collective worship and RE lessons, Sunday Schools, youth groups and camps, Boys' Brigade, Church Lads' and Church Girls' Brigade, CYFA, youth Alphas, children's holiday weeks and so on. I then made a second list of all the youth and children's workers who are employed by parishes and deaneries in our diocese. There is no doubt that we have more contemporary Christian music that ever before, more hi-tec equipment and more DVDs. We also have more young people's camps, adventure holidays and festivals, whether it be Greenbelt, Soul Survivor, the Walsingham Youth Pilgrimage or Taizé. I ended up with several long lists, but also a question. Even with all these resources, why are we not being very successful at passing on the faith to the next generation?

The role of the family in the Scriptures

These factors made me pause to ask some fundamental questions. In particular, it made me go back to see what the Bible has to say on the subject of working with the younger generation and passing the faith on to them. When we turn to the Old Testament we discover that the place where faith is shared with the next generation is in the context of the home and the family. Deuteronomy 11 illustrates this clearly. Moses speaks to the people of Israel and spells out to them bluntly that their children are too young to remember the way that God had led them from slavery into freedom. It was only the adults who could look back and see the way that God had been with them and had saved them. Therefore, he says, there is an important task for parents:

> Remember today that it was not your children (who have not known or seen the discipline of the Lord your God), but it is you who must acknowledge his greatness, his mighty hand and his outstretched arm, his signs and his deeds that he did in Egypt to Pharaoh, the king of Egypt, and to all his land; what he did to the Egyptian army, to their horses and chariots, how he made the water of the Red Sea flow over them as they pursued you, so that the Lord has destroyed them to this day; what he did to you in the wilderness, until you came to this place; and what he did to Dathan and Abiram, sons of Eliab son of Reuben, how in the midst of all Israel the earth opened its mouth and swallowed them up, along with their households, their tents, and every living being in their company; for it is your own eyes that have seen every great deed that the Lord did.[1]

Moses reminds the Israelites that God had delivered them by leading them out of Egypt through the Red Sea. This is a formative experience that they need to remember and to reflect on. This is the faith that is to be recounted to the next generation. They did not have the luxury of blaming teachers, church school or the youth club for their children's lack of understanding or faith. But Moses does not leave it there. He then goes on to explain that it is not just about the past and their roots. He turns to the present to uncover the values and the motivations that lie behind their current decisions:

> Keep, then, this entire commandment that I am commanding you today, so that you may have strength to go in and occupy the land that

you are crossing over to occupy, and so that you may live long in the land that the Lord swore to your ancestors to give to them and their descendants, a land flowing with milk and honey. For the land that you are about to enter to occupy is not like the land of Egypt, from which you have come, where you sow your seed and irrigate by foot like a vegetable garden. But the land that you are crossing over to occupy is a land of hills and valleys, watered by rain from the sky, a land that the Lord your God looks after. The eyes of the Lord your God are always on it, from the beginning of the year to the end of the year.[2]

It is not sufficient to have a faith that just looks back to some formative experience in the past if it has no implications or relevance for today. The Israelites are facing some stark choices as they look across the Jordan into the Promised Land, with its 'seven nations mightier and more numerous than you'.[3] Will God give them the land or not? Does this faith actually mean anything now? Are they going to retreat in fear because of an unknown future, or at this point of crisis are there wells they can draw on to give them the courage to walk by faith? What young people want to see in adults is whether their faith makes a real and tangible difference now. Can they see a faith that helps them make sense of and inform their living today? Does it provide a set of values and core beliefs that is sustaining their lives, families, communities and society?

Moses not only questions the positive values and beliefs of the Israelites, but he also asks whether they have the sort of faith that will help them identify what they are going to reject and avoid. He points out that it will be easy to be seduced by all sorts of temptations, which are ultimately idolatrous:

If you will only heed his every commandment that I am commanding you today—loving the Lord your God, and serving him with all your heart and with all your soul— then he will give the rain for your land in its season, the early rain and the later rain, and you will gather in your grain, your wine, and your oil; and he will give grass in your fields for your livestock, and you will eat your fill. Take care, or you will be seduced into turning away, serving other gods and worshipping them, for then the anger of the Lord will be kindled against you and he will shut up the heavens, so that there will be no rain and the land will yield no fruit; then you will perish quickly from the good land that the Lord is giving you.[4]

Moses highlights the sort of faith that is so clear and principled that it will cause its adherents to reject those sorts of behaviour that are wrong or compromising. They are called to live their lives according to a different set of standards and values, which may prove to be costly. In other words, they are called to live a prophetic style of life. This is one of the most pressing questions for Christians today. How should we live in the light of society's idolatries? In theological terms, this is the issue of incarnation. How can the life of God be lived out and shown forth in the life of the Church today? I remember at the beginning of the Decade of Evangelism Bishop John Davies put his finger on this issue: 'The most fundamental question is not whether others are going to be converted during the decade. The first question is whether we are going to be converted.'

Moses tells the Israelites that they must not only live in the light of God's deliverance, but they are also to celebrate what he has done:

> You shall put these words of mine in your heart and soul, and you shall bind them as a sign on your hand, and fix them as an emblem on your forehead. Teach them to your children, talking about them when you are at home and when you are away, when you lie down and when you rise. Write them on the doorposts of your house and on your gates, so that your days and the days of your children may be multiplied in the land that the Lord swore to your ancestors to give them, as long as the heavens are above the earth.[5]

Where is the story to be told? Moses does not mention the temple, the synagogue or any other public place of worship.[6] It is to happen in the home. Nor is this the responsibility of the priest or the elders to tell the story of what God is like and what he has done. This is the task of the parents and the wider family. When Moses is speaking to the Israelites he is speaking in the plural. This is a corporate activity. However, we must not fall into the trap of equating the Hebrew view of family with our modern nuclear family. In the Hebrew scriptures we do not have an exact equivalent to the word 'family'. We have *bêth,* the word that is used in verse 19 in Deuteronomy 11, which means 'house' or 'household'.[7] In the New Testament the equivalent word in Greek is *oikos/oikia*, again meaning 'household'. In both cases the 'house' includes the immediate family of spouse and younger children, grown-up sons and their families, unmarried daughters, kinsmen, servants, and even friends. It is what we mean by 'extended family'. This is the place that the faith is to be lived, celebrated and recounted. Now we cannot reintroduce the extended family and try to mimic the way that our forebears lived, but we can still learn from the underlying principles.

For a considerable period the focus of Christian worship and devotion was in the home. In fact, separate church buildings did not become common until the time of Constantine, who ruled from 306 until 337.[8] Initially those living in Jerusalem worshipped both in the temple and in the home,[9] but soon virtually all Christian worship took place only in the home. We read of believers meeting to pray in the home of John's mother, Mary,[10] and of the young man, Eutychus, going to sleep during Paul's teaching and falling from the upstairs window.[11] Elsewhere in the New Testament there are references to churches meeting in the homes of Prisca and Aquila,[12] Nympha[13] and Philmon.[14]

The role of the family today

If we are going to take the Scriptures seriously, then the question is 'How is Christian faith to be nurtured in the home today?' I am unaware of any research on the subject and I cannot comment on what other Christian denominations do. However, the anecdotal evidence among Anglicans is that in the majority of Christian families today there is very little explicit nurturing of faith in the home. Few homes say grace at mealtimes or pray together, let alone read even the briefest passage of Scripture together. We have separated out the sacred from the secular in the home and have relegated prayer and worship to the Church (or possibly to schools if our children go to a school where Christianity is actually a part of its life). We've left much of the nurture to teachers and Sunday School teachers, and basically it has failed. Why?

There is a great deal of research to show that it is the people with whom one lives and deals with on a daily basis who have the greatest influence (although not the *only* influence) on us, and particularly on children's and young people's attitudes. Between the ages of five and sixteen most children will spend 15,000 hours at school and 125,000 hours at or around the home.[15] The time spent in church (whether it be a 'fresh expression' one or not), Sunday School or a confirmation class will be little more than an hour a week. What empirical evidence we have suggests that attendance at Sunday School makes a 'small significant contribution to the promotion of a positive attitude towards Christianity'.[16] But if they then return to a home where faith is not clearly practised and articulated they are far less likely to follow that faith in adult life. Even more usual is the scenario where a church runs an excellent children and youth work programme that attracts young people from families that have no other contact with the Church. The youngsters return home to parents who never come to church and may even deride the Christian faith. No wonder the 12-year-old who is in the process of becoming an adult is influenced primarily by the home and gives up on God as he or she enters into the teenage years or adulthood.

Nevertheless, there are some young people who find their way into Christian faith despite their parents, or sometimes even in direct opposition to them. Indeed I have noticed an odd phenomenon. When I was in my teens one of the ways that some of us rebelled against our parents was by refusing to go to church. Perhaps four or five times a year I now meet young people who have come to be confirmed and who have no family members to support them. On enquiry, it turns out that their parents are not believers. For that small group of teenagers, one of the ways of rebelling against parents is by going to church and getting confirmed. It would be fascinating to follow up these young people and see how many of them sustain an active, committed faith through their adult lives.

The vital role of the parents' faith and support may also be a reason why so many members of University Christian Unions are reported to fall away from the faith when they leave university. Some young people arrive at university and make a Christian commitment. They have the support of the other members of the Christian Union, with its regular meetings, Bible studies and prayer meetings. However, only some of them were brought up in Christian families, and during their time at university not all of them join a local church. When they graduate and move away to a new area they leave their peers. Most parish churches cannot provide the same level of intensive support and fellowship that they had in the Christian Union. There may be hardly any other young people of a similar age in the congregation. Some lose touch with their Christian friends and fall away from the faith.

Contemporary evidence for the importance of the family

It is easy to make claims about the influence of parents on the faith of their children. For example, there is an evangelical organization which works with men, which claims on its website:

If you lead a child to Christ, 3.5% of their families follow
If you lead a mother to Christ, 17% of their families follow
If you lead a father to Christ, 93% of their families follow[17]

So is there any empirical evidence to back up these claims (and also the insights from the Book of Deuteronomy)? In fact, there is a great deal of research available, much of it from the USA, but also from the UK, on the influence of parents on the faith of their children. The consistent picture that emerges is that of all the factors that have been tested, parental faith is the strongest predictor of teenage religiosity.[18] For example, Weigert and Thomas found that 'adolescents receiving a high degree of both support and control tend to have the highest self-esteem, to conform most to parental expectations, and to adhere most strongly to traditional forms of religiosity'.[19]

Kay questioned pupils who attended Anglican, Catholic and state schools in England and Ireland (Eire and Ulster) to look at the influence of the home and school on attitudes towards Christianity. He concluded: 'The home was shown, in all instances but one, to be more influential than the school on shaping children's attitude towards Christianity.'[20]

Francis and Gibson analysed the responses of 3,414 teenagers in Dundee about their personal religious practices and attitudes. They found that they were more likely to attend church if both their parents were churchgoers, although it was the 'mothers' church attendance which was the more powerful predictor of adolescents' church attendance than fathers' church attendance'. They also discovered that

> the differential balance between paternal influence and maternal influence varies slightly between sons and daughters. In relation to both age groups, the comparative influence of the father is weaker among daughters than among sons, whereas the comparative influence of the mother is stronger among daughters than among sons. This is consistent with the view that, although mothers are more influential in religious socialization than fathers among both sons and daughters, sons still identify with fathers rather more strongly than daughters identify with fathers.[21]

Kay and Francis developed this point by suggesting that: 'On the brink of the teenage years the support of the father within the churchgoing home is important if the religious socialization is to go smoothly.'[22]

Okagaki *et al.* arranged for 58 females and 36 males aged 18 to 25 to complete questionnaires on their religious beliefs and their perceptions of their parents' beliefs, their parents' childrearing goals and behaviours, and their relationships with their parents. Some 79 mothers and 75 fathers also answered questions about their own religious beliefs and their childrearing goals and practices. They found that

> parents' socialization efforts [by which they mean how the parents transmitted their faith to their children] are related to the accuracy of their young adult offspring's perceptions of their beliefs. Analysis of young adults' spontaneous responses to how they learned about their parents' beliefs revealed that the most common response was learning through discussions with their parents. Parents explained their beliefs to their children, discussed what they were learning in their own reading of the Bible, and shared what they 'took away' from church services. Parents engaged in various faith-building activities with their children. In addition to taking their children to church, parents prayed with their children, took them along when they were doing volunteer work at church, and told the children Bible stories before they went to sleep at night. The young adults also observed that their parents influenced them by exposing them to material and activities that encouraged the development of their faith (e.g. giving them books about their faith, encouraging them to participate in church youth groups). Our data demonstrated that the degree to which parents used multiple approaches to teach their children about their religious beliefs, supervised their children's religious development, wanted their children to embrace their faith, and modelled participation in religious activities was positively related to how accurately young adults understood what their parents believed.[23]

In other words, the children who were most likely to follow their parents' faith were those with parents who not only lived their Christian faith by their good example, but also positively encouraged their children to practise the faith and articulated the content of their faith to their children and explained why they believed. Gunnoe and Moore also found that parental influence was highly significant in the transmission of faith among children and teenagers:

> . . . religiosity during young adulthood is best predicted by the presence of religious role models during childhood and adolescence. Religious youth tended to have religious friends during high school and religious

mothers. In keeping with social learning theorists' tenet that learners are more likely to imitate role models they positively regard, highly supportive religious mothers were particularly likely to foster religiosity in their children.[24]

However, they also noted that there was an interesting change when the young people reached their late teens and early twenties:

> Whereas research with high school students (Hoge and Petrillo, 1978) has identified parental religiosity as the primary predictor of adolescent religiosity, peer religiosity emerged as the better predictor in the present study of youth aged 17–22. Our finding may reflect an actual inversion in the relative influence of parents versus peers as youth move out of their parents' residence, or it may be a methodological artefact.[25]

As they point out, the greater influence of peers on religiosity for those aged 17–22, if it is correct, may show that peers become increasingly important in sustaining religiosity during the transition from home to university and to independent living.

Voas and Crockett looked at data from the British Household Panel Surveys from 1991–2 until 1999–2000. The study, which began in 1999, involved 10,264 individuals who lived in 5,538 households. Three questions were asked: 'Do you regard yourself as belonging to any particular religion?', 'How often, if at all, do you attend religious services or meetings?' and 'How much difference would you say religious beliefs make to your life?' They concluded: 'The natural interpretation is thus that religious decline is principally the result of differences between generations: each age cohort is less religious than the last.'[26] An examination of a subgroup of 1,500 young adults aged 16–29 and their parents reveals some stark statistics:

> If neither parent attends at least once a month, the chances of the child doing so are negligible: less than 3 percent. If both parents attend at least monthly, there is a 46 percent chance that the child will do so. Where just one parent attends, the likelihood is halved to 23 percent. What these results suggest is that in Britain institutional religion now has a half-life of one generation, to borrow the terminology of radioactive decay. The generation now in middle age has produced children who are half as likely to attend church, and the trend does not depend on marriage patterns: the net effect was the same whether people married in or out.[27]

Conversely, 'If neither parent is religiously affiliated, 91 percent of the children likewise describe themselves as having no religion.'[28] One further insight is also of interest to us here:

> Where both parents belong to the same denomination, the proportion of children maintaining that allegiance and the proportion listing themselves as 'none' are equal at 46 percent each. Interestingly, there is no disadvantage for religion if the two parents choose different denominations: 48 percent of children follow with their mother or (a little less often) their father. As with attendance, so with affiliation: if only one parent is religions, the probability of the child following suit is around 22 percent. There is a fairly constant 7 to 9 percent risk that the child will become religiously different, whatever the parental configuration. No religion, different religions, the same religion, mixed religious/non-religious, it makes no difference: roughly one child in 12 will choose a denomination not mentioned by either parent.[29]

Voas and Crockett then turn to beliefs (as opposed to churchgoing). They write:

> . . . the conclusion for belief seems to be much the same as for attendance and affiliation. Two non-religious parents successfully transmit their lack of religion. Two religious parents have a 50/50 chance of passing on the faith. One religious parent does only half as well as two together.[30]

Having laid stress on the vital importance of parental faith and support, I would not want to give the impression that all the other work that the churches undertake with children and young people is not worthwhile. It is simply that the strongest foundations, and those that have the greatest influence, are laid in the home. If this has been done, then all the church initiatives, such as children's groups, Sunday School, youth groups, new forms of emerging church and confirmation classes have their place. Indeed, these groups have a vital role for two reasons. First, because the support of peers is vital, especially during the teenage years. Second, because the vast majority of young people will need space to examine the faith that they have inherited from their families and to decide whether they can own if for themselves.

Some years ago I was taken to meet members of the Amish community in Pennsylvania. The Amish are the descendants of the Swiss Brethren who emigrated to the USA in the eighteenth and nineteenth centuries.

Today they are known for wearing traditional dress, eschewing such things as cars and machinery, and offering one another personal, practical and financial support. Their lifestyle is all encompassing, and I was told that when the young people reach their late teens they are allowed (or even actively encouraged) to have a time away from the Amish community. Families and peers are both important in this process. Some leave and never return. Others choose to return to the Amish community, having discerned that this is the faith and the way of life that they wish to follow.

So what can we do?

We cannot reinvent the extended family. For the foreseeable future, the extended family has gone and it is hardly likely that we are going to return to the scenes portrayed by Victorians of the large family (plus servants) gathered around to listen as the head of the house reads the Bible and leads family prayers each day. Nevertheless, I suggest that any church that wishes to reconfigure itself into a mission-shaped church will have to put imagination, time and resources into supporting families as they find new and appropriate ways of sharing and celebrating the faith in the home. I suspect that many parents find this difficult, so they need support and ideas.

The first thing that needs to be done is to help parents understand that they have a vital role in sharing and embodying faith in the home. Some parents are already stressed by the demands put on them and may think that this is an extra burden to make them feel even guiltier. Therefore such groups need sensitive leadership. It needs to be underlined that no one can make a child have faith and parents are not failures if their children do not follow their example. Support groups can be helpful as they provide a forum where parents can help each other and reflect on what has worked well and what has not been so successful. One of the particular areas that needs support is for fathers. All the statistics and anecdotal evidence suggests that there are fewer fathers who are practising Christians. This should not lead us to give up, but rather to see that when we have fathers around they may need extra support.

Second, we need to identify people in our congregations who can be trained and authorized as family ministers. We have Sunday School teachers, youth leaders and pastoral visitors in many parishes. Why not identify and commission people who are gifted at working with families?

Organizations such as the Mothers' Union have a great deal of expertise in this area and could play an important role. In some churches the work can be undertaken as part of an existing parents and toddlers group. A number of churches have found that they can draw on professionals to help lead short courses on potty training, parenting, discipline, play or diet, all of which can be an effective starting point for such ministry.

Third, there is a great deal of material available, such as DVDs and videos, picture books, autobiographies and adventure tales recounting the stories of the Christian faith. Why not have a church library of such material which can be borrowed? In rural areas the resources may have to be taken around to the different churches on a rota, but at least parents will have access to well-produced material that they can make available to their children and teenagers.

Fourth, each parish needs to commend a variety of ways in which faith can be celebrated in the home, perhaps as part of the baptism preparation or through toddlers groups or Sunday School. Sadly, in many places Advent Calendars have become little more than chocolate dispensers (which is an extraordinary thing to happen in what was traditionally a period of abstinence), but it is still possible to buy calendars that tell the Christmas story and these can be made available on church book stalls. Advent wreathes can be used in the home as well as in church, and can form the central feature on the table in the lead-up to Christmas. Likewise, the Mexican tradition of *Posada,* where the events of Christmas are re-enacted in homes, is rapidly growing in popularity.[31] We also need to help families by providing resources and ideas for praying together. Some families symbolically light a candle, or join hands as they say grace before a meal. Other families have a special 'birthday' prayer of thanksgiving which is said after the singing of 'Happy Birthday to you'. These are simply ideas, yet can become a normal part of family life together, celebrating faith and belonging.

Notes

1 Deuteronomy 11.2–7.
2 Deuteronomy 11.8–12.
3 Deuteronomy 7.1.
4 Deuteronomy 11.13–17.
5 Deuteronomy 11.18–21.
6 If, as many scholars believe, the Book of Deuteronomy was written during the Babylonian exile, the Israelites would not have had access to the temple, although there may have been some early synagogues.

7 So *bêth ʿab* means 'father's house'.

8 The earliest known church building (at Dura Europas, which is dated *c.* AD 231) was a private residence that had been adapted for Christian worship.

9 Acts 2.46–47.

10 Acts 12.12.

11 Acts 20.9.

12 Romans 16.5 and I Corinthians 16.19.

13 Colossians 4.15.

14 Philemon 3.

15 Rutter *et al.*, 1979, quoted in Kay and Francis, 1996, p. 59.

16 Kay and Francis, 1996, p. 66, reflecting on data published in Francis *et al.*, 1991.

17 www.CVMen.org.uk. This quotation is from the 'Four Level Evangelism' section on their home page and refers to an article in *Evangelicals Now*, July 2003. I have not been able to track down the source of this claim to see if it is based on research or simply anecdotal evidence.

18 Ash, 1969; Hunsberger, 1976; Acock and Bengston, 1978; Hoge and Petrillo, 1978; Dudley, 1978; Hoge *et al.*, 1982; De Vaus, 1983; Hunsberger, 1985; Dudley and Dudley, 1986; Kieren and Munro, 1987; Clark *et al.*, 1988; De Hart, 1990; Erickson, 1992; Francis and Gibson, 1993; Sherkat, 1998; Martin *et al.*, 2003.

19 Weigert and Thomas, 1972, p. 389. When Weigert and Thomas used the phrase 'receiving a high degree of both support and control' this included the sense of the parents having high expectations of their children.

20 Kay and Francis, 1996, p. 68.

21 Francis and Gibson, 1993, p. 249.

22 Kay and Francis, 1996, p. 66.

23 Okagaki *et al.*, 1999, p. 292.

24 Gunnoe and Moore, 2002, p. 620. This was an interesting American study because the young people were studied when the participants were aged 7–11 and 11–16. The 1,046 people were assessed again between the ages of 17 and 22.

25 Gunnoe and Moore, 2002, p. 621.

26 Voas and Crockett, 2005, pp. 4–5.

27 Voas and Crockett, 2005, p. 11.

28 Voas and Crockett, 2005, p. 11.

29 Voas and Crockett, 2005, pp. 11–12.

30 Voas and Crockett, 2005, p. 12.

31 The Church Army has been promoting *Posada*, and has material available. Church schools can also organize *Posada* among the pupils, either at home or in the classroom.

IO

Apologetics: Is the Gospel True?

A presupposition behind *Mission-Shaped Church* is that one of the most important (if not *the* most important) challenges facing the Church is how to respond to our culture:

> If the decline of the church is ultimately caused neither by the irrelevance of Jesus, nor by the indifference of the community, but by the Church's failure to respond fast enough to an evolving culture, to a changing spiritual climate, and to the promptings of the Holy Spirit, then that decline can be addressed by the repentance of the church.[1]

This presumes that Jesus is still as relevant as ever and people are spiritually receptive, so all we have to do is to find culturally appropriate ways of living and sharing the Christian gospel which will resonate with this generation. For example, some of those involved with 'alternative worship communities' have been exploring different ways of praying, the use of silence and new styles of music, and some of the café churches have experimented with the use of film clips and discussions, and sitting around tables in a relaxed atmosphere (see Chapter 6). It is encouraging that some of these approaches have been the means by which people have become Christians.

However, for other people the problem is not primarily with the culture of the Church, the irrelevance of the faith to modern-day living, or how much Christians contribute to the betterment of the human lot. Indeed, they may be happy to concede that Christians make a positive contribution to the world. The problem for many is that they think that Christianity is superstitious nonsense. To put it starkly, that it is not true. However welcoming or culturally relevant the Church is, they do not believe since they think that Christians are mistaken and there is no God.

When I was a curate I made friends with a couple who lived in the next street. He was a regular worshipper at church, but she did not attend. As our friendship grew and we got to know each other better, she told me that in one of the places they had lived the vicar had persuaded her to come to church and to attend a confirmation class. She enjoyed being part of a group with other adults, discussing issues of life and faith. Eventually she was confirmed and started to attend church regularly. However, after a time she realized that there was a gap between what she heard in church and, if she was totally honest with herself, what she actually thought. It was crystallized one day as she sat in church and, as she put it to me, 'I realized I didn't believe it, so from that day I stopped going to church.' The 'friendship evangelism' that had brought her into the life of the Church was not built on a firm foundation that could stand when hard questions arose. As a deeply thinking person she needed to know how and why it was possible for an intelligent person to believe today.

There have been atheists and agnostics for centuries (although the way that the word 'atheist' is used nowadays is relatively recent, and the word 'agnostic' was coined by Thomas Huxley as recently as 1869). Read, for example, the eighteenth-century Scottish philosopher David Hume's *Dialogues concerning Natural Religion* (1779), the philosopher Bertrand Russell's book *Why I Am Not a Christian* (1927) or Michael Martin's *Atheism: A Philosophical Justification* (1990). More recently, the Oxford scientist Richard Dawkins has written *The God Delusion* (2006).

For another group of people the problem with Christianity is that there are so many competing voices in the religious marketplace, other world faiths as well as a wide variety of New Age beliefs, that everything has become relative. Why should one embrace the Christian faith rather than any other belief? Surely Buddhism or yoga will do, if it fulfils my needs.

The problem of credibility is further exacerbated by an odd phenomenon in our contemporary world. When the media reports on science or medicine they invite acknowledged experts in the field to elucidate the subject and to give a considered assessment. However, when it comes to religion it seems that anyone's opinion will do. This is well illustrated by the coverage in the media in April 2006 of the 'discovery' of the Gospel of

Judas, which was made public at a news conference at the National Geographic Society in Washington. There was minimal attempt, even in the more serious media, to set the document in its historical context, nor to explain third-century Gnostic literature. Instead we were treated to sensationalist headlines, which suggested that this in some way showed that the canonical Gospels were untrustworthy. Add to this the confusion created by such books as Dan Brown's *The Da Vinci Code*,[2] and even some well-educated, widely read people find themselves in a complete fog about, for example, the historicity of the New Testament or even whether Jesus Christ was a real person.

If the Church is going to engage with society, then it is vital that we do not just look at the *way* we do things (as laid out in *Mission-Shaped Church*), but we also examine the *content* of the faith and the claims it makes. At the moment there is a real danger that we are putting more effort into showing the relevance of the gospel than arguing for the truth of the gospel. We need to do both. Our forebears knew the importance of seeking the truth; indeed, many were willing to die for it.

No less a figure than St Augustine recounts how he overheard a debate between a Christian and a pagan that was a significant factor in his conversion. C. S. Lewis, one of the most popular apologists of the twentieth century, observed that 'nearly everyone I know who has embraced Christianity in adult life has been influenced by what seemed to him to be at least a probable argument for Theism'.[3] I think it is regrettable that apologetics is not dealt with at any level in *Mission-Shaped Church*. The question of the credibility of the Christian faith in today's world is only referred to once, in the section describing the 'closed de-churched', a category of people from Richter's and Francis's book *Gone but not Forgotten*. We read of 'leavers speak of loss of faith in the face of scientific claims and other world religions'.[4] But this important insight is not picked up or developed in any way by the report's authors. Admittedly, the report *Mission-Shaped Church* could not include everything. Indeed, it sees its primary task as describing and reflecting on some of the new ways of being church that have emerged over the past 15 years.[5] However, we are fooling ourselves if we ignore the question of credibility. I am convinced that if the Church is going to be truly mission-shaped, then we will have to address issues of truth.

Frank Morison's book *Who Moved the Stone* tells how, as a young man, he knew the basic facts about the life of Christ but the influence of critical scholarship and science had left him confused. Later in life he decided to write a book on the last week of Christ's life and had gone back to read the Gospels for himself: 'The opportunity came to study the life of Christ as I had long wanted to study it, to investigate the origins of its literature, to sift some of the evidence at first hand, and to form my own judgement on the problem which it presents. I will only say that it effected a revolution in my thought. Things emerged from that old-world story which previously I should have thought impossible. Slowly but very definitely the conviction grew that the drama of those unforgettable weeks of human history was stranger and deeper than it seemed. It was the *strangeness* of many notable things in the story which first arrested and held my interest. It was only later that the irresistible logic of their meaning came into view.'[6]

The apologetic task is not new: the challenge exists for every generation. However, the reason Christians need to be engaged in apologetics at the present moment with increased vigour is because we are living in a world and at a time where there are serious intellectual battles raging about truth and what it is to live an authentic human life. For example, Freud argued that 'Religion is an illusion and it derives its strength from its readiness to fit in with our instinctual wishful impulses'. Marx asserted that 'Religion is only the illusory Sun which revolves around man as long as he does not revolve around himself'. More recently, Dawkins has spelt out his manifesto: 'If this book works as I intend religious readers who open it will be atheists by the time they put it down.'[7] Such claims need a robust response and serious engagement if Christianity is going to continue to play a part in public debate.

At a more mundane level, advertisers are busy shaping our expectations and trying to persuade us how we should live. Underlying much advertising is the assumption that if we wish to be a fulfilled human being we need to be consumers, forever fulfilling our every whim ('You are worth it'); a world where every human being has a right to happiness (a Masters degree on happiness has just been launched at the University of East London); and where relationships are utilitarian and disposable if they do not meet 'my needs'. These are highly questionable assumptions that need to be countered. We should not be afraid of trying to persuade people that there are other ways of viewing the world and human flourishing, which arise from ancient Christian wisdom. Part of the Christian task is to paint a picture, through apologetics and by example, of human living that is nourished by worship and strengthened by mutual dependence; and of a society that has a symbiotic relationship with the environment. As we shape the apologetic task for this generation, what can we learn from the past and the way our Christian forebears engaged their contemporaries?

Apologetics: a New Testament imperative

Apologetics is the branch of theology that seeks to give 'a rational defence of Christian faith'.[8] The word apologetics comes from the Greek meaning 'to explain or to give a defence' and it is used when someone is in court and has to give an account of themselves. For example, Felix uses the word in this sense when he brought St Paul face to face with his accusers,[9] and shortly after we read of Paul 'making this defence' (*apologoume-nou*).[10] There are several places in the New Testament where believers are enjoined to engage in apologetics. In the words of Peter's first letter, Christians are called to 'to give a reason (*apologian*) for the hope that is in them'.[11] St Paul tells the Christians in Corinth 'This is my defence (*apologia*) of those who would examine me',[12] and 'We demolish arguments and every pretension that sets itself up against God, and we take captive every thought to make it obedient to Christ'.[13] He explained to the Christians at Philippi that he had to 'defend (*apologia*) and confirm'[14] the gospel. He claimed that he was in prison 'for the defence (*apologian*) of the gospel'.[15] In the letter of Jude, believers are exhorted to 'contend for the faith that was once for all entrusted to the saints'[16] and in the letter to Titus it states that each elder in the church should 'hold firmly to the trustworthy message as it has been taught, so that he can encourage others by sound doctrine and refute those who oppose it'.[17]

Whenever St Paul visited a synagogue he used the opportunity to set forth the truth of the Christian gospel: 'Every Sabbath he would argue in the synagogue and would try to convince Jews and Greeks':[18]

He entered the synagogue and for three months spoke out boldly, and argued persuasively about the kingdom of God. When some stubbornly refused to believe and spoke evil of the Way before the congregation, he left them, taking the disciples with him, and argued daily in the lecture hall of Tyrannus. This continued for two years, so that all the residents of Asia, both Jews and Greeks, heard the word of the Lord.[19]

Paul was so concerned to communicate the truth of the gospel that Agrippa, before whom he was making his defence, asks, 'Are you so quickly persuading me to become a Christian?'[20]

Another interesting example of apologetics in the Bible is found in the Acts of the Apostles, chapter 17, when Paul arrives in Athens. The place itself is highly significant, since it was one of the three great centres of learning in the ancient world (along with Alexandria and Tarsus). Paul finds, not unlike our own age, that Athens is a city that hosts a wide variety of religions and philosophies. He goes to the synagogue and 'as was his custom' (verse 2) he debates with the Jews, using logic and rhetoric.[21] This is the obvious starting place since Paul knows that he would get a hearing in the synagogue. But he then goes to the marketplace to argue with Epicurean and Stoic philosophers (verse 17). As a result, Paul is taken to the Areopagus where he is invited to speak. Bruce writes:

> The Council of the Areopagus . . . was the most venerable Athenian court, dating from legendary times. Its traditional power was curtailed as Athens became more democratic, but it retained jurisdiction over homicide and moral questions generally, and commanded great respect because of its antiquity . . . It had supreme authority in religious matters and seems also to have had the power at this time to appoint public lectures and exercise some control over them in the interest of public order.[22]

The significance of Paul's sermon is only really seen when it is contrasted with the earlier sermons in the Acts of the Apostles which were preached to a Jewish audience. In Athens he does not quote the Jewish scriptures, since he was speaking to a Gentile audience. Instead, Paul begins by appealing to common ground ('Athenians, I see how extremely religious you are in every way'). He explains that as he travelled through the city he noticed an altar 'to an unknown god' and he wants to explain to them who this unknown god is. To do this he uses arguments from nature (verses 24–25), just as he did when he wrote to the Christians in Rome.[23] His language draws on Epicurean and Stoic ideas and he even quotes two pagan poets, Epimenides and Aratus (verse 28), to support his case.

Finally, his authority is derived from revelation (verses 30–31) and from the resurrection of Jesus Christ.[24] The response of the audience was that some scoffed, others wanted to hear more, but a small group became believers.

Another early example of apologetics in the New Testament is found in Paul's first letter to the Corinthians, chapter 15, where Paul is expounding the central truths of the gospel. He wants to assure his readers that the resurrection of Jesus Christ was an historical event:

> . . . he was raised on the third day in accordance with the scriptures, and that he appeared to Cephas, then to the twelve. Then he appeared to more than five hundred brothers and sisters at one time, most of whom are still alive, though some have died. Then he appeared to James, then to all the apostles. Last of all, as to one untimely born, he appeared also to me.[25]

Paul lists the eyewitnesses who saw the risen Christ to back up his claim, pointing out that it would still be possible to speak to many of them.

Apologetics in the early church

The task of apologetics was vital in the early years of the Church as the Christians were a tiny minority who had few rights. They were under threat both from the Roman and the Jewish authorities and for decades they were struggling to survive. Sometimes the attacks were overt and followed by persecution, at other times they had to contend with false accusations or misrepresentation. For example, they were accused of being 'atheists' because they had no visible gods, like the Romans.[26] At other times they were accused of being cannibals. This arose because at the time the Eucharist was celebrated in private, and only baptized and communicant Christians were present. It was rumoured that Christians ate the body of Christ and drank his blood.[27] In response to these and other attacks, a group of Christians, known as 'The Apologists', emerged in the second and third centuries. They became powerful advocates for Christianity in the face of opposition from some of the greatest thinkers of their day. Among the most famous of the Apologists were Aristides, Justin Martyr, Athenagoras, Theophilus and Tertullian.

Dulles argues that

the work of the Apologists can be divided into two main categories: political apologies, designed to win civil tolerance, and religious apologies, designed to win new converts to the faith. The religious apologies can in turn be divided into those aimed at paganism and those aimed at Judaism.[28]

A century later, between 416 and 422, St Augustine wrote his famous treatise entitled *The City of God*. Its main purpose was to counter the claims being made by pagan opponents of Christianity that Rome had been sacked in 410 by the Visigoths because the Romans had abandoned the old gods. Augustine contrasts the City of God with the City of Man, both to refute these claims and also to offer a critique of pagan religions and philosophies.

We are today living in a period not unlike that of St Augustine, when some people are quick to blame religion for the problems that society is experiencing. In particular, religion is readily seen as the handmaid of inflexibility and terrorism. We cannot bury our heads in the sand and hope that such critics will go away. We have to listen to what they have to say and respond to it. In some cases, there may be truth in their accusations, in which case we need to admit it and learn from it (and even try to do something about it to make the situation better). But we also need to refute false accusations.

Apologetics in the medieval church

Anselm, the Italian Abbot of Bec and later Archbishop of Canterbury (*c*.1033–1109), was the most important apologist of his day. Among other works, he wrote his *Proslogion*, which contained his famous onto-logical argument (based on 'something than which nothing greater can be imagined') for the existence of God. Ever since this has been argued over and re-worked by various scholars, such as Leibniz at the end of the seventeenth century and Hartshorne in the twentieth century.

One of the greatest apologists for the Christian faith of all time was Thomas Aquinas (*c.* 1225–74). He wrote his *Summa Contra Gentiles* to support members of the Dominican Order in their missionary endeav-ours. He claimed that he was 'making known, as far as my limited power will allow, the truth that the Catholic faith professes, and of setting aside the errors that are opposed to it'.[29] He also produced the *Quinque Viae* (the 'five ways'), based on philosophical arguments, which presented a rational defence for the existence of God. Some people have described these as his 'proofs', but this is to misunderstand them. Aquinas knew perfectly well that it is not possible to prove the existence of God and that the ultimate basis of faith lies in revelation. These 'five ways' are just one aspect of his apologetic which supports his overall position, but they are not the basis of belief or even his starting point. In Chapter 4 I discussed the nature of God, and in particular his hiddenness. Our inability to provide a knock-down argument for the existence of God is not due to intellectual flabbiness. It is simply that if such an argument were to be available, then humankind would have to believe in God and there would not be the freedom to enter into a loving relationship with him.

Apologetics in the modern age

As well as the great apologists mentioned above, such as St Augustine, Anselm and Aquinas, who overturned the prevailing philosophy of their day, there have also been apologists who have been more modest in their aims and achievements. In the last century, two of the best-known British apologists were Alan Richardson (1905–75), who wrote *Christian Apologetics*, and C. S. Lewis (1898–1963), who wrote a number of apologetical works, including *Mere Christianity*, *The Problem of Pain* and *Miracles*. They were widely read by many thoughtful people of their day and offered a philosophical and theological rationale to complement revelation.

An historical perspective

One of the reasons why I have mentioned some of the great apologists of the past 2,000 years is that it is helpful to remember that in every age there have been powerful voices arguing against Christianity. At the time these opponents must have appeared very daunting, and it may have been tempting to wonder whether Christianity could weather the storm. One only has to remember that in the middle decades of the twentieth century, logical positivism (which originated in Vienna in the 1920s and was popularized in Britain by the philosopher A. J. Ayer in his book *Language, Truth and Logic*) asserted that all metaphysical statements are meaningless – that is, any language about God is nonsensical. It is interesting that few philosophers nowadays are trying to develop the ideas of the logical positivists. Today we are confronted with post-modernism and its proponents such as Karl Popper and Thomas Kuhn who argue, among other things, that it is impossible to give any description of reality, and that no theory can ever be proved true or can explain all things. Yet still today, billions of people find that belief in God does help them make sense of their daily lives.

Looking to the past, we can see that, despite what felt like profound threats from brilliant philosophers, the Church survived and, in the words of Beza, 'the church is an anvil which has worn out many a hammer'. For those that are able to do so, we need to read contemporary philosophy; we still need to take the criticisms and questions of our contemporaries with utmost seriousness and it is necessary for theologians to engage with them, but we do not have to be shaken the moment someone comes up with a new philosophical idea that questions religious belief.

What's the problem with apologetics?

There are a number of objections that Christians make about apologetics. At its most basic level, some people argue that it is unbiblical. Jesus Christ told his followers not to worry about what to say when they were brought up before the authorities: 'Make up your minds not to prepare your defense in advance.'[30] Others are uncomfortable with the idea of Christian apologetics and question what it is for. Surely apologetics cannot prove the existence of God or the truth of the Christian gospel? Apologetics, though, does not suggest that it is possible to provide irrefutable proofs for the existence of God. The Scriptures are quite clear that we cannot find God through our minds or intellects,[31] as if to suggest that we could ever understand God. However, to live by faith is not to abandon our minds. Apologetics sets out to show that belief is not irrational and that intelligent, thoughtful people can believe without suspending their critical faculties.[32] More than that, apologetics tries to show why Christian belief offers a way of seeing the world that is consistent with our experience and can make sense of our deepest hopes and longings.

Third, some are worried about apologetics since they fear that it is about trying to force their faith on others. At its heart, apologetics is about the search for truth, and for Christians this means that we should positively embrace every opportunity to debate and discuss with people from different religious or philosophical outlooks. It does not mean that we abandon our convictions; indeed, apologetics begins from our beliefs. Such searching for truth means that we find ourselves in a dialogue with others that will almost inevitably change us as it causes us to re-examine our presuppositions and ideas. But it can also change others as they are forced to examine their presuppositions and assumptions.

Finally, some people are concerned that if we engage in apologetics all we will be doing is getting into arguments that lead nowhere. I imagine that many of us have found ourselves in unfruitful exchanges with people who do not appear to be seekers after truth, but simply enjoy having a good argument. But Christian apologetics is not about being argumentative and, if it is, then it will fail in its purpose. When Peter's first letter invited believers 'to give a reason for the hope that is in them', he told them that they should not do it in an aggressive way. Instead they are to do it 'with gentleness and respect'. Some of the most powerful ways of helping others think, as every teacher knows, is by asking pertinent questions or even by the use of stories.

Different aspects of apologetics

Apologetics takes place at a number of different levels. At an academic level there is a vital role for the theologian to explain the Christian faith using the thought forms of the day. This is important, even though only a very limited number of people read serious theology or philosophy so it may not reach a wide group of people. Nevertheless, it is the philosophical and theological debates of this generation that filter down to become the common currency of the next generation. Most Christians will not be able to contribute at this level in the sense of lecturing or writing books, but many can at least read what is being written and reflect on the debate. More than ever before, we need an educated clergy and laity who are able to speak about the faith in a meaningful and persuasive way.

There is a place for apologetics through lectures and talks. Although these may not attract large numbers of people, they are a reminder that as Christians we are interested in and committed to the truth.[33]

Even before I had moved to Shropshire I had known that Shrewsbury was the birthplace of Charles Darwin. What I did not know was that in 2000 an annual Darwin festival had been launched to celebrate his contribution to human understanding. Following discussion with the Revd Mark Thomas, Vicar of St Chad's, Shrewsbury (the church in which Darwin had been baptized), and the organizers of the festival, it was agreed that we could sponsor an annual lecture on science and religion, hosted by St Chad's Church. Each year we have invited scientists, such as John Polkinghorne, Arthur Peacocke and Simon Conway-Morris, to give an open lecture. The aim of the lecture has not been to convert anyone, but rather to show that it is quite possible for Christians both to believe the gospel and to engage with the latest scientific discoveries. Each lecture has attracted a sizeable audience and stimulated much interest and discussion.

A different method of apologetics is to engage in contemporary issues from a distinctively Christian standpoint. This is the approach taken by Archbishop Rowan Williams. He has spoken on a wide range of issues such as education (both on faith schools, but also on 'what is a university?'), Islam, the environment and childhood. This approaches apologetics from an oblique position and has the advantage that it stirs up and contributes to a debate, questioning secular assumptions and offering Christian perspectives. It takes place in national and local media and keeps the faith dimension alive in the public consciousness.

Another important type of apologetics is through the arts. The National Gallery Exhibition and subsequent television series presented by Neil McGregor (who at that time was Director of the National Gallery), called *Seeing Salvation*, was a good example of this, inviting viewers to see the world through the eyes of artists who were Christians.

At a more local level we need all those who preach to be able to commend the faith *because it is true*. As well as from the pulpit, this can also go on quietly in every process evangelism course, such as Alpha or Emmaus, where questions are posed and discussed. There is good evidence of a correlation between churches that run process evangelism courses and growth,[34] so we need to encourage every church (or in the case of small rural churches, each benefice or deanery) to run such courses on a regular basis.

Occasionally one comes across someone who has taken the trouble to read Christian theologians and philosophers as part of a genuine search for truth. More often, however, I find myself engaged with people who present me with 'objections' to belief as if no one had ever thought of them before. The Christian faith has never claimed that it can produce answers that will persuade the most hard-bitten atheist. Nevertheless, it is important that thinking, educated Christians have thought through their responses to some of what McGrath calls 'intellectual barriers to faith', such as God as wish-fulfilment, suffering, religious pluralism, the resurrection, the divinity of Christ and sin and salvation.[35] A recent example of such an apologetic is Bishop Richard Harries's *God Outside the Box*, in which he set out to answer some of the common objections, in four main sections: the case against God, difficulties in belief, the case against religion, and the case against Christianity. The book ends with a final section 'towards a spirituality for today'.[36]

The apologetic task is multi-faceted. As well as defending Christian truth, apologetics will sometimes go on the offensive and question some of the claims that are made by non-believers. For example, it is often said that religion is to blame for much (or even most) of the suffering in the world. There is truth in the accusation that some religious people have done terrible things, but we also need to point out that it is highly questionable that religion is the cause of most suffering. Indeed, the case could be made out that the worst genocides of the last century have been committed by those who have consciously rejected religion.[37] Simply to make a bald statement that it is non-religious people who have caused more suffering than religious people may not lead to a very fruitful exchange with a non-believer. However, we should be ready to ask non-believers to justify their claims and not make wild generalizations.

Christians can also ask (on the principle of 'by their fruits you will know them') which religions and philosophies have resulted in charitable and good works. It is significant that it is difficult to identify schools, orphanages and hospitals that were set up and are run by atheists or agnostics. Yet for centuries the Christian faith has inspired men and women to go to some of the most remote parts of the world and to make the most extraordinary sacrifices for people from whom they can never benefit in return. There is plenty of empirical evidence that Christians are one of the largest contributors to charitable work and to social capital in the UK today.[38]

It is also possible to ask unbelievers how they account for the approximately two billion people in virtually every country in the world who claim to be Christians and who meet week by week to worship God. Such Christian worship has continued for 2,000 years.[39] It is not a 'proof' of the truth of Christianity, but it may well make someone pause for thought.

How should we go about the apologetic task?

We need to find ways of doing apologetics in the public domain. In an age when people are bombarded with free newspapers and 24/7 news bulletins, how is our voice going to be heard? Some Christians have responded by setting up Christian radio stations, others have set up a charity to place Christian books in public libraries; and still others have focused on the worldwide web as the key place to stake our claims. But will the programmes be listened to, the books read, and the web pages be found? While it is good to be involved in these places, we need to find the modern-day equivalent of the Areopagus if we are going to make our voice heard. Where might this be? Well, it is probably not one place, but a variety of places. The opportunities will vary in different contexts. As well as Alpha and Emmaus courses, some churches run lectures, courses such as 'Agnostics Anonymous' or 'Everything you wanted to know, but were afraid to ask'. Others run open discussion groups such as 'Pints of View', held in a bar in Birmingham.[40] Some churches have experimented with book clubs and with the use of films and, as we saw earlier, there are a number of places where they've found that café churches and film evenings are popular venues for discussion. Elsewhere groups of churches may be able to sponsor an 'Any Questions' session. We need to make the very best use of the media, especially local newspapers – which are often widely read and are happy to receive good local copy. We need to take stands at Body, Mind and Spirit Fairs, which are now regular events in many towns and cities.[41] All of these are examples of the Church engaging in the public arena.

Notes

1 Church of England's Mission and Public Affairs Council, 2004, p. 14.

2 Brown, 2005.

3 Lewis, 1993, p. 173.

4 Richter and Francis, 1998, p. 38.

5 'What is Mission-Shaped Church?' by George Lings, http://www.encounter-sontheedge.co.uk.

6 Morison, 1983, p. 12.

7 Dawkins, 2006, p. 5. He appears to be a living example of the evolutionary

principle: a Darwinian scientist who has evolved over a few years into a proselytizing atheist.

8 Geisler, 1999, p. 37.

9 Acts 25.16.

10 Acts 26.24. See also Acts 25.8, Acts 19.33 (where Alexander 'tried to make a defence before the people'), Acts 24.10 ('Paul replied: "I cheerfully make my defense".') and 2 Timothy 4.16.

11 1 Peter 3.15.

12 1 Corinthians 9.3.

13 2 Corinthians 10.5.

14 Philippians 1.7.

15 Philippians 1.16.

16 Jude 3.

17 Titus 1.9.

18 Acts 18.4.

19 Acts 19.8–10.

20 Acts 26.28.

21 For a discussion of the way Paul presented his arguments and sought to persuade his audience, see Witherington, 1998, pp. 504–6.

22 Bruce, 1951, p. 333.

23 Romans 1.19ff.

24 Scholars have also done a great deal of work on the style of Paul's speech, demonstrating that he uses all his powers of rhetoric to persuade his hearers. Witherington comments that his speech 'is carefully crafted with considerable alliteration, assonance, and paronomasia' (1998, p. 520).

25 1 Corinthians 15.4–8.

26 Justin Martyr, *Apology*, 1.5–6.

27 Pliny, *Epistle 10*.

28 Dulles, 1971, p. 23.

29 *Summa Contra Gentiles*, 1.2.9.

30 Luke 21.14.

31 1 Corinthians 1.18–25.

32 The disagreement over the nature of Christian apologetics, and even whether it is right to practise apologetics, has divided some eminent theologians. Both Barth and Kierkegaard argued that there is no place for apologetics since all we need is God's revelation. On the other side of the debate, both Brunner and Tillich felt that it was important to establish points of contact in order to provide a rational basis as to why people should be invited to consider the claims of Christianity.

33 There are a number of centres that promote Christian apologetics: for example, the Faraday Institute for Science and Religion in Cambridge (www. faraday-institute.org) sponsors lectures and seminars on science and religion. See also www.christianheritageuk.org.uk.

34 Booker and Ireland, 2003, pp. 14–16.

35 McGrath, 1992, pp. 132–87.

36 Harries, 2002.

37 Ferguson summarized the number of people killed in war in the twentieth century:

Estimates vary widely for the number of deaths in China attributable to Mao's policies, but they must certainly have run to several tens of millions. The total victims of Stalinism within the Soviet Union may have exceeded 20 million. Mortality rates in excess of 10 per cent have also been estimated for Pol Pot's reign of terror in Cambodia, as well as for the civil wars in Mexico (1910–20) and Equatorial Guinea (1972–79), and the Afghan War that followed the Soviet invasion of 1979. By one estimate, sixteen twentieth-century conflicts – war, civil wars, genocides and sundry mass murders – cost more than a million lives each; and a further six claimed between half a million and a million victims; and fourteen killed between a quarter and a half a million people (Ferguson, 2006, p. 651).

The worst genocides of the twentieth century were not caused by religion but mainly by people who had rejected religion.

38 An article in *The Economist*, 17 February 2007, reported 'A separate study, by the Institute for Philanthropy, a lobbying group, shows that the bulk of all [charitable] giving is done by a discrete group who go to church, identify with one of the political parties and read a broadsheet (quality) newspaper, all of which have become minority pursuits.'

39 Estimates of the numbers of Christians in the world vary greatly. However, *The Encyclopaedia Britannica* estimates that there are about two billion Christians today. Barratt *et al.* (2001a, p. 3) estimate there were 1,999,564,000 Christians in AD 2000.

40 Howell-Jones and Wills, 2005.

41 See Chapter 3 for the example in Oswestry.

Part 4

Principles for Mission in the Rural Church

Listening, Learning, Acting, Refocusing

Listening

The vital importance of listening is highlighted in many parts of the Scriptures. The prophet Isaiah spoke of people whose ears are open but who do not hear;[1] Jeremiah called out in frustration to the people 'who have eyes, but do not see, who have ears, but do not hear'.[2] Jesus Christ picked up the same thought and concluded a number of his parables with a reminder that people needed to hear what he was really saying,[3] and lamented that the Pharisees and Sadducees would not interpret the signs of the times.[4] The messages to the churches in the second and third chapters of the Book of Revelation each end with the refrain 'Let anyone who has an ear, listen to what the Spirit is saying to the churches'. Clearly, real listening is important.

Listening to God

Christian discipleship comes from hearing the call of God and responding to it. We often use the word 'vocation' (from the Latin word *vocare*, meaning 'to call'), but we tend to limit its use to those who have a specific calling, such as to be a priest, a missionary or a religious. However, in the New Testament all Christians are called by God to live out their faith in their daily lives at work, in their families and their local communities. Part of baptism and confirmation is about being commissioned for service (indeed, the laying on of hands at confirmation for the filling of the Holy Spirit might be described as a sort of lay ordination as a servant of God). In recent years there has been a renewed emphasis on the ministry of all believers,[5] although there is still much to do to recapture and nurture a broad understanding of vocation, which is about God's presence and action in the whole of life. However, without this understanding, Christian faith is likely to be limited to church services and Bible study groups.

Nevertheless, there are times when people are called to specific tasks or challenges. One of the classic instances of this in the Old Testament is the young Samuel who served in the temple under Eli the priest. God calls to Samuel in the night, and Samuel presumes that the voice he hears must be Eli. He runs to his side, only to find that Eli had not called him. This happens a second time. On the third occasion Eli realizes it must be God calling, and tells him to reply, 'Speak, Lord, for your servant is listening'.[6] The point of the story is that we can miss what God is saying if we do not learn to recognize his voice.

Another example is found in the New Testament where we see Paul and Barnabas setting off on a missionary journey because the church heard God's guidance:

> While they were worshipping the Lord and fasting, the Holy Spirit said, 'Set apart for me Barnabas and Saul for the work to which I have called them.' Then after fasting and praying they laid their hands on them and sent them off.[7]

It is easy to gloss over injunctions about listening to God, not least because many Christians feel uncomfortable about the idea of the Holy Spirit leading in such a direct way. However, we are not given any details of how these early Christians heard God's speaking. We know from our own experience that the sense of being guided comes in many different ways. The crucial thing in this passage is that they are worshipping, fasting and praying because they know that unless they are guided by God, all their efforts will be in vain. The same might be said of the Church today. No bishops, synods or grand strategies will motivate people to work for the coming of God's kingdom, unless there is a sense of vision and call from God. I have often wondered if it would be more profitable if a substantial part of each meeting of General Synod were a silent retreat, meditating and reflecting on the agenda in silence, before any discussion began.

Listening to the local community

One of the greatest dangers following the publication of *Mission-Shaped Church* and the ensuing discussions across the Church of England is that parishes may simply adopt some of the latest ideas (for example, organizing a café Church or an after-school club) in the hope that they can bridge the gap between the Church and the 60% of the British population who have no significant contact with the faith. Such initiatives may indeed be good things to do (and it would certainly be better to do something rather than do nothing), but they would be missing out on one of the most important aspects of *Mission-Shaped Church*, which is listening. Unless we have listened to and understood the hopes, fears and aspirations of people in our area, it is unlikely that we will respond in the most effective way. This is one of the reasons why I spent the first three chapters of this book trying to understand what is happening in rural areas, in rural churches and in rural spirituality, and a further three chapters (Chapters 6 to 8) describing some of the fresh expressions in rural churches in recent years.

However, even this has a danger, since there is no such thing as a typical 'rural church'. Each church and each area is unique and although some of them may share a number of characteristics, if we make presumptions about what they are like we may fail to listen carefully and to really understand them. *Mission-Shaped Church* talks about 'double listening' – that is, to the culture and to the 'inherited tradition of the gospel and the church'.[8] This is certainly a good starting point, but it seems to me that we need to create a culture of listening that is even wider than this. We need to cultivate the practice of listening so that it is a fundamental part of our Christian discipleship. We need to be people who are always curious, receptive and open to new insights.

Most churches live with unquestioned myths about themselves. When I was a Diocesan Missioner I often asked members of PCCs to tell me about the church. Almost invariably they would say that they were a friendly and welcoming bunch of people. On more than one occasion I questioned whether this was actually the case and suggested that we should go and knock on the doors of some of the adjacent houses and say 'I am sorry to bother you, but I am from the church and we are doing some research of how people view us. Do you have any opinions about the congregation?' Once the PCC members had got over the shock and had agreed to try it out, we found that there were always interesting responses. On no occasion did a neighbour volunteer that they thought the congregation was friendly. One commented that members of the congregation appeared to be friendly with one another because they stood on the pavement in groups chatting and she could not always get past them with her child's pushchair. Another neighbour in a large village said that he did not know any of the churchgoers. Still another person wanted to complain about the church bells and the congestion on Sunday mornings on the road outside the church. On each occasion it turned out to be a salutary and thought-provoking exercise. The members of the congregation were friendly with one another, but they did not appear to be friendly to those who lived nearby.

Listening to rural cultures

The early chapters of this book describe how the countryside has always been changing. I also explored some of the ways that the Church and spirituality in the countryside have evolved and are still evolving. These trends will affect the way that we think about the future and how we respond to the opportunities that are presenting themselves, such as:

- The population in rural areas is set to rise, which raises questions about the staffing of rural churches and church planting.
- The number of children and young people is growing, but they have fewer leisure opportunities than their counterparts in urban areas.
- There are proportionately fewer people aged 18 to 40 in the countryside, which makes it harder for them to find mutual support.
- There will be a larger proportion of older, retired, better-off people who the Church may wish to target as having skills and energies to give to their local communities.
- As the population of England increases, so the demand for land and for access to the countryside will increase.
- House prices in rural areas are set to rise above the average, leading to a growing problem of affordable housing.
- The number of people working in farming is declining and therefore they are likely to feel more vulnerable. At the same time the number of immigrant workers in rural areas will probably increase. How can the Church respond to their social and spiritual needs?
- Employment in rural areas is changing from agricultural industry to leisure, which includes tourism and heritage, of which churches are a major part.

- Increasing numbers of people are likely to visit rural areas for leisure. Are there ways that rural churches can provide for their spiritual needs?

It is easy to fall into the trap of making simplistic generalizations about the rural scene, from which myths develop. For example, the myth that most churches used to be packed full every Sunday can leave today's generation feeling a failure. A church that develops a culture of enquiry and listening will be aware of its history and alert to the social changes, some good and some bad, that are going on around them.

Such listening quickly reveals the extent to which the rural context is different from the urban, and indeed that there are many shades of difference within rural areas. The challenge for those who are experimenting with the principles of *Mission-Shaped Church* in rural areas is to understand the dynamics of country communities and to build on their strengths, rather than to transplant uncritically what is working in urban areas. Larger urban churches may have the resources to offer a wide range of forms of worship and may sponsor all sorts of mission and evangelism, but small rural congregations are unable to do the same. Because populations are smaller and resources are scarcer in the countryside, we need to identify the natural regions or areas (which may be multi-parish benefices, group ministries, team ministries or even deaneries) and work across them strategically. Instead of seeing neighbouring churches as competitors, we need to see them as allies in developing a shared approach to worship, ministry and mission, serving a wider area.

We have to listen to the cultures of the rural areas in which we live, for even the most sparsely populated parishes will have a range of different cultures. There is plenty of research available to help us understand what is going on. Material from the 2001 UK census is freely available on the web and provides a mass of information about local authorities and neighbourhoods on a wide range of subjects – such as age, employment, housing and long-term illness. It can reveal whether there are particular needs, problems or opportunities in the area.

As well as using statistics, it is possible to set up groups for listening. It is easy to be snooty about 'focus groups', which have become associated in some people's minds with the idea of 'spin', but they can be very helpful. They use well-tried techniques to enable people to hear what others are saying, rather than what we wish they were saying. It is arguable that to *really* listen to people and to understand their needs is a profoundly Christian activity, since it takes others seriously and does not presume that we know what makes them tick. It is also one of the first steps of understanding how we can enter into other people's worlds and serve them.

Listening to the Church

If a church is going to serve the area in which it is set, and if it is going to grow, then it is important to understand the history of rural Anglicanism. On a broad canvas it is useful to know what is happening in rural churches across the UK. There are a number of resources that bring together research on rural churches and that are helpful in understanding the range of problems and opportunities that most rural churches have in common. One of the best resource books is by Francis and Martineau, *Rural Mission: A Parish Workbook for Developing the Mission of the Rural Church.*[9] Each of the 25 chapters provides suggestions for an audit, in the light of the history of the church and parish. There are statistics that set the discussion in a wider context and that provide bench-marking. There are questions for discussion, leading to planning and action.

As well as understanding the general rural context, we should not forget that each church has its own unique story, which explains something of its present life, its ministry and its mission. Some churches are thriving because they have had many years of first-class ministry from their clergy, and the congregation has been deeply involved in the community. This care and service has borne fruit and there is a positive relation between church and parish. By listening to our past, we may be able to build on those foundations more effectively.

Conversely, a church may have had a troubled history. It may be that there have been long-standing conflicts within the congregation or that some events in the past have soured particular relationships with the local community. There are also plenty of examples of where a church was built not by someone motivated by the desire to worship God, but because they argued with a previous incumbent and set up a rival church. In such cases where a church was founded in anger or selfishness, there may be deep memories in the corporate life of the church and community that need to be dealt with through prayer and repentance.

One rural church (which asked to remain anonymous), set in a large village, told how it had nearly been closed 20 years earlier. The Sunday congregation had averaged eight to ten people for many years. They had tried many different things, but nothing ever improved. A new vicar arrived and was puzzled that a church that appeared to have so much potential was so weak and divided. He took the four members of the PCC away for a day of listening and reflection. They prayed for guidance at the beginning of the day and then spent the morning looking at maps and statistics about the parish. When they discussed the long-standing turbulent relationship between the village and the church they began to see that various groups had been alienated – in particular the farming community, the Baptists, and the residents of the council housing on the edge of the village. People disagreed as to who was at fault, but the vicar was adamant that it was the church's responsibility to take the first step. They decided to send a letter to all the residents of the village, acknowledging that there had been problems, offering an apology if offence had been caused and inviting people to a 'Songs of Praise' service at which prayers would be offered for healing. Only six extra people came to the service, but looking back some years later it is clear that this was a turning point. Within three years the congregation had increased to 24 people and there was energy to begin a children's group and a monthly lunch for the older people in the community. Instead of being in debt and under threat of closure, the congregation now gives 10% of its income away to charity.

Listening to the Christian tradition afresh

There have been many times in the past when the Church has faced new and challenging situations. For example, in 1799 Bishop Cleaver of Chester visited a highly industrialized part of his diocese where there was a parish of 4,000 people, yet *nobody* attended religious services of any kind.[10] It is not surprising that at such times there have been strident voices of doom, predicting the Church's imminent demise. It was said that in 1747 Bishop Joseph Butler refused the offer of becoming the Archbishop of Canterbury on the grounds that it was 'too late to try and support a failing church'. Thomas Arnold was reputed to have said that, 'The Church of England, as she now stands, no human power can save.' During these periods of profound change there have been siren voices urging caution and arguing that the only safe and prudent thing to do is to consolidate what is already going on. Others, in contrast, have felt that change and innovation were needed.

At such times the way forward is rarely clear-cut. However, the challenge is to talk, pray, argue, listen and then begin to walk by faith. But integral to this process is the need to go back to our roots, and in particular to listen afresh to God through reading and studying the Scriptures: 'Look to the rock from which you were hewn, and to the quarry from which you were dug.'[11] The motivation and the energy for the Church to move forward comes from a renewed sense of God's grace and his call.

The Community of Sant' Egidio (the Italian for St Giles) in Rome was founded in 1968 by Andrea Riccardi. When he was a young man he gathered together a group of students in order to read the Gospels together. Soon God led them to work in the slums on the edge of Rome, running afternoon schools ('Scuola Popolare'). Their life focuses on three main areas: prayer (by which they mean joining together to listen to the Scriptures and to offer themselves to God and to others), communicating the good news of Jesus Christ (by living and sharing the gospel), and friendship with the poor. Every day they gather together for worship and to hear the word of God. Today there are more than 30,000 members living in over 30 countries. Their life is a powerful witness to the love of God, lived out in costly service, which began because they started to read the Gospels and to ask God to help them live out their teaching.

Listening to one another

We also need to listen to one another from different traditions within the Anglican Church and also to other Christian denominations. We are now long past the time when Christians of different churches can afford the luxury of ignoring others or presuming that they have nothing to learn from them. Each style of churchmanship has its strengths and weaknesses.

- The stress by evangelicals on grappling with the Scriptures (even when it is difficult and we would rather they said something other than what they say) can save the Church from simply becoming a reflection of the values of the society in which it is set. The emphasis on a personal response to God is a powerful reminder that each one of us is accountable to God.
- The Catholic focus on worship can save us from a frenetic activism, since we are brought face to face with the timelessness and otherness of God. The sense of the corporate nature of the Church is a counterbalance to an unhealthy individualism.
- The liberal concern to take the experience of individuals and contemporary scientific discoveries with utmost seriousness can help the Church be earthed in the real world and protects us from an otherworldly pietism.
- The charismatic experience of the immanence of God reminds us that he comes to meet us and that we can abandon ourselves to him in joy and confidence.

In saying this I am not suggesting that we give up our convictions and become a sort of bubble-and-squeak Church where everything is mashed up in the frying pan. But it can be immensely powerful to gather a disparate group of Christians together to listen to one another, to our communities, and to identify points of contact and the best ways to share in mission and ministry.

It is no accident that the first word of St Benedict's monastic *Rule*, which was so formative of the culture of medieval Christianity, was 'listen'. His description of a monastery as 'a school of the Lord's service' provided an educational metaphor that had an impact way beyond the cloisters of medieval Europe. He saw the Christian community gathered to attend to God and to one another in mutual obedience. Here was the arena for discerning the will of God and for being transformed by his Spirit. However, he avoided two things. He did not set the monastery up as a democracy, but nor did he leave all the power in the hands of the abbot or prioress:

As often as anything important is to be done in the monastery, the prioress or abbot shall call the whole community together and explain what the business is; and after hearing the advice of the members, let them ponder it and follow what they judge the wiser course. The reason why we have said all should be called for counsel is that the Spirit often reveals what is better to the younger. The community members, for their part, are to express their opinions with all humility, and not presume to defend their own views obstinately. The decision is rather the prioress's or the abbot's to make, so that when the abbot or prioress of the community has determined what is more prudent, all must obey. Nevertheless, just as it is proper for disciples to obey their teacher, so it is becoming for the teacher to settle everything with foresight and fairness.[12]

Surprisingly, when gathering the community for counsel, Benedict directs the abbot particularly to listen to the voice of the youngest, because he says, 'God invariably reveals his will to them'. There is an extraordinary freshness in Benedict's wisdom.

Things have changed so quickly in the Church of England that it is easy to forget that in the 1990s the subject of evangelism could still be a controversial and divisive matter. On more that one occasion I had watched a clergy chapter divide into two hostile groups who could hardly begin to discuss the matter in a civilized manner. I was appointed as a Diocesan Missioner at the beginning of the Decade of Evangelism. Before I had taken up my post, the diocesan bishop had asked two senior priests in the diocese to run a series of workshops for all the clergy. One of these was John Lang, the Dean of Lichfield Cathedral, who was very much on the liberal end of the spectrum. The other priest was John Widdas, who described himself to me as 'a catholic charismatic'. Diverse groups of clergy were invited to the Cathedral to spend a day talking about the Decade of Evangelism. It sounds like a recipe for disaster, but the two Johns were wise and began each day with a brief explanation of what was going to happen, followed by a prolonged period of corporate silent prayer. This proved to be extraordinarily disarming. No one was able to set any personal agendas through their choice of language, prayers or hymns. We were all equal before God in the silence. The result was a great deal of real listening to one another took place on each occasion.

Listening to the worldwide Church

After centuries of sending missionaries to other parts of the world, the paternalism of the Church in the West is being challenged. Much of the dynamism and growth of the worldwide Church is now to be found in Africa, Asia and South America, and many of these churches are sending mission partners to the West. In some places these exchange programmes have led to new insights and have become a way for churches to redis-cover aspects of the gospel.

At the time of the 1988 Lambeth Conference, the Diocese of Lichfield signed covenants with four overseas dioceses: Sabah, Kuching, West Malaysia and Qu'Appelle. Like many diocesan links, they began with exchange visits, organized by the World Mission Officer, the Revd Dr Michael Sheard. However, it soon became clear that if these were going to be mutually beneficial we had to move beyond 'religious tourism' and discover how we could become part-ners in mission and ministry.

The Bishop of Lichfield invited our Companion Dioceses to share in a month of mission in June 1997, called 'The Feast', culminating in a celebration on Stafford County Showground. It was hoped that the overseas dioceses would send about 100 people in total, and this was what was planned and budgeted for. Much to everyone's surprise, nearly 250 visitors came: from West Malaysia (82), Kuching (51), Sabah (32), Canada (46), Africa (8), India (3), Poland (13), Germany (8) and the USA (1). Most of these visitors paid their own airfares to come, although the diocese provided some subsidies.

More than half of the 430 parishes in the diocese responded to the invitation to engage in a week of outreach and service between Pentecost and mid-summer. One hundred and seventy-nine of these parishes invited teams from overseas to share with them in 89 'centres' or groups of churches, approximately a third of which involved Christians from other denominations. They were divided into teams and each team shared in two parish missions, each last-ing for a week. The range of activities and initiatives was extraordi-nary: numerous school and hospital visits, flower festivals, talent shows, barn dances, men's breakfasts, prayer breakfasts, lunch clubs, discos for youth, picnics and barbeques at which visitors met and chatted with church members and outsiders. In a number of places the overseas guests gave presentations – dance, song, video, drama or just a brief talk.

The impact of the month of mission was felt in five different ways. First, the lively faith of the visitors revealed to many parishes just how inward looking they were. It renewed and deepened the faith of many church people, who returned to their home communities and workplaces witnessing more openly and effectively.

Second, there were a number of converts. For example, 15 people at Stoke Heath Young Offenders Institution gave their lives to Christ. Some people became Christians at Bucknall. Moxley reported 'some effective outreach', and one young man gave his life to Christ at Meole Brace. Shrewsbury Abbey reported that, during the mission, it had 'made contact with some new people and had renewed contact with some from the past'. At Albrighton the mission enabled the church to make contact with a number of new families, several of whom became involved in the life of the church over the following months. There was also a dramatic increase in the numbers at Wellington Mums and Toddlers as a result of the Teddy Bears' Picnic, one of the special events of 'The Feast' week of outreach. In several places, 'The Feast' had the effect of drawing a number of people from the 'fringe' further into the life of the Church.

Third, several other places also attributed new work to the impact of mission: initiatives with men and youth at Whittington and Weeford; a monthly evening of prayer and healing at Yoxall; men's breakfasts at Colwich and Great Haywood; greater attention to children's ministry (an after-school club), and a family service for the 'un-churched' to which baptismal families are invited at Albrighton; a 'God spot' begun in the youth club at Castlechurch; a new house group, 'Open Book', and a children's group, 'Kingdom Kids', in the Bucknall and Bagnall Team. Above all, as the final evaluation of all Feast events indicated, the month of mission 'focused the minds of many parishes on evangelism for the first time'.

Fourth, the effects of The Feast were perhaps most evident among those who came to help, and many testified to growth in confidence and Christian maturity as a result of The Feast. Many correspondents described how they had gained a deeper appreciation of the diversity of the Church, and had become more aware of God's presence with them, 'discovering the joy of prayer and of learning to depend on the Holy Spirit'. A Canadian participant summed it up this way, 'I feel there were so many benefits in growth for individuals, spiritually stepping out in ways they may never have thought they could, and doing things they would never have imagined themselves doing here at home. What happened to me in Lichfield will help to provide direction for the rest of my life.'

Fifth, this exchange taught people about the difference between gospel and culture. Spending a period of time with Christians who live in another country made many of us realize that much of what we take for granted as an integral part of the faith is in fact just cultural additions. Discussions with Malaysian Christians about Islam were enlightening, as some of the visitors from West Malaysia live as a minority community and experience persecution. In some areas churches had been forcibly demolished. They found it hard to understand our attitudes towards the Muslim minorities in the UK. The Malaysians also had to learn about culture. Some of them had arrived thinking that the problem with the Church of England was that it did not really preach the gospel, and if only we did what they did in Malaysia then we would have many converts. It was a profoundly disturbing and thought-provoking experience for some of them to come on mission to England and find themselves in a culture that was so unreceptive to the gospel. The worldwide Church is vitally important to those of us in the West if we are to recover a sense of being a mission-shaped Church.

All these aspects of listening – to God, society, church, Christian tradition, each other and the worldwide Church – are vital if we are to rediscover our sense of vocation, to be revitalized in the service of our communities, and in sharing the good news of Christ in word and deed.

Notes

1 Isaiah 42.20.
2 Jeremiah 5.21.
3 Mark 4.9; 4.23; 7.16; 8.18.
4 Matthew 16.3.
5 Board of Education of the General Synod, 1985, 1987 and 1999; John Paul II, 1989; Methodist Church, 1988.
6 1 Samuel 3.9.
7 Acts 13.2–3.

8 Church of England's Mission and Public Affairs Council, 2004, p. 104.
9 Francis and Martineau, 2002.
10 Schlossenberg, 2002.
11 Isaiah 51.1.
12 RB 3.

Learning

As a Church, we spend too much time on internal matters and squabbles, and one of the greatest challenges facing us is to find ways to harness church members' diverse gifts and passions to help us respond to the many opportunities facing us. Sadly, there often appears to be a lack of realism about just how wide the gulf is between the Church and contemporary society. Thus there is an urgent need for the Church to engage in listening and learning at a profound level.

In recent years the way that the Church has tended to respond to opportunities or difficulties is by top-down initiatives. For example, one of the problems that the Decade of Evangelism encountered was that most dioceses did not realize that one cannot inspire action or change the culture of an organization simply as a result of a corporate decision taken at a synod. Lambeth Conference resolution 44 (which proposed setting up the Decade) read, 'This conference calls for a shift to a dynamic missionary emphasis going beyond care and nurture to proclamation and service.' In response to this resolution, various reports were written, such as *All God's Children* (1991) and *Breaking New Ground* (1994).[1] They were debated by most dioceses and approved, although it is difficult to know what real impact they made in the long term. There was little sustained or systematic reflection on how the Church at every level would need to change and develop in order to fulfil its calling.

Instead of the radical reorientation proposed by the Lambeth Conference, most dioceses delegated the responsibility to a missioner or evangelist, and set up one or two committees in the hope that this would stimulate the wider Church to engage in its missionary task. In the end, however, the Decade was seen as an extra, an 'add-on', to the work of the Church, much of which went on exactly as before and made little difference to its meetings, agendas, budgets or structures. Not surprisingly, the Decade of Evangelism had little impact on many areas of church life or on the nation as a whole.

Despite this, some good things *did* come out of the Decade of

Evangelism. John Finney's *Finding Faith Today* (1992) showed that evangelism happened in many different ways; and for the majority of people conversion was not a Damascus Road experience, but a process that took place over a period of time. The growth of Alpha (and later Emmaus) courses, building on the insights of earlier courses such as *Good News Down the Street* (which had been used widely since the 1980s), demonstrated that friendship and discussion are important elements of evangelism. However, at the close of the Decade of Evangelism a typical parish church looked and acted pretty much the same as it did in 1990. It continued to function as if it were still part of Christendom, when it was presumed that everyone belonged to the Church (unless they specifically opted out), and when the vast majority of people would still turn up for baptisms, weddings and funerals, despite the fact that in reality this had not been the case for many years.

Another reason for the lack of a concerted response to the Decade of Evangelism was that no consensus existed over the causes of decline in Christianity in the West, and consequently there was no agreement on how the Church should respond. You have only to browse through the books in the mission section of any Christian bookshop to find a bewildering, and often contradictory, range of publications on the subject. There are many reasons for this, but it is partly to do with the fact that most of us operate with models of the Church and the world that arise from a combination of our cultural background, our experience, or even our personality type. We find it difficult to 'think outside the box'. For example, someone who was converted by hearing a sermon may think that the best way (or even the only way) to evangelize is through preaching. Another person who came to faith because they were prayed for when they were ill might think that prayer or the ministry of healing is the key. Someone else's outlook may be determined by the friendship offered by someone in a congregation. Yet another was drawn into faith by the beauty of the worship or music. It is all too easy to universalize our own experience and think that everyone should see things in the same way.

Most of us are clear about what we think is likely to bring people to faith and therefore what the Church ought to do. The difficulty is that those within the Church have totally different diagnoses. To illustrate this and to help us understand the complexity of the Christian family, I want to divide many of the popular diagnoses and solutions into four groups. They are not necessarily exclusive of one another; indeed, some of the approaches may fall into more than one category, which is why I picture them as overlapping circles.

First group

The first group thinks that issues of truth are of paramount importance, and this is the driving force behind the work of the apologists – who we looked at in Chapter 10. Such people would acknowledge that it is God the Holy Spirit who is the great evangelist, but nevertheless would assert that it is vital that the faith be explained better and communicated more clearly. Thus the fundamental challenge is to demonstrate that the Christian faith is credible and relevant. A contemporary example of this is to be found in Alister McGrath's book called *Bridge-Building*.

Allied to this group are those who believe that the most important thing is evangelistic preaching, such as that done by Billy Graham or Michael Green. This would be the approach adopted by, for example, the Proclamation Trust,[2] where great emphasis is placed on reading and teaching the Scriptures, especially expositional preaching on biblical texts. Its exponents argue that if this ministry were to be exercised faithfully, then the Church would grow, as 'the word of God is living and active'.[3]

In total contrast to this group are those who think that one of the reasons that people do not believe today is that the traditional formulations of the Christian faith are not credible for those who live with a post-Enlightenment worldview. 'How can people today believe that Jesus could have been raised from the dead bodily?' they might ask. They would argue that they too are concerned about truth and the Church's mission, but the task for Christian theologians in their view is to reinterpret traditional Christian beliefs, particularly in the light of contemporary scientific knowledge or philosophy. At the more conservative end of this spectrum was John Robinson (of *Honest to God* fame) and David Jenkins, the former Bishop of Durham. At the more radical end are Don Cupitt and John Hick. What all the people in this group share is the

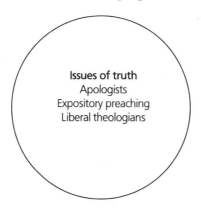

Issues of truth
Apologists
Expository preaching
Liberal theologians

conviction that we should approach mission and evangelism from the perspective of what is true.

Second group

A second group of Christians approach the challenge of sharing the gospel via spirituality. They are concerned to begin with people's religious experience, or lack of it, and to explore their sense of God. It is clear that the way people come to faith varies greatly, but we know that most do not have a sudden conversion experience that makes them change their minds overnight and immediately join a church and begin worshipping. Most people are drawn gradually into the community of faith and, as a sense of belonging emerges, they begin to take on board Christian truth and beliefs. In this perspective, belonging precedes believing. John Finney's empirical research has demonstrated that the vast majority of Christians point to a process of conversion and that on average took people four years.[4] There is no doubt that the experience of being drawn into the community of faith is one of the factors behind the success of such groups as Alpha, Emmaus, Cursillo and some forms of charismatic renewal.

Another quite different expression of this approach, but one that is theologically related to it, is that of those who believe that the most important thing we need to attend to is prayer; therefore, such people put an emphasis on spiritual direction and retreats. There are numerous religious communities and conference centres that run retreats, ranging from the formal (such as the 30-day Spiritual Exercises of St Ignatius of Loyola) to those based on a quiet day of walking, poetry, painting or the environment.

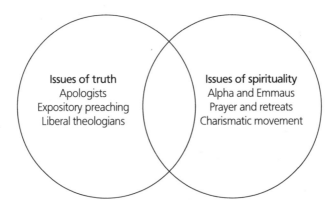

Issues of truth
Apologists
Expository preaching
Liberal theologians

Issues of spirituality
Alpha and Emmaus
Prayer and retreats
Charismatic movement

In the 1980s the American pastor John Wimber came to the UK to run a series of charismatic conferences with an emphasis on speaking in tongues, healing and deliverance from evil powers. A number of people were converted through witnessing or experiencing these 'signs and wonders'. Allied to this approach is the holiness tradition that believes that God cannot bless a nation or a church where there is sin and where there has been no repentance. This was one of the strands that was at the heart of the Methodist movement in the eighteenth century, the Welsh Revival of 1904, and the East African experience of the 'Balakole' in the mid-twentieth century, and is still part of some Pentecostal and charismatic traditions. What all of these have in common is a stress on spirituality.

Third group

The approach of the third group is what I call organizational, and several sub-groups fall into this approach. One of the best-known exponents is Jackson in his *Hope for the Church* and *The Road to Growth*, based on studies of statistical trends. He advocates a range of strategic changes, such as shortening the length of clergy vacancies, ordaining younger clergy, reforming the way that the Church is financed, and so on. The church planting movement also comes into this category, based on the assumption that we need many more churches (not necessarily more church buildings), so that there is a Christian presence in each immediate locality. The work of the Catechumenate network is also an example of a group seeking to re-form the Church around one particular development. This approach argues that what we need to do is to identify, train and resource strategic leaders (which is one of the reasons why books on Christian leadership are such a growth area). There are plenty of people around who lament that the biggest problem we have in the Church today is hopeless bishops or ineffective clergy.[5]

For others, the organizational problem is that the Church has excluded groups and that until we sort this out we will not have any credibility. For example, some point out that the bar on women being ordained to the priesthood was a stumbling block to people becoming part of the Church (although there has not been a noticeable return to the fold of the feminists who left the Church over the ordination of women). Others believe that gay rights also fall into this category, since it is argued that people are being excluded from the Church.

This group also includes those who believe that divisions between

Christian denominations are a barrier to belief and that if we were to fulfil Jesus Christ's prayer that 'they all may be one',[6] then more people would come to faith ('that the world may believe'). For them, the ecumenical movement is about bringing credibility to its proclamation of the gospel and about saving precious resources.

Finally, there is the conviction in some circles, especially at grassroots, that the problem is that the clergy do not do enough pastoral visiting, summed up in the age-old proverb, 'A house-going parson make a church-going people'. What all of these approaches have in common is a conviction that we need to organize or do things differently.

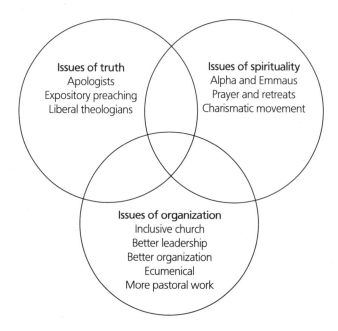

Fourth group

The approach of the fourth group is to do with culture. *Mission-Shaped Church* works on the basis that throughout the ages churches have expressed their worship, mission and ministry in different cultural forms. The report does not, for example, envisage that we ought to think about how to restate the content of the historical gospel or to update the creeds to bring them in line with contemporary scientific thought. Indeed, in this aspect it is an extremely orthodox document.

We should note that those who prefer traditional forms of worship and argue for the retention (if not a return to) the formularies and worship of the Book of Common Prayer are also saying something about culture; namely, that Cranmer's sublime language communicates through its beauty of language. In contrast, it has sometimes been argued that the banality of the language of contemporary liturgies can never lift the heart and soul to God as effectively as the older liturgies. One residentiary canon told me that the cathedral congregation was growing because of the high quality of the (traditional) worship the cathedral offered, combined with 'intelligent preaching'. Other Christians claim that it is the liveliness of contemporary music that is most helpful, while for others it is the aesthetics of church architecture, music and ritual that speak of the 'otherness' of God and inspire worship. All of these are concerned with different cultural expressions of the gospel.

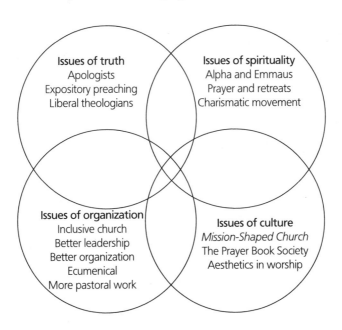

The above model, based on four approaches/groups, is simply an illustration, and it would be possible to classify the approaches in different ways and under other headings. Many people would place themselves in one of the various overlapping categories or perhaps towards the middle of the above layout. However, I am using the model to make the point that there are a wide variety of approaches, all held with conviction by intelligent, committed members of the Church, some of which are complementary and some of which are contradictory. For example, those who like traditional worship will have an opposing perspective to those espousing modern worship and vice versa. Nevertheless, we owe it to one another to try to listen and understand why other people see things so differently, and often so passionately.

Church as a learning organization

Faced with such a wide range of approaches, one might be tempted to think that it is an impossible or even an unfruitful task to try to forge a common understanding of the problems, challenges and opportunities facing the Church. However, it is not only the Church that has had to deal with a complex organization in which many people hold conflicting views – the same can be said of the government, the NHS, universities, businesses and charities. Similar problems have been recognized and addressed by many other organizations too.

Governments have now come to see that many problems cannot be solved simply by passing laws, which is why they have set up Strategic Partnerships, comprising the statutory and voluntary sectors. In Shropshire, one of the Partnership's priorities is to tackle the worrying growth in obesity that threatens to make this the last generation that can expect to live longer than their parents. Simply telling people that obesity carries high health risks and that people should lose weight is important, but is not likely to solve the problem, as every doctor knows. The issue has to be addressed in as many ways as possible so, for example, there are now more explanations about health on the packaging of food; advertising 'junk' food is being banned; the food served up for school dinners is being changed to make it more healthy, vending machines selling sweets in schools are being removed in some places; some schools have been encouraging parents to walk to school with their children; better sports and recreation facilities are being built; bicycle lanes are being built; youth groups are being encouraged to organize physical activities, and so on. Obesity is a complex problem which, if it is going to be solved, will need a comprehensive, multidisciplinary response.

One of the foremost thinkers about the way that complex organizations work is Peter Senge, based on his concept of 'Learning Organizations'. Interestingly, his work has many resonances with the experience of the early church and with insights from the New Testament. When Jesus called people to follow him they were drawn into a teacher–student relationship in which the disciple became a learner and a follower (the Greek word 'to follow' is a key concept of discipleship in the New Testament). The first disciples quite literally travelled around with Jesus, responding to those they met by proclaiming the 'good news of the kingdom', which was accompanied with signs of healing. In the New Testament discipleship is not just a once-off experience of learning: it is a way of living. One of the fundamental changes that we need to encourage if we are going to be a missionary church is to rediscover what it is to be a community of learners or disciples.

Senge identifies five basic areas or 'disciplines' that are fundamental to a Learning Organization and that are essential if it is going to fulfil its highest aspirations. Each of these five areas can be applied to the situation we are currently facing in the Church.

Getting a holistic picture[7]

Most organizations and the problems they face are extremely complex. For example, anyone who has been involved in trying to effect change in the NHS realizes how difficult it is to achieve. In a similar way the current problems facing the Church as it seeks to re-engage with contemporary society admit no simple analysis or solution. Unfortunately, many people in the Church fail to understand the complexity of the situation confronting us and jump to premature and often mistaken conclusions about what the problems and the solutions are.

Traditional analysis works by breaking down a problem into smaller elements and looking at each one. Indeed, the word 'analysis' means 'to break down into the constituent parts'. The danger is that we can miss important insights into how all the elements work together. Instead we need to help one another ask fundamental questions and seek long-term solutions, by piecing together all the parts of the jigsaw and viewing the whole. Such an approach tends to undermine a culture of blame, where it is easier to project all our problems on to someone else. This is sometimes the problem that faces the Church, where various factions blame one another rather than listen to what that particular group has to say.

In the 1980s the Revd Roger Arguile, who was then a team vicar in Stafford, undertook some statistical work that showed that there was a direct correlation between long-term vacancies in parishes and a decline in the size of the congregation – a finding that has been endorsed by Bob Jackson.[8] As a result it was decided that we need to shorten the length of vacancies. It was agreed that the archdeacon would visit the parish as soon as it was known that the priest was leaving. The process could be explained and a timetable set. However, even with this improvement vacancies were still averaging more than six months. We decided to look at the problem differently. A major part of the delay was the time it took for a PCC (or in the case of multi-parish benefices, six or more PCCs) to produce its parish profile. It was one of the factors that persuaded us that Mission Action Plans could have additional benefits. A well-prepared and updated Mission Action Plan was virtually a ready-made parish profile. All a PCC had to do was to tweak it, add a person profile, and pass it at the Section 11 meeting, which saved weeks of extra work and delay, thereby shortening the process.

Engaging in lifelong learning[9]

Most professions expect people to keep up to date through a programme of continual training. However, lifelong learning is about cultivating an attitude of openness and curiosity. Senge writes about 'continually clarifying and deepening our personal vision, of focussing our energies, of developing patience, and of trying to see reality objectively'.[10] He goes on to argue that:

People with a high level of personal mastery share several basic characteristics. They have a special sense of purpose that lies behind their visions and goals. *For such a person, a vision is a calling rather than simply a good idea.* They see 'current reality' as an ally, not an enemy. They have learnt how to perceive and work with forces of change rather than resist those forces. They are deeply inquisitive, committed to continually seeing reality more and more accurately . . . [they] live in a continual learning mode, they never 'arrive'. . . . It is a process. It is a lifelong discipline. People with a high level of personal mastery are acutely aware of their ignorance, their incompetence, their growth areas.[11]

If the leadership in a parish (the priest and members of the PCC) is going to help the Church engage in its mission, then they will need to encourage a culture that lifts people out of simplistic solutions and frees them to be curious and imaginative. It prevents them from lapsing into victim mode, forever lamenting that 'things aren't what they used to be', and blaming decline on factors which are outside of their control.

St Paul was called by God to be a missionary. On a number of occasions he found that his plans were thwarted – for example, when he was travelling in Asia Minor and was unable to enter Bithynia (Acts 16.6–10). Rather than see this as a problem and give up, Paul saw it as God's opportunity. On another occasion he was arrested and imprisoned. He used the time to talk to the guards (who were a captive audience) and to write letters of encouragement to the churches that he had founded. In the words of Senge, he 'saw "current reality" as an ally, not an enemy'.

Allowing the conversion of the mind[12]

Many of us interpret the world through the ideas and concepts that we have inherited from our parents or from foundational experiences in our past. Our understanding of, for example, God the Father, will be based at least in part on childhood stories about God and our experience of our own father. As we grow older, these images are modified by our reading of the Scriptures and our experiences in life. These are the 'deeply ingrained assumptions, generalizations, or even pictures and images that influence how we understand the world and how we take action':[13]

> The discipline of mental models starts with turning the mirror inward; learning to unearth our internal pictures of the world, to bring them to the surface and hold them rigorously to scrutiny. It also includes our ability to carry on 'learningful' conversations that balance inquiry and advocacy, where people expose their own thinking effectively and make that thinking open to the influence of others.[14]

One of the reasons why it is helpful for leaders and congregations to map out all the different views and opinions that each person holds is that it

167

demonstrates the diversity of people who are members of the Church, and by implication the diversity of people outside the Church. It stops any thinking person from universalizing his or her experience and presuming that the solutions are obvious. What Senge is describing is strangely akin to the experience of the believer whose worldview is being changed from 'my-world which revolves around me and my needs' to 'God's-world, where I find that I have a part to play in working for the coming of his kingdom'.

A colleague decided to write a course to be used with enquirers to the Christian faith. He discussed the project with a number of people in the Church but was challenged by one person who insisted he was talking to the wrong people. Surely, she argued, you should be listening to the people for whom you are writing the course. After much hesitation, he decided to invite a number of non-churchgoing acquaintances and neighbours to three evenings in his house. He explained that he needed their advice on the sort of issues that would be relevant and important to people exploring the faith. He pointed out that they would be in the majority. He was surprised and encouraged to find that six people agreed to come. As a result of listening to them and their questions, he reworked much of the material and introduced a totally new session. A further, unexpected consequence was that two of the people began to attend church within the following year. It appears that the process had the effect of changing several people's worldview.

Building shared vision

Following the resurrection, the early centuries of the Church witnessed extraordinary growth – a growth that was not centrally organized and co-ordinated, but simply gathered momentum as ordinary people were inspired by an irrepressible sense of God's victory over evil. This was so powerful that these men and women gave sacrificially of their time and energy – and, in some cases, even their lives. Individual Christians today, and even whole congregations, are unlikely to look outwards and engage with the world unless they are grasped with a similar sort of vision. Senge writes:

When there is a genuine vision (as opposed to the all-too-familiar 'vision statement'), people excel and learn, not because they are told to, but because they want to. But many leaders have personal visions that never get translated into shared visions that galvanize an organization . . . given a choice, most people opt for pursuing a lofty goal, not only in times of crisis but at all times. What has been lacking is a discipline for translating vision into shared vision – not a 'cookbook' but a set of principles and guiding practices.[15]

In a time of retrenchment the tendency of many people is to retreat into the past and indulge in nostalgia. Yet looking backwards rarely inspires actions that help an organization move forward in a new and rapidly changing context. In contrast, when a group of people begin to share a sense of what the future might hold, there is an emergence of commitment and urgency, which draws out the best in people and elicits their time and energy to work for common goals.

Some years ago I was privileged to be part of a group of people who were grasped by a shared vision. In the late 1970s, St Stephen's Church, Selly Hill in Birmingham, began to explore the possibility of starting a new congregation in the Church Centre on the Pershore Road, which was a part of the parish that was furthest away from the parish church. Some preliminary research was undertaken and the matter was discussed at PCC meetings. Then a small group of Christians began to meet for prayer. Nothing spectacular happened, but gradually a sense of rightness and excitement grew. The curate, David Veness, was appointed to head it up. We did not have to bully or cajole people to join in. Those who felt called were happy to move down the road to the hall. Some people were willing to give sacrificially, others were committed to visiting or leading the music. It was the sense of sharing in something new together that drew people. The church is still thriving today and has seen considerable growth more than 25 years later.

Encouraging team learning

The New Testament understanding of discipleship is that every believer is a lifelong learner and each person has an indispensable contribution to make if the Church is going to be true to its calling:

> The discipline of team learning starts with 'dialogue', the capacity of members of a team to suspend assumptions and enter into a genuine 'thinking together'. To the Greeks *dia-logos* meant a free-flowing of meaning through a group, allowing the group to discover insights not attainable individually . . . The discipline of dialogue also involves learning how to recognize the patterns of interaction in teams that undermine learning. The patterns of defensiveness are often deeply engrained in how a team operates. If recognized and surfaced creatively, they can actually accelerate learning.[16]

A group of young people on a mission team were asked to rewrite and then re-enact the parable of the Good Samaritan in modern language for a secondary school assembly of 400 young people. The challenge provoked heated debate and discussion. Who are today's equivalents of the priest, the Levite, the Samaritan and the innkeeper? Where would it have taken place today – and what sort of language would Jesus have used if he was telling the parable in the school? All the young people had different views and insights that they contributed in order to communicate with their peers. Many of the initial ideas were jettisoned as they worked away together, seeking to tell the old story in a contemporary way.

I will return to the subject of building shared vision and team learning in Chapter 14, but at this point I want to make one specific observation. For Christians, there is an extra dimension: the gift of the Holy Spirit. The Old Testament view of leaders is that God selects, calls and anoints a leader with the Holy Spirit, such as one of the kings or the prophets. He or she knows what the will of God is and tells the people what they have to do. However, in the New Testament there is a profound change. On the Day of Pentecost the Holy Spirit falls on *all* the believers, so that everyone can hear the word of God:

... I will pour out my Spirit upon all flesh,
and your sons and your daughters shall prophesy,
and your young men shall see visions
and your old men shall dream dreams.[17]

St Paul presumes that each believer will have an insight to contribute from God,[18] and the role of the leaders is to ensure that all the contributions are weighed up and tested. The Church is called to be a learning community, based on real and continual listening and reflecting, undertaken by the whole body of the Church. The question we need to ask, therefore, is how do we create this culture of listening and learning in the Church, which will strengthen Christians in their mission and ministry in the world? It is to this we turn in the next chapter.

Notes

1 However, despite much enthusiasm in certain quarters, church planting did not achieve what many hoped it would. For an analysis, see Lings and Murray, 2005.

2 http://www.proctrust.org.uk.

3 Hebrews 4.12.

4 Finney, 1992, p. 25.

5 This complaint is not confined to church leaders. It is also made of politicians, business leaders and health service managers.

6 John 17.21.

7 Senge's name for this is 'systems thinking'.

8 Jackson, 2005, pp. 25–9 and 129–32.

9 Senge's name for this is 'personal mastery'.

10 Senge, 1990, p. 7.

11 Senge, 1990, p. 142.

12 Senge calls this 'mental models'.

13 Senge, 1990, p. 8.

14 Senge, 1990, p. 9.

15 Senge, 1990, p. 9.

16 Senge, 1990, p. 10.

17 Acts 2.17.

18 1 Corinthians 14.26.

13

Acting

In this chapter I describe an approach to listening, learning and acting, called Mission Action Planning. I then go on to reflect on four areas of church life that need special attention if we are to engage in mission in rural areas.

A methodology: Mission Action Planning

In the last two chapters on listening and learning I suggested that as Christians we need to listen to a wide variety of different voices in our society if we are to grasp the complexity of the situation that confronts us today and learn from these voices. It is easy to pay lip-service to the importance of listening and learning, and it is not particularly difficult to organize a meeting or conference with a church to facilitate the process. It is, however, much more difficult to effect a broader change in the culture of the church so that we become a community of faith that is constantly striving to listen and learn. Unless we enable individuals and congregations to do so we will never develop a mission that is both appropriate to their area and sustainable.

There are a number of resources available to help churches listen and learn, such as Springboard's *Discerning Church Vocation* or the five-step approach set out by Gill:

- Analyse – identify the points of weakness in the church that foster decline and isolate those that are capable of being changed.
- Planning – draw up a careful plan based on this analysis, setting out objectives for growth that are capable of being attained.
- Responsibility – identify ways in which churchgoers may be encouraged to take more responsibility for attaining these objectives for growth.
- Develop – identify opportunities from growth that are not fully realized at present.

- Testing – having fostered responsibility and implemented development, test, and keep testing to make sure real growth is being attained.

These five steps form a cycle.[1]

However valuable these resources are, the danger is that they can be treated as a once-off initiative. The important question for us is how can we change the culture of the Church so that listening becomes a way of life. Mission Action Planning (with its useful acronym 'MAP') has tried to address this problem. It was first developed in the early 1990s by David Hope when he was Bishop of London. Subsequently a number of other dioceses, such as York, Blackburn, Gloucester and Exeter, have also adopted Mission Action Planning as a tool, although the basic concept has been developed in slightly different ways. In the Shrewsbury Episcopal Area within the Diocese of Lichfield we have been using Mission Action Planning for several years as a way of helping us to listen, to reflect, to plan and to act. In an ideal world such planning is best undertaken ecumenically and we have tried to do this with our sister churches wherever possible.

Mission Action Planning is based on the Lichfield diocesan strategy of 'Growing the Kingdom', with its four focus areas of

- Worship and Prayer
- Teaching and Nurture
- Outreach and Evangelism
- Justice and Care

These remind us of different aspects of the gospel, all of which are fundamental to the mission and ministry of the Church. Each parish or ecumenical group has been asked to work out its own Mission Action Plan, in the light of the communities they serve, their resources and their concerns. There are five main stages to Mission Action Planning:

Listen to the community

The first step is to listen to the community, using some of the ways laid out in Chapter 11. Drawing up a history (not in the sense of writing a history of the town or village, but creating a time chart, marking the important events of the past and their impact on the life of the area, including that of the church) gives a sense of the story of a locality placing the current situation in its historical context. Drawing up a contemporary community map can also be an illuminating exercise. Using large sheets of paper, all the groups, businesses and organizations in the community are recorded and links are made by arrows or overlapping circles. Exercises such as these can create a better and more holistic understanding of the local community.

Churches have sometimes listened to members of the community via focus groups or by formal or informal systems of interviews, trying to record accurately what has been said. Focus groups may ask questions about the things that really concern people; how they hope the community and its facilities could improve; and what part the church might play in this. It is significant that even this piece of work alters the church's relationship with the parish, since it takes us out of our comfort zone and helps us to listen to the people around us.

Listening to national and global issues broadens the horizons still further and saves a Christian community from becoming unhealthily self-preoccupied or narrowly parochial. Many of the issues raised in this listening process will not be able to be resolved by the church, but even understanding them represents a movement into a bigger world and will enrich the life of the church. It is important that this process of listening is shared by as many people as possible. It defeats the object of the exercise if one person or a small group does all the work and then tells the members of the PCC what the outcomes are. The process is strengthened further when 'critical friends' from other churches, or even from overseas, are involved and are given permission to be really honest with us.

Reflect on the local church

The second stage of Mission Action Planning is to reflect on the local church, its people, its buildings, its history and its resources. It can be enlightening for a congregation to reflect on its own history, to understand where it has come from and draw lessons from it. It is also often encouraging to be reminded of how much the church is already doing.

However, it is strange that the Church of England spends so much time collecting statistics about church attendance, the occasional offices, children, finance and so on, and so little time analysing the trends and what we can learn from them.[2] Jackson has done a great service to the Church by studying statistics on a national, diocesan and deanery level,[3] but few individual churches have kept records of their statistics and used them for planning. Indeed, none of the churches in the north of Shropshire included such statistics in their Mission Action Plans until I started to provide them. This is all the more sad since in many cases churches discovered for the first time that they had been growing slowly, but were unaware of it. By examining trends churches are able to identify what has not worked well (and therefore not continued with it), but also to build on what is growing.

Make a list of priorities

Third, having listened and reflected, there is a process of prayerful discernment on our calling as a Church. What does this mass of data say to us? And, more importantly, what is God saying to us through it? Discernment of priorities is vital at this juncture because sometimes churches can create such long lists of needs, concerns and 'things to do', that they are exhausted just by looking at it and feel defeated before they have even started:

> Many parish churches overwhelm themselves with actions, meetings and projects that are not necessarily directed by careful theological reflection, and may in fact be a squandering of their energies and resources rather than a faithful commitment to engage incarnationally with God in the world.[4]

Prioritizing is what many churches find most difficult. They can become so concerned not to hurt people's feelings by neglecting their ideas (or hobbyhorses) that they end up including everything in the plan, which then becomes burdensome and self-defeating. By asking questions about priorities, a PCC or a leadership team can begin to uncover the underlying issues and decide which ones have to be tackled (and, conversely, which ones can be left for the time being – or even what should be stopped altogether).

Plan focused action

Fourth, there is a need to agree on some specific actions. When it comes to translating priorities into actions, there is a tendency for churches to produce a series of vague aspirations ('We must be more loving' and 'We must do something with young people') so they are asked to make their plans 'SMART'. There are a number of different variations of what this acronym stands for, but they are usually:

- Specific: do we have a common view of exactly what it is we want to do?
- Measurable: how will we know if we have fulfilled what we set out to do?
- Achievable: is this 'pie in the sky' or something we can really do?
- Realistic: can we achieve these things within the constraints of our resources and our knowledge?
- Timed: is there enough time to complete, or too much time so there is no urgency?

Most small rural congregations make the mistake of putting too many things in their Mission Action Plan. It is far better to undertake just one action in the coming year and to do it well, than to set an over ambitious target that is bound to fail.

Another vital part of planning action is also having the courage to stop some things in the life of the church that have been productive and valuable in the past but that are no longer working well. Very often clergy and lay people feel they have an obligation to keep propping up something, usually out of personal allegiance to the person who has kept it going for many years, when it needs to be helped to die and the energy redirected to a more fruitful area.

Reading the process I have just outlined is enough to make most rural clergy want to give up. Anyone who has ministered in the countryside (perhaps excluding commuter villages) knows that rural folk do not think like this. One excellent rural parish priest in Shropshire told me that in the first year he had to write every part of the Mission Action Plan himself. He could not find anyone willing to work with him on it. He tabled it at his three PCCs and received virtually no response. The same thing happened in the second year when he revised the three Mission Action Plans. However, in the following year he received some comments and contributions from members of the PCC. It can take a long time in the countryside for new ways of working and thinking to begin to impact. Mission Action Planning is a tool to be used for the long term and in some rural parishes will take many years before it begins to get into the culture of the church. The important thing is to work with the principles, adapting them to the context.

Ensure regular follow-up

One of the most important aspects of Mission Action Plans is the annual follow-up meeting, which is fundamental to their success. From the very start, we have stressed that this is not a once-off initiative that can be undertaken, then filed away and forgotten about. An integral part of the process is that each year the PCC of every parish or united benefice reviews and updates their Mission Action Plan and sends a copy to the bishop and rural dean. They then get a visit from either the bishop, the archdeacon, the rural dean or one of the sector ministers who comes to listen, to discuss and to pray with them. It is a means both of support and accountability. The parishes know that they have been listened to. The person who is conducting the follow-up meetings learns new things and is also able to share good experience from other parishes. Some of the key questions for the person conducting the follow-up meeting are: 'What stories or insights do you have to share with other parishes?' and 'What do you want to learn from others?'

Mission Action Plans are not a panacea for the Church's ills. They have not suddenly turned churches into communities of vibrant believers, willing to try anything or go anywhere for the sake of the gospel. Nevertheless, they are gradually creating a new culture where people are seeking to listen, where they are not afraid to ask hard questions, where a vision for the future is nurtured, and where every member of the Church is discovering that he or she has a vital role if the Church is going to grow.

The parishes of Llanymynech, Morton, Llanybodwell and Trefonen are the western most parishes in the Diocese of Lichfield and lie on the Welsh border. They have a combined population of about 4,700 people and were brought together as a group in the late 1990s. They are currently served by a stipendiary priest, the Revd Christopher Penn, two active retired priests, two readers and one of the churches, Trefonen, has a mandated ministry team. As the PCCs worked on their Mission Action Plans they became aware of the many families, young people and children in the parish. They consulted widely and decided that if they were going to maintain long-term contact with young people, then it was vital to work with families, not just with the children and teenagers. Having applied for money from the Diocesan Growth Fund they were able to

---

appoint a full-time youth and families' worker in 2006. The job description was broad in its scope to allow the worker, Ian Evans, freedom to get to know people and work out the best way to engage with them. He has used the baptism registers in order to contact families who have had some involvement with the churches. He is working in the schools and is also involved in running film clubs for young people in two of the churches, which provide opportunities for discussion groups. This holistic approach is designed to develop strong links with families in the parishes over the long term.

Having worked with a wide variety of rural churches on their Mission Action Plans over the last five years, I have identified four areas that merit special attention: welcome, worship, ministry and evangelism.

Rethinking 'welcome'

The dominical command at the end of Matthew's Gospel was not to make converts or churchgoers, but rather to 'make disciples'.[5] Disciples are people who are constantly learning and who are following the example of their master – Christ himself. Disciples are out and about in the world working for the coming of God's kingdom by living out the gospel values as taught by Christ and by preaching the good news in word and deed. This is what we mean by vocation. Most Christians would agree that we want churches full of disciples who are concerned to work for the coming of the kingdom. The difficult question is 'How do we encourage this?'

Mission-Shaped Church has helpfully reminded us that in today's generation there is much less emphasis on duties and obligations. Research shows that levels of social capital are declining in the UK and across Europe.[6] There is some truth in the generalization that people today approach the world (and the Church) from the perspective of individuals who demand the right to choose and who expect to be served. They see themselves as customers rather than citizens with responsibilities, as individuals rather than subjects with obligations. We may wish that they approached life from a different perspective, but that will not change the situation. For many years, cathedrals have used the phrase 'turning visitors into pilgrims'. Perhaps the challenge for the Church today is how to turn 'consumers into disciples', which will require a deep understanding and appreciation of the contemporary mindset.

One of the starting points for the Church, whether it is in a traditional-style church or in a fresh expression, is to understand how to welcome people, since this reveals whether their primary concern is for themselves or for those outside. Most people confuse greeting with welcoming. Greeting is about a smile, saying 'hello' at the beginning of the service or event, and 'goodbye' at the end. Welcoming is the long process that takes place after greeting. Welcoming has happened when a person realizes that they are valued for who they are and, if they wish to, are allowed to offer their gifts and energies to make a contribution. Welcoming has taken place when someone knows they belong and have a role to play.

One of the interesting experiences on my recent sabbatical was staying away from home and worshipping in different churches in mufti. I was greeted with a smile as I entered most (but not all) churches. Several churches announced that there were refreshments after the service, and on one occasion a sidesman mentioned it again as I left. I am sure that all of those churches think that they are friendly and are good at welcoming, but on no occasion was I shown to a seat or did anyone offer to go with me into the refreshment area. No one approached me to start a conversation. This contrasts strongly, for example, with the practice of most supermarkets today where if you ask a member of staff for the location of an item in the store, he or she will walk with you to show you where it is. They work on the principle that every customer matters and needs to be made to feel valued and important. It takes a confident person to be willing to make their way into a church hall after a service for a cup of coffee and wait around in the hope that someone will come to talk to them. Many people fear, rightly, that they may well land up standing by themselves in the corner with no one to chat to them.

Robert Warren likens the process of someone joining a church to the birth of a child. There are months of hidden activity during the pregnancy, the pain of the birth, and the disruption of having the newborn in the home. It can be a long, complex and messy process. Most people in church do not have the gifts and the confidence to approach a stranger to greet them and to begin the process of welcoming. However, there are usually one or two people in the church who do have this gift, and it needs to be recognized and the person encouraged to see that it is of vital importance for the church. We need to be systematic about welcome, especially in larger communities and congregations.

I was about to conduct a confirmation service in a small village church. The churchwardens had led me around the outside of the building and we were standing at the west door waiting to enter as a young couple arrived with a baby in a pushchair. They had recently moved into the village and it was their first visit. At the end of the service I greeted them and (although I was not one of the locals) encouraged them to go to the reception in the village hall. When I arrived some 15 minutes later I found there was a happy buzz in the hall with people sitting around tables chatting to one another. There in the corner was the couple sitting by themselves with no one talking to them. I managed to have a few words with them before meeting the confirmation candidates. I watched out of the corner of my eye. The vicar went and had a talk for a few moments, but no one else approached them. After another ten minutes they slipped out of the door. I am sure that the congregation would have been horrified if anyone had said they were unfriendly – but they were.

One of the most basic lessons that every thriving business has taken on board today is that people matter and that every customer is important. As I have already intimated, most people in the Church would echo this, although it is not always what newcomers experience. However, the point is not to leave people as dependent 'customers' in the Church, but to allow the gospel to transform them into kingdom-focused, mission-shaped people who want to participate in God's work in the world. But it is no good hoping that kingdom-centred people are going to turn up out of nowhere to join our churches. When most people first try out a church or are considering the Christian faith they come for a variety of reasons and with different motivations. They may arrive because they are genuinely seeking God, or because they are looking for friends, or because they want to join in with the church in trying to make the world a better place. It will probably be for a mixture of selfish and altruistic reasons. We need, therefore, to be the sort of community that enables each of us to be changed and become more outward looking.

This will come about through a variety of things. The preaching and the prayers are two areas where worshippers can be helped to look outwards to the community and to the world. The charitable giving of a congregation is another point at which our concerns and sympathies can be nurtured with a kingdom-shaped vision. The agendas of PCCs need to ensure that they are concerned with more than maintenance of a building and to reflect on the wider world and the local community. Christians can be encouraged to get involved in practical forms of service in the community, and even the elderly and the housebound can play their part by praying or writing letters. In rural areas there are a number of specific opportunities available, such as increasing awareness of countryside issues and relating to the farming community. This is particularly important in those villages that have become dormitories for people from urban areas and who may have little opportunity to talk face to face with those who are working on the land. The church is sometimes one of the few organizations that can broker meetings between, for example, the commuters and farmers in an area.

Rethinking worship

A small village congregation cannot offer a wide range of services like a large urban church. Indeed, in most villages there is likely to be just one service each week or, in a few cases, one a fortnight. As stipendiary clergy have taken over responsibility for more and more churches, we have inadvertently structured decline by building the life of the church around the availability of the clergy. So we have organized the times of services to allow the priest to move from church to church. On the first Sunday of the month there may be Common Worship Holy Communion at 9 a.m., on the second Sunday there is Evensong from the Book of Common Prayer at 6 p.m. (but brought forward to 3.30 p.m. in the winter), on the third Sunday there is an All Age Service at 11 a.m., and on the fourth Sunday there is a fresh expression in the village hall at 5 p.m. On the fifth Sunday all the congregations combine and the service moves around the churches. This is fine for the regular attenders, but is designed to create a club mentality within the congregation who attend most weeks, take the parish magazine, and are committed enough to check where and when the service will be.

But today we are living in a consumer culture. If we phone a shop or a bank and are not answered within a few rings, we put the phone down and give up on them. No other organization allows its main shop-front activities to be so hit and miss as the local church, and casual or infrequent worshippers are less likely than regular attenders to be able to work out the times of services. Such people only have to make the effort once or twice to arrive at church and find that they have the wrong time or place to decide not to bother to come again. Francis identified this problem in his *Church Watch*, which took an in-depth look at 121 rural churches:

> So many rural churches now seem to exist as tightly knit inward-looking communities. They see no need to open their building to visitors. They see no need to provide Christian literature or aids to prayer to help visitors on their spiritual pilgrimage. They see no need to identify who it is within the community who can proclaim the gospel of salvation and meet with those in need. They see no need to advertise their services. They feel able to change the times of services or to cancel services, simply by telephoning round the faithful few.[7]

The ideal we need to work towards is to have a weekly service in every church at a regular time. This will necessitate the development of teams of lay leaders for the services and may mean in some rural areas that we do not have so many services of Holy Communion. Francis and Martineau (2002, p. 122) argue that it is vital that there is regularity of worship in each church and think that 'united' services in a benefice lead to reductions in the numbers of people who worship.

One deanery in a very rural area of Shropshire has been experimenting with holding an annual joint service on a Sunday morning. All the churches in the deanery were encouraged to close their normal Sunday service and to come together for a celebration. Part of the rationale was that it was a great encouragement for people who worship in small congregations to get together and worship in a full church. On a normal Sunday morning there would be about 350 people in the churches in the deanery. The joint service was attended by about 250 people. The net result was that those who came (most of whom formed the committed core of each rural church) were encouraged, but as many as 100 regular worshippers simply took the Sunday off. These may well have been the less committed, who were either getting *into* the habit of regular worship or who were in fact gradually dropping out. In addition there were probably some other people from the fringe of the Church who turned up at their local church to find there was no service that Sunday. Such an experience makes it more likely that they will think twice before trying church again. It is important that we find ways of encouraging small rural congregations, but it is better to do so by holding united services at other times which do not detract from the normal Sunday morning worship.

There is a place for joint services in rural benefices, but these should be the services that only the committed core are likely to attend anyway, such as Ash Wednesday, Maundy Thursday, Good Friday and Saints' Days or special one-off services such as an open-air Songs of Praise on a summer's evening.

The Revd David Baldwin, the vicar of Edstaston, Whixall and Tilstock, inherited a pattern of services that meant that the times of services were different in each church every Sunday. Three years ago he persuaded the PCCs to rethink the pattern and timing of services. Now each church has a service at the same time each week. The numbers of worshippers has increased slightly each year, and even those who were not keen on the changes admit that the regularity of worship is the factor that has helped the congregations to build.

Another factor that encourages decline is the practice of alternating styles of worship on offer each Sunday. This is usually done for the best of reasons, since in many villages it is only possible to have one service on a Sunday. In an ideal world, every worshipper would be understanding and would be willing to put up with styles of worship that they themselves do not particularly like. In practice, many families are only prepared to come once a month to the all-age worship, and some of the regular churchgoers only attend the traditional styles of service. It is for this reason that I believe groups of rural churches have to co-operate, so that a wide variety of worship styles are on offer across the different churches. Instead of competing with one another, rural multi-parish benefices (or even whole deaneries) need to advertise one another's services (avoiding jargon such as 'BCP' or 'CW', which will only be understood by people who are familiar with church culture). Some people will gravitate to one parish because they want something more traditional, others will go elsewhere because they want something with a more contemporary feel. This, of course, is not without its problems, since the existing congregations will include people who want different styles of worship and will not want to move to another church. However, in the long run it is more likely that congregations will be sustained and grown if there is regularity in time and style of worship. It is crucial that each congregation is helped to see that it is part of the worldwide Church, as are the other churches in the locality, even if they have a very different style of worship and church-manship.

For some years the parish of St Michael's Child's, Ercall, has had a pattern of fortnightly services on Sunday mornings at 9.30 a.m. using Common Worship. The clergy, the Revd Jeremy Stagg and the Revd Linda Chapman, wanted to encourage families to attend but found that most of them felt that 9.30 a.m. was too early. Unfortunately, it was difficult for the clergy to be there at any other time, without altering the times of worship in several other churches. Eventually a compromise was reached. Once a month the Common Worship Holy Communion was radically shortened and immediately followed by a Family Service at 10 a.m. This has worked well and the regular worshippers have stayed on for the Family Service.

There had not been any evening services in the church for a long while, but on a hunch it was decided to try a monthly Sung Evensong. Surprisingly, this has attracted a congregation of between 20 and 30 worshippers, some from the village and some from the surrounding area. About half of these people were not worshipping in the church on a regular basis before. It is unlikely that in the long run this will attract totally new people to the faith. Nevertheless, it is serving an important role in providing worship for as wide a group as possible in the villages. In rural areas, the 'mixed economy' church means listening to old-timers and newcomers and trying to find the best way forward.

We also need to think carefully about re-ordering rural churches. Gill's research suggests that tiny congregations meeting in large churches are one of the main reasons why churches are perceived to be failing. He quotes approvingly from Cox:

> The empty church is the single most important piece of evidence brought forth by people who argue that religion has become unimportant. They are right, but not for the reasons they think.[8]

There is still a hidden assumption that proper worship is what happens in a large congregation with an organ and a full choir. Our church buildings give out the same message as week by week the congregations of most rural churches sit in front of empty choir stalls whose subliminal message is that something is missing. The lectern and pulpit are designed for a declamatory style of reading and preaching that may be suitable for a packed church, but is inappropriate where there are 12 people in the congregation. Most hymnbooks continue to be compiled with large congregations and a choir in mind. For example, many hymns are pitched for a four-part choir, which means that the melody is usually too high for most people to sing comfortably (interestingly, the pitch of people's voices has gone down in recent years, which has made the problem even more acute).

But small can be beautiful, and we need to create acts of worship that are designed for small groups. Sometimes a side chapel is a better setting for worship than the nave, especially if it can be heated separately. A moveable nave altar may be more appropriate for a small congregation. It is not necessary to sing all the verses of a hymn, and it is possible to pitch them at a level where they are easier to sing. This is not about bringing worship down to the lowest common denominator, but finding what works well with a small congregation and building on it. In some cases, it is not possible to adapt the medieval church building to modern needs, and we may have to worship in a hall or community centre that is warm, light and has all the facilities that families expect nowadays.

Rethinking collaborative ministry

One of the points I argued in the previous section is that in some rural multi-parish benefices we have structured decline by organizing Sunday worship around the availability of the priest. The committed core of the congregation deal with this well (indeed, they usually like it) since they know what is going on and do not mind travelling to a neighbouring village, but the people on the fringe of the church find it more difficult to become part of the regular worshipping community. I am convinced that it is essential that we maintain high-quality worship in every church at a regular time each week.

However, there are a number of areas in the life of the church where collaboration between several small rural congregations has tangible benefits, and this is particularly the case in the sphere of ministry. When groups of rural churches begin to work together it is sometimes possible to have a deanery office, staffed by paid or voluntary help to organize rotas and deal with baptism, wedding and funeral enquiries. Groups of rural churches can achieve economies of scale by producing a benefice magazine. Several of the multi-parish benefices in north Shropshire have lay ministry teams made up of people from different congregations. In one village there may be a person who has a particular gift with caring for the bereaved, in another village church there is a reader, and in yet another there is someone who is good at children's work. These lay ministers can be part of a team that works across the whole benefice. Likewise, a single rural church is unlikely to have enough people to justify putting on a training course for leading intercessions in church, baptismal preparation, or on faith in the workplace. However, across a united benefice and in co-operation with Christians of other denominations, there may be sufficient people to run such training and offer ongoing support.

Rethinking mission and evangelism

In many smaller villages there may be too few people to organize support for the community, such as lunches for the elderly, holiday activities for children, or welcome and support for migrant workers on farms. This is where groups of rural churches (wherever possible, working ecumenically) or even deaneries can find a role. By careful listening to local needs and pulling together whatever resources can be found, it has been possible in some places for churches to make a significant contribution to the well-being of the people in the area.

In 1991 the vicar of Oswestry, the Revd Preb David Crowhurst, challenged Bill Bowen, one of the members of the congregation of St Oswald's Church, by asking what he was going to do for the Decade of Evangelism. Bill was aware that there were seven women's groups in the parish, but nothing specifically for men, so he decided to start a monthly breakfast.

The first breakfast was held in September 1992 in St Oswald's Parish Centre, and it has been held regularly since then on the second Thursday of the month. From the beginning it was decided that it should be an ecumenical event, so he invited people from the Methodist Church, the Community Church and five people from St Oswald's, with David Crowhurst as the speaker. It was well received and it was decided that on the following month each person would bring a friend. When October arrived there were 16 men present. Name labels were put at each place to mix people up. Bill did the cooking and others helped with the clearing up.

Nowadays the breakfast starts at 7 a.m. and there is a speaker who has a short slot from 7.45 a.m. to 8 a.m. after which the meeting concludes with prayer. The Breakfast Fellowship has grown now to an average monthly attendance of just over 70 men from all sorts of denominations, many of whom come from the surrounding villages. Part of the secret of the breakfast's success is that the catering is so good. A full English breakfast is served, starting with a choice of cereals, fruit juices and Florida cocktail. It is followed by grilled bacon and sausage, fried eggs, hash browns, black pudding, tomatoes and mushrooms. It is finished with toast and marmalade, washed down with plenty of tea and coffee. Most of the catering equipment has been bought over the years from the surplus money raised and anything left over is given away to charity.

Few of the local village churches have enough men around to organize any sort of regular activity. However, this breakfast has enabled people to come from the town and from the surrounding villages to find fellowship, teaching and good food.

When it comes to evangelism, Finney found that there were a variety of factors in people coming to faith, with the influence of spouses, friends and the priest/minister being the most influential.[9] However, other factors could also be identified – such as evangelistic events, church activities, reading the Bible, Christian books and films. Most village churches will not have sufficient people to run a variety of forms of evangelism, but if they co-operate across a benefice, or even across the whole deanery, all sorts of things become possible. For example, most villages could not possibly use a full-time children's or youth worker – even if they could afford it – but a group of rural churches are sometimes able to do this. Many multi-parish benefices run Alpha or Emmaus courses across a wider area. In some places there are men's evenings in pubs or men's breakfasts, drawing on people from several miles around. Elsewhere there are evenings of apologetics based on talks or discussions. These are all areas that are unlikely to be viable in a small village, but that can thrive if planned across a multi-parish benefice or ecumenically.

Notes

1 Gill, 1994, p. 83.

2 Fortunately, this gap is now starting to be filled by such books as Barley, 2007a, 2007b and 2007c.

3 Jackson, 2002 and 2005.

4 Green, 1990, p. 103.

5 Matthew 28.18.

6 See, for example, Halpern, 1995, p. 383, Wilkinson and Mulgan, 1995, pp. 99–106, and Park, 2004, pp. 37–9.

7 Francis, 1996, p. 242.

8 Gill, 2003, p. 31, quoting Cox, 1982, p. 276.

9 Finney, 1992, p. 36.

14

Refocusing for Mission

Throughout Part 4 of this book I have been arguing that every constituent part of the Church needs to be examined if we are going to re-engage with each local community. It is no good leaving the task to a national network of 'fresh expressions' officers and church planters. If we are to be a missionary church again, it will need to affect every part of church life. In this chapter I return to the theological starting point that everything needs to be built on God and that the nature of leadership and the structures of the Church need to be remodelled in the light of this.

Maintaining a clear focus on God

It is all too easy for churches to lose sight of what they are about. The relentless pressure to keep the show on the road, to maintain the church building, and to deal with the ever-growing mountain of paperwork mean we can forget what is at the heart of our calling. In Chapter 4 I argued that the focus of all that we are and all that we do is God. It is not, in the first instance, church – or even mission. When other things become our main focus we will be little more than a campaigning group (along with every other anti-poverty or pro-environment group), a heritage lobby, a self-help group catering for the needs of its members, or simply an outdated organization looking for those beyond its membership to delay the arrival of its sell-by date.

There is also an important question about the underlying motivation of our mission and ministry. It is possible for churches and individuals to be driven by their fears of the future or of change. Such congregations are hardly going to be places where the grace of God will be experienced and lived. Christian mission and ministry arises from a vision of God and is sustained by prayer and an inner stillness that is the gift of the Holy Spirit. It is in response to the grace and call of God, rather than in reaction to threat or fear.

I do not think that there is a church in the land that would not sign up to the need to maintain a clear focus on God. However, it is interesting that our church buildings, our services and websites often send out different messages about our real values and concerns. An examination of a church's weekly news-sheet, the parish magazine or the noticeboard soon reveals whether the spiritual life of the church is at its core and is the motivating force behind all that goes on. A look at the church accounts will disclose the values of a congregation and illustrate its priorities. An analysis of the PCC minutes will show what it is ultimately concerned about, and an examination of the way that the PCC works may also be revealing. There are those who are content to push through difficult decisions on a narrow majority, while others want to spend time in prayer and listening in order to discern the guidance of the Holy Spirit.

The fundamental work of leaders, whether ordained or lay, is to ensure that the worship of God is central, that as far as possible we are motivated by God's call and grace, and that we are growing in holiness and service. This will be worked out in different ways. In some traditions this will mean making spiritual direction, quiet days and retreats the priority. In others, it may mean focusing on encouraging people to use Bible reading notes and attend prayer meetings. In addition, for some people pilgrimages, Taizé, Cursillo, Focalare, Spring Harvest or Soul Survivor will be the means to sustain and encourage them in the faith.

This focus on God also needs to be translated into the way that we welcome visitors and how we tell the story about the church building. In recent years there have been about thirty-four million visits made to our churches each year (excluding cathedrals, minsters and abbeys). People come for a wide variety of reasons, including an interest in history, searching for their roots, or even just an opportunity to sit down in quiet for a few moments. What messages do we give when they come to visit? Most churches have guidebooks that focus almost exclusively on history. However, it is equally possible to explain the significance of the building from the perspective of faith and worship, to have photographs of the congregation (making the point that the church is the people of God), to describe the church's involvement in the community and in supporting charities. While it is good to have Bibles available, most people will not be able to find their way around them. It may be better to have some helpful biblical passages printed out and put in the pews or in a side chapel. Literature can be available to suggest ways to pray. Intercession boards and the opportunity to light candles may also be helpful. Some churches have produced a booklet, written by members of the congregation, reflecting on how their faith has grown and been nurtured, especially in times of suffering or difficulty. These are all things that communicate that our ultimate concern is about God.

Mission-shaped bishops

When I was ordained bishop in 2001, I set about reading (and, in some cases, re-reading) books on episcopacy and the theology of episcopacy. I soon discovered that nearly all of the theological reflections on leadership and episcopacy, as well as the examples of how particular bishops have chosen to use their time, come from the periods when the Church was an established institution in Christendom.

In the early centuries of the Church we see the role of bishops evolving in relation to the rapid spread of Christianity and in response to the changing attitude of the Roman state to the Church. Following the death of the apostles, the bishops became the prime teachers and defenders of the faith, pastors of their congregations and presidents of the liturgy. With the cessation of the persecutions, however, came a huge influx of converts who did not necessarily have a mature faith, and from the end of the fourth century onwards we can plot the gradual but progressive fragmentation of the Roman Empire. The bishops found themselves navigating unchartered waters, increasingly having to cope with unrealistic expectations from an anxious populace, propelled into the political vacuum created by the demise of civic life. This, more than anything, fundamentally altered the shape and character of their ministry and, with a few notable exceptions, eclipsed the missionary task that lay at the heart of their ministry. As the Report of the Archbishops' Group on the Episcopate, entitled *Episcopal Ministry*, put it:

> The missionary role of the bishop as minister of the Word altered after the first generations, as his principal function came, on the whole, to be the service of the needs of the life of the existing community. Augustine of Canterbury was sent to England at the end of the sixth century as a monk-missionary, by Pope Gregory the Great, and consecrated Archbishop of Canterbury at Arles only when the mission was well established. During the period of decline of the Roman Empire and the early mediaeval centuries Christianity spread throughout Western Europe partly by conquest and partly by private enterprise, on the part largely of monastic missionaries such as Boniface (680–754) and

Willibrord (658–739). Willibrord was consecrated Archbishop of the Frisians by the Pope in 695, and thus became a 'missionary bishop' rather in the way that Augustine had been. In the later Middle Ages the emphasis was upon the winning back of Christians who had strayed into heresy, with fresh missionary endeavour a conscious second to that. Bernard of Clairvaux argued in the twelfth century that Christendom ought to put its house in order before it sought to convert Moslems or Jews to the faith. Again, we see some individuals achieving conversions. But it cannot be said to have been seen as a major responsibility of the episcopate to foster, or indeed to lead, mission in a mediaeval world where every soul in the greater part of Europe was baptised and all could be deemed to come already within the Church's fold.[1]

The formative model of leadership within Christendom (and which we still take for granted today) arises from the convergence of two contemporary sixth-century streams of thought: St Benedict's *Rule* (governing the religious – monks and nuns) and Pope Gregory the Great's treatise entitled *Pastoral Care* (governing secular – that is, parish clergy). These two models have been hugely influential in shaping Christian leadership for more than 1,000 years. As with virtually all sermons on leadership in the patristic period, Benedict and Gregory drew upon the imagery of the shepherd, specifically on the charge of the risen Christ to Peter recorded in John 21.15–22.[2] This is, of course, a foundational image of Christian leadership. While the Church continued to grow, or was at least strong enough to survive, the principal role of bishops was oversight. However, this assumes there is a flock to lead. With the relentless decline in committed, practising Christians in the UK, the pressing question for us today is not just how to look after the existing sheep, but how to breed new flocks.

Most bishops are deeply involved in the wider mission of the Church. For example, the bishops who sit in the House of Lords seek to influence public policy in a Christian direction. They preside at confirmations (although these only usually attract people who have some significant connection with the Church) and attend public functions in the diocese (although one can attend hundreds of social events and not be in the least sense 'missionary'). There is much talk about the bishops being a 'presence' or 'a sign', and many of them are excellent at using the media.

Despite all of this, I suspect that if you asked an Anglican bishop to log his diary over a month, you would find that the bulk of his time is consumed in what are essentially bureaucratic tasks – such as a vastly increased workload in making clergy appointments, dealing with correspondence, complaints, or planning and attending meetings. It would be fascinating to see how much of a bishop's time was spent in actually teaching the faith; or in face-to-face encounters with non-believers discussing faith and belief; or in real, tangible apologetics; or even in strategic planning about how other clergy might be involved in such work.

If there is going to be a concerted and sustained engagement with our contemporary culture, as called for by the 1988 Lambeth Conference and the *Mission-Shaped Church* report, then it will need clear and consistent leadership by the bishops and clergy as well as the synods. Having said that, I am not suggesting that it is the bishops who will make this change happen. Church history gives little comfort to those who think that such new initiatives happen top-down. Indeed, most of the great movements of spiritual renewal have taken place despite the Church – or sometimes even in the face of opposition from church leaders. One only has to think of the rise of monasticism in the fourth century; or the radical lifestyle of St Francis and his followers in the twelfth century; or the passion and energy created first by the Evangelical Awakening of the eighteenth century; or the Oxford Movement in the nineteenth century. The accounts in *Mission-Shaped Church* show that a wide variety of groundbreaking experiments are already going on at a grassroots level across the UK, sometimes with little support from bishops – or even unknown to them.

Although bishops and synods are unlikely to generate new movements of mission and evangelism, they can (and sometimes do) block them, stifle them or hinder them. This is not so much a deliberate strategy; it is just that most leaders have emerged from a culture that is cautious and conservative. Few leaders in the Church are chosen for their ability to be entrepreneurs. This is the point that Jackson makes when he argues that bishops have to move into strategic mode.[3]

When I first became an archdeacon I was told that if I was not sure about any legal questions I could phone the diocesan registrar who would tell me what I could or could not do. Within a few months I learnt that you never start by asking a diocesan registrar 'Can I do this?' since most of them are naturally cautious. I discovered that the key question to the registrar is 'How can I do this within the constraints of the law?' Canon law should not be seen as an immoveable edifice, hanging over us and preventing us from taking new initiatives. Its purpose is to help us regulate and order our common life in the light of the gospel and society, and it needs to evolve as we find ourselves in new situations. This is why the *Pastoral Measure 1983* will shortly be replaced by the *Dioceses, Pastoral and Mission Measure*, which is currently passing through General Synod.[4]

The task of bishops in this generation is to create space where a vision of society that is about human justice and human flourishing can be nurtured and articulated; where listening can happen; where experimentation is encouraged and blessed; where new initiatives in mission and evangelism are tried and tested; where theological reflection on new developments takes place; where the stories of what is happening are told more widely, so that others may learn and build on them.

Recapturing a positive vision

Too much of our time is taken up with running a shrinking organization ('keeping the show on the road') and our internal politics that there is little time or energy for the most important priorities facing us. As a Church, we need a shift of emphasis from the institution to discover a compelling vision of what the world might be. Sadly, many Christians and churches are trapped in the past rather than excited by this challenge. Consequently we find ourselves locked into a defensive posture. This is not to trivialize our traditions or history. Indeed, without them a form of dementia can affect communities and nations, for without a corporate memory society can easily lose its way. Bereaved of the past, including the lessons and wisdom of previous generations, the Church becomes imprisoned in the present, vulnerable to the claims of expediency and the whims of the latest fads. Bishops are rightly seen as guardians of the tradition. However, the past is not to be used to limit what God is calling us to be and to do. When a church finds its identity solely in its traditions and ancient buildings, it can become obsessed by them. As a result the overwhelming impression that is given to the world of the Church is a religious version of the National Trust, whose only concern is raising money to maintain its ancient buildings.

The other danger is that in a fast-changing world the Church becomes defined by being against things: against women, gene and stem cell research and so on. Organizations that are defined by what they are *against* find it almost impossible to grow. In the short term they recruit people who are dissatisfied with the way things are going, but when the agenda moves on or public perceptions change, they are left stranded. For example, this is the problem for the UK Independence Party which is best known for its stance against British membership of the European Community. In a similar vein, Forward in Faith (despite its name) is unlikely to thrive in the long run if one of its most fundamental purposes is to be *against* something (women bishops and women priests).

There are, of course, times when the Church has no option but to take a stand on some issues. This was the stark choice faced by the Confessing Churches in Nazi Germany in the 1930s and 1940s. Church history shows that Christians have related to society in various ways. For example, there are those who have made a radical separation from society, such as the Desert Fathers and Mothers, who felt called to leave society and live an alternative lifestyle. Their presence soon attracted people into the desert and challenged them to reflect on their beliefs and values. In other periods Christians have immersed themselves in the problems of the world and have tried to change them. In the words of William Booth, the founder of the Salvation Army:

> While women weep as they do now, I'll fight; while little children go hungry as they do now, I'll fight; while men go to prison, in and out, in and out, I'll fight; while there is a poor lost girl upon the street, I'll fight; while there remains one dark soul without the light of God, I'll fight – I'll fight to the end.

But in other periods of history the Church has resonated with society and found that it can act as the channel of the fears and aspirations of the communities in which it is set. This happened in the nineteenth century during the Methodist revival when alcoholism and poverty were endemic in many urban areas. Conversion, faith and the class system provided a way out of the problems and opened up a new life for many people.

In today's complex world there is no single way for Christians to share in God's mission. The challenge will be different in multicultural areas of inner cities, in areas of rural poverty, and among the wealthy parts of cities. The important thing is for Christians in each area to discern how they are going to engage with their community and how they can embody and share a positive, life-affirming vision of society and human flourishing.

There have been many times when the Church has been grasped with a vision of the kingdom and risen above its self-interest – such as in the fight against slavery and child labour in the eighteenth and nineteenth centuries. More recently the Make Poverty History campaign has also had the effect of taking us out of our survival mentality and working for a greater vision of what the world might become. It is significant that both our archbishops are committed to this sort of positive public engagement, if in different ways. Archbishop Rowan Williams in many of his inaugural interviews and sermons spoke forcefully about the need 'to re-imagine' what it means to be human and, in the light of it, to forge a more just and compassionate society. He has been able to engage with the intelligentsia and policy-makers as part of the apologetic task. In contrast, Archbishop John Sentamu seems to have the knack of embodying a positive message liturgically (consider his services of welcome at Birmingham and York) and in engaging with the media (living in a tent in York Minster for a week). There is a vital role for bishops, clergy and lay leaders to stimulate this process of 're-imagining' in and beyond the Christian community.

But are these small signs enough? Although the Church of England is quite good at a number of aspects of mission,[5] the evangelistic element of mission is still seen by the majority of leaders (and congregations) as an 'add on', as a side-interest for a group of enthusiasts, to be fitted around all the usual business that makes up the life of the (rapidly declining) Church of England. But *Mission-Shaped Church* is prescriptive on this point:

> This is in line with other pressures to ensure that bishops are sufficiently free from administrative overload to be able to invest time in a more apostolic role, developing mission strategy and taking the lead in the discernment of priority mission initiatives.[6]

The problem with the report is that it has no suggestions about how this might come about. Is there any evidence to suggest that either the leaders, or those who are being led, have the appetite for such fundamental change? Are church leaders so desirous of growth (and here I specifically include *numerical* growth) that they are ready to make the necessary changes and sacrifices? There are a number of reasons why this is likely to be difficult.

First, like all the major denominations, the Church of England has bought in deeply to an institutional and bureaucratic model of church that so dominates our thinking and our praxis that even those of us who try to be missionary leaders still focus the vast majority of our time and effort inwards. The institutional model of the Church is undergirded by a long and honourable theological tradition, drawing upon selective parts of the New Testament to give it validity. At a practical level, this puts bishops (and, to some extent, clergy) into privileged positions, which means that we have a vested interest in maintaining the status quo. It is said that in the early church the bishops wore green for growth, not the Roman colour of purple which denoted privilege.

'The Irish drew heavily on an Egyptian tradition – or one could call it a monastic tradition – of the bishop's office, to which Martin of Tours had belonged. The nature of this tradition was that holy orders and Episcopal consecration were among the weapons with which the devil attacked the humility of holy men.'[7]

Second, in a time of change the danger for Christian leaders is that, purely at a practical level, they can find more than enough to challenge and stimulate (as well as consume their time) within the organization of the Church and therefore not give sufficient time and energy to engage with the mission task in any strategic or sustained way. Bouyer, in a critique of Roman Catholic bishops, lamented:

What then are we to think of diocesan bishops who nowadays ask for an auxiliary from Rome, not because illness or old age prevents them from fulfilling their proper duties, but in order to devote their full time to work on commissions, to make or study reports, or the like? As the late Secretary of State, Cardinal Villot, said to me, showing bishops' files accumulating on his desk, 'They just do not realize what they are or should do! They want auxiliaries to do their own task, whilst they devote all their time and interest to the duties proper to a vicar general. In the best periods in the life of the Church, nobody would have thought such duties were even those of a presbyter, but only of a deacon!'[8]

If we wish to see the Church reconnect with the contemporary world then the leaders will have to stand back from the inherited models of episcopal leadership (that is, people whose primary task is to run an institution), and re-imagine the task for our generation. It will be a costly undertaking that will necessitate letting go of many of the trappings of privilege. If we are going to respond to the challenges and opportunities of our present age, we may need to examine models of episcopal leadership from other periods (in particular, that during the pre-Constantinian period, in the Celtic church, and during what used to be called the 'mission field') when the leadership of the Church was faced with the question of whether or not the Church would even survive. In the early centuries bishops were normatively evangelists and apologists. Frend, describing the mission in Osrhoene in the second century, noted that 'Bishops and clergy seem often to have been itinerant, preaching from village to village travelling with merchant caravans.'[9]

St Aidan was a bishop, based in the monastery at Lindisfarne, yet he travelled extensively as an evangelist. John Finney, writing about the Anglo-Saxon church, argues, 'The early bishops were evangelists. Whether Roman or Celtic they see their prime task as bringing the gospel to the pagans, baptising them into Christ and bringing them up in the faith.'[10] Many of the Celtic saints, such as Patrick, Chad and Wilfred, were consecrated and sent out to do their missionary work, often basing themselves in minsters.[11] In the seventh century Paulinus was consecrated in order to accompany the daughter of King Ethelbert to the north when she married Edwin. He then became a missionary, travelling extensively to spread the faith.

In the nineteenth century a number of bishops were consecrated as missionary bishops. In 1861 John Patteson was made bishop of Melanesia and Charles Mackenzie was made bishop of 'an undefined diocese somewhere in Central Africa'.[12] This was the first time an Anglican bishop was consecrated to head up a mission. Samuel Crowther was consecrated in 1864 to be a missionary bishop in East Nigeria. None of them had established dioceses to go to, but they were sent out to make converts and to create dioceses. In similar fashion, throughout the 1990s the Nigerian church consecrated a number of missionary bishops to work in the north of the country. Each of them was assigned an area to work in, but there were no diocesan structures in place. Perhaps the time has come for the Church of England to make mission and evangelism a higher priority in the selection of its bishops.

Mission-shaped clergy

As far as I know, there has been little work undertaken on the sort of changes that we might need to make to the selection (and even the training) of bishops. This is significant since extensive work has been done on the selection and training of the parish clergy. In the new guidelines for the selection of clergy, the changing culture of society and the Church is noted:

> In previous generations ministry was exercised in a culture where Christian beliefs and behaviours were the norm; today's context is more of a spiritual and moral market-place.

> Ministers in the Church of England must pursue their vocation increasingly aware of the missionary context in which the Church is set.

> In the New Testament unity is important and is always for the sake of mission.[13]

One of the most significant changes in the guidelines is the addition of a new criterion, 'Mission and Evangelism', and the fact that they argue that all those being ordained should have a basic commitment to the way that the Church needs to look more outward in mission:

> Candidates should demonstrate an openness to being part of re-envisioning and reshaping the Church for mission.[14]

However, the guidelines state that for those who are going to lead churches there needs to be more than general support for mission. Such leaders have to be able to lead a congregation to become a missionary community:

> In candidates whose ministry is envisaged to be at incumbent level or equivalent, there should be some evidence of potential to be leaders in mission within a community of mission.

Candidates should be able to point to ways in which the challenge of evangelism has had an impact on their own lives and in their local Christian community. They should be able to articulate, within their own theological and cultural context, what it means to share or proclaim the good news so that others might respond to Jesus Christ.

From their own background candidates should be able to say how they would journey with an enquirer seeking to respond to Jesus Christ and have a sense of how they would help others to do so.[15]

This guidance is helpful and timely. However, it is still modest in scale. For example, in some other Christian traditions, including some of the Pentecostal churches, candidates for ordination are expected to have planted a church before they can be ordained. It is based on the premise that ordination is the process whereby the Church recognizes and therefore authorizes the exercise of the charism of leadership that the candidate has already been given by God.

What is the role of leadership?

In the light of this discussion I would now like to return to reflect Senge's five areas or disciplines, which I described as:

• Getting a holistic vision
• Engaging in lifelong learning
• Allowing the conversion of the mind
• Building shared vision
• Encouraging team learning

The role of leadership is to use these disciplines to create and sustain the context in which the Church can thrive, and to do this, leaders need to develop new skills. Senge contrasts hierarchical models of leadership with new styles. Traditional styles of leadership are, he argues, 'based on assumptions of people's powerlessness, their lack of personal vision and inability to master the forces of change, deficits which can be remedied only by a few great leaders'.[16] In contrast, leaders of learning organizations need a different set of skills, as designers, stewards and teachers. As a designer, the leader has to attend to the governing ideas that are the purpose, vision and core values by which people should live.[17] As a steward, the leader has to give 'the overarching explanation of why they do what they do, how their organization needs to evolve, and how that evolution is part of something larger'.[18] Leaders do not own the vision, but are stewards of it.[19] Third, leaders are teachers: 'much of the leverage leaders can actually exert lies in helping people achieve more accurate, more insightful and more *empowering* views of reality'.[20] This is about 'fostering learning for everyone. Such leaders help people throughout the organization develop systemic understandings. Accepting this responsibility is the antidote to one of the most common downfalls of otherwise gifted teachers – losing their commitment to the truth.'[21]

Using their skill as designers, stewards and teachers, bishops, along with the clergy, have several key tasks:

To help the Church to understand and articulate the changing context of contemporary society

By and large, bishops and priests are good at articulating the gospel week by week in their sermons. It is, however, more difficult to unpack and reflect on the changing context in which we are living. Yet this is essential if the Church is going to engage with contemporary society. Indeed, the greatest threat to any organization or business is to fail to understand the changes that are going on around it. Gill and Burke, writing about the Church and drawing on insights from the restructuring of universities in recent years, suggest that the first task of leadership is to respond to change. They point out that few companies that have *not* responded to change have survived.[22]

Enabling a vision to be discerned

It is not the responsibility of the bishops to have a vision and impart it to others, since bishops share leadership with others ('Receive this Cure of Souls, which is both mine and yours'). It is the task of the whole Church to capture God's vision, which is the discipline that Senge calls 'building shared vision'. This is different from consultation. Gill and Burke comment that:

> Strategic ownership means joint discussion about objectives that are to be implemented and jointly monitored. Consultation, on the other hand, seeks people's views, but makes no commitment about the final outcome. Strategic ownership accepts that all parties are involved in finding, agreeing upon and testing a solution.[23]

Can we free up our bishops and clergy to give them time to create the contexts where this can happen? This is about hearing what is good (and which can therefore be affirmed) and that which is bad (and therefore needs to be challenged). Can we articulate a vision of where we are going? Can we paint a picture of human flourishing? This will certainly re-shape the clergy's role of teaching and is also likely to require the gifts and skills of artists, poets, musicians and authors.

We will only have the time and energy to do this if we separate out episcopal, priestly and diaconal ministries. This was the stark choice faced by the early church (Acts 6). The apostles were absolutely clear that their main task was concerned to preach the word. Therefore they appointed deacons to ensure that the pastoral and administrative work of the church was undertaken. Moorman noted that the duties of a bishop as set out in the ordinal 'do not say anything about running a diocese or organizing the church life of the place. They do not mention any of the activities which will take up most of the bishop's time and energy in the ensuing years.'[24] Dare we empower the archdeacons to run the institution of the Church on a day-to-day basis to free up the bishops?

By implication, this poses the same sort of question for priests. Can we release them from the never-ending administrative burden to concentrate on the task for which they were ordained? The Church of England has debated whether or not to have a permanent deaconate, but has been unable to resolve the issue. Meanwhile, many large urban churches, and even many multi-parish benefices, have responded to the challenge by appointing parish administrators, who act, in effect, as deacons, undertaking the day-to-day running of the parishes.

Embodying the vision

Leaders have to live out the vision by their example, leading from the front. People pick up the values and priorities of leaders not primarily from what they say, but by their style of leadership and the choices they make about the use of their time and energies. If they model a top-down hierarchical model, that is what people will tend to emulate. If they model an empowering, enabling style of leadership, this will set the tone for the whole Church.

Helping churches live out the vision

A prime task of leadership is to engage with local churches, through teaching, praying and listening, so that they are caught up with the vision of the kingdom. Bishops need to resist being drawn into the management of the Church and focus instead on its spiritual renewal. This cannot be done through the occasional sermon at a confirmation service, but requires a bishop to spend dedicated time with the clergy and congregations. Where he cannot do it alone, he needs to build up a team to help him with this episcopal task. One of the recommendations in Gill and Burke is based on the observation that:

> there is strong evidence that small, supportive groups are an essential feature of many growing churches . . . church groups are highly influential both in church planting and in encouraging outsiders to join more fully in church life . . . the tendency of too many church leaders is to spend a great deal of their time instead making appointments, chairing committees, and meeting church groups to resolve one problem or another. Strategic leaders might decide to delegate many of these functions to others and devote a significant amount of their time to visiting groups amongst the churches in their care.[25]

It is not enough to establish a vision, identify priorities and launch it. To make fundamental changes to the culture and practices of an organization, there needs to be constant reinforcement through example and through regular and sustained engagement.

Mission-shaped synods

I referred, at the beginning of Chapter 12, to the Lambeth Conference motion calling for 'a shift to a dynamic missionary emphasis'. This will not happen if we leave everything at parish level. We need to re-think every part of the Church, including its structures.

The synodical system in the Church of England, particularly at the level of Diocesan Synods and General Synods, has considerable strengths. For example, it is an excellent way of allowing a large number of people to examine the annual financial accounts and to decide on future budgeting. It is a good tool for passing new legislation. Drafts are put forward and members of Synod may propose amendments that have to be scrutinized and that must be responded to. The synodical system is a useful way to reach a decision on a complex issue, as essentially what it does is to set the parameters within which the Church is allowed to operate. However, there are at least three reasons why the synodical system is not a good instrument to help the Church become more mission-focused.

First, synods are not good at helping groups of people reach a consensus. This is because of the way they operate. A motion is put forward, which you either have to vote for, vote against, or attempt to amend. Essentially it is an adversarial system that has the tendency to divide people into factions. This is all too evident during General Synod where various faction groups have their fringe meetings. Outside of the debates there are meetings of Fulcrum, Reform, Affirming Catholicism, Forward in Faith, the Open Group and so on, and a great deal of energy is spent talking about other groups rather than talking with them. Discussions take place about tactical voting to get the 'best' result. This is a million miles away from getting the 'holistic picture' that Senge and others advocate, where patient listening enables real understanding of opposing views and where common ground is identified and built on.

In many traditional societies there are different ways of working together to reach a decision. In some aboriginal societies there is a consensual approach to decision-making. It may take more time, since space needs to be given for everyone to speak and to be heard. There may be prolonged periods of discussion, and even times of silence. It does not necessarily mean that total unanimity will be reached, but there is an attempt to reach a point where everyone feels they can live with the consequences. The objection made to such an approach in the Western world is that we do not have enough time, but what this fails to take into account is the time spent in the aftermath of a decision that was made on a 45–55% majority where a large section of the Church feels disenfranchised, alienated or, in some cases, decides to leave.

The second weakness of synods is that they act like a black hole and create a church culture that is primarily concerned about its future and its survival. An essential task for each synod (whether Deanery, Diocesan or General Synod) is to undertake an annual audit of how it has used its time. My own analysis (which is impressionistic and not systematic) is that the most synodical time is spent on housekeeping matters, a small proportion is concerned with 're-engaging with society and the world', and virtually nothing on how we can support apologetics or evangelism.

The third weakness of the synodical system is that it is essentially permissive. It authorizes new liturgies and changes in legislation, such as the ordination of women to the priesthood. All of these are vital things – and it is essential that part of General Synod's time is spent doing this – but it does not foster some of the most important things that we need, such as the shared vision that inspires people to service and mission.

'Synod' in the New Testament

When we turn to the New Testament we find that the Greek word from which we derive 'synod' is found in several places, including the account of Joseph's and Mary's annual visit to Jerusalem:

> Now every year Jesus' parents went to Jerusalem for the festival of the Passover. And when he was twelve years old, they went up as usual for the festival. When the festival was ended and they started to return, the boy Jesus stayed behind in Jerusalem, but his parents did not know it. Assuming that he was in the group of travellers [*sunodía*], they went a day's journey. Then they started to look for him among their relatives and friends. When they did not find him, they returned to Jerusalem to search for him. After three days they found him in the temple, sitting among the teachers, listening to them and asking them questions. And all who heard him were amazed at his understanding and his answers. When his parents saw him they were astonished; and his mother said to him, 'Child, why have you treated us like this? Look, your father and I have been searching for you in great anxiety.' He said to them, 'Why were you searching for me? Did you not know that I must be in my Father's house?'[26]

The word 'synod' is derived from two words (*sun* and *hodos*), which means 'being on a journey together'. That is what a synod should be: a group of believers making a shared journey as we travel towards God and as we share our lives in the world.

When I was at junior school we had a series of pictures on the wall depicting this account of the journey of Jesus and his family to and from the Temple in Jerusalem. On one of the sheets there was a large group of people travelling together, of all ages, young and old. At the front of the group there were some people, including a number of young children dashing ahead, exploring the way, climbing the trees. They were the explorers, learning by experience. Then there was the main group – adults and young people walking together. At one point an adult is bending down explaining something to one of the children and pointing. At the back were people who needed help – one or two children who needed to be carried by an adult, an elderly person riding on a donkey. They were the ones who needed help in making the journey and needed someone alongside. They were all making the journey, but at their own pace and in their own way. The explorers had to slow down sometimes to let the others catch up, and the ones at the back couldn't sit down and say 'I'm not going any further'. It was costly for all of them, but by bearing with one another they shared the journey. That's what *sunodía*, a synod, should be like.

Mission-shaped Diocesan Synod

In response to this understanding of synod as 'sharing the journey', we have experimented with restructuring the meetings of the Diocesan Synod of the Diocese of Lichfield. On occasions we have suspended the standing orders and set up a listening process in which everyone can participate. Instead of sitting in rows facing the chair at the front, we have set the room out with tables at which six or eight people sit. It is important that this is organized in such a way that people do not sit with their friends or with groups of likeminded people. Everyone is asked to undertake preparation for the session before they come, and this is a vitally important part of the process. For example, on one occasion we set out to review the progress that we had been making with our diocesan strategy 'Growing the Kingdom'. Every member of the Diocesan Synod was asked to prepare for the session by approaching five members of their home church and asking them a set of questions. They were specifically requested to select a wide range of people, not just their immediate circle of friends. The questions were about the diocesan strategy and how it was being worked out in their parish: 'Do you know what "Growing the Kingdom" is?', 'What have you found to be the best thing about it? And the worst? How might we build on your strengths and successes?'

This meant that every person coming to the Synod had some raw data about what was going on in the diocese, and what a wide range of people thought about it. I do not know the exact figures, but if we assume that approximately 200 people attended the Synod on that day, then together we had heard the views of about 1,000 people.

The first part of the process was to ask the people on each table to share with one another what they had heard, to write it up on a flipchart, and to discuss the findings. They were asked to refrain from writing up their own opinions. Their task was to listen as carefully as possible to the views that they had collected. They were then asked to summarize what was working well and what was not working well. Out of this discussion they were asked to decide what were the three most important things that

- The diocese needed to do
- The deaneries needed to do
- The parishes needed to do
- They themselves ought to do

Their summaries were written up on flipcharts, and during the coffee break a small team of facilitators consolidated them. Not surprisingly, many of the groups had identical or nearly identical comments. They were posted on the walls around the room, and when people returned they were asked to keep silent as they walked around and prayerfully read the ideas on the sheets. They were then given three 'votes' for each of the four areas, to indicate which of the ideas they believed were the most important. One of the advantages of the system was that everyone in the room contributed, everyone's ideas were included, although the voting meant that they were prioritized. Those ideas that had found their way on to the walls, but which represented one person's hobbyhorse, received fewer votes.

What was significant was the way that the process energized people. Because this was an experimental way of working, we distributed questionnaires as people were leaving to assess if the members of synod had valued this approach. A minority of the members were critical, but the vast majority were positive. Several people commented that they felt they had contributed more than usual, and one person said that it was a change 'from having to listen to all the usual people who speak at every Synod'. More importantly, some people who had participated in the process left the Synod committed to implementing what we had decided. A traditional debate does not usually have this effect on Synod members.

Mission-shaped Deanery Synod

The current discussion has been about Diocesan Synods, but an argument can also be made for rethinking at least part of the way that Deanery Synods work.[27] Since most Deanery Synods do not hold significant budgets and therefore have less power, they can easily becomes talking shops for people who like sitting on committees. Indeed, I have heard of standing committees discussing how to fill the programme in the coming year – 'What can we do on that evening?' If it is a case of filling up the statutory number of annual meetings, then we may actually be detracting from the mission of the Church by consuming energy on unnecessary meetings.

But suppose Deanery Synods also used Mission Action Planning? They could become places where prayerful listening and discerning take place. They might be the arena in which parishes take it in turns to reflect on what they are planning, on what has worked well and what did not work well. They may be able to spot places where adjacent parishes have particular opportunities to co-operate in, for example, a secondary school. We have found that rural deaneries (by which I mean those that are actually in rural areas) are excellent units for the running of Bishop's Certificate, Alpha and Emmaus groups for all the parishes. Several deaneries have organized training for parish visitors and worship leaders on a deanery basis.

Due to the serious concerns about the lack of activities and facilities for children and young people in North Shropshire, it was decided to put some money into each of the deaneries. We put together a package that offered £4,000 a year for three years for each deanery to do something new with children or young people. We asked the deaneries to find matching funding and to ensure that whatever was done it should include the training of local lay volunteers. We also said that if they did not take up the grant it would be given to another deanery. The offer generated a great deal of debate and finally all eight deaneries responded to the challenge. For example, two raised enough money to employ full-time youth workers; another decided to employ someone to run workshops during the school holidays; another employed a freelance Christian musician

---

to work with groups of children across the deanery in preparing participative worship for the churches; another put the money into an extra assistant Youth for Christ worker and so on. These are examples of deaneries discerning what they should be doing to further God's mission and implementing the plans.

I am convinced that we need a 'mixed-mode' approach to the way that we use and structure our synods. There will of course be times when they need to be in debating mode, as budgets still have to be passed and sometimes we have to come to a decision over a difficult matter and do not have the luxury of unlimited time for debate. At other times, however, we may need to work in a listening, collaborative, brain-storming mode. We need both flexibility and discernment. The criterion must always be how best we can facilitate the prime objective of a synod to 'share the journey' and so advance the kingdom of God.

Notes

1 *Episcopal Ministry*, 1990, pp. 24–5.
2 This Gospel reading has always been used at the ordination of a bishop.
3 Jackson, 2002, pp. 179–80.
4 For a helpful discussion of the relation of canon law and mission, see Rees, 2006.
5 From bishops in the House of Lords, to the chairing of Local Strategic Partnerships, or John Sentamu's role as adviser to the Stephen Lawrence enquiry, and Richard Harries's chairing of the Human Fertilisation and Embryology Authority.
6 Church of England's Mission and Public Affairs Council, 2004, p. 135.
7 Mayr-Harting, 1972, p. 87.
8 Bouyer, 1982, p. 37.
9 Frend, 1984.
10 Finney, 1996, p. 111.
11 Finney, 1996, p. 113.
12 Neill, 1986, p. 323.
13 *Criteria for Selection for Ministry in the Church of England (Ordained and Lay Ministry)*, 2005, pp. 36, 37.
14 *Criteria for Selection*, p. 38.
15 *Criteria for Selection*, pp. 38, 39, 40.
16 Senge, 1990, p. 340.
17 Senge, 1990, p. 340.
18 Senge, 1990, p. 346.

19 Interestingly, Senge thinks that leaders have to inspire (literally 'breathe life into') the vision. His use of language has powerful New Testament resonances of the work of the Holy Spirit.

20 Senge, 1990, p. 353.

21 Senge, 1990, p. 356.

22 Gill and Burke, 1996.

23 Gill and Burke, 1996, p. 74.

24 Moorman, 1982, p. 116.

25 Gill and Burke, 1996, p. 90.

26 Luke 2.41–49.

27 Cundy (2006) has some interesting suggestions of how the deanery can further the mission of the Church.

Afterword

In spite of the enormity of the challenges that confront the Church today, not least in rural areas, there is a spiritual thirst at the heart of our generation's searching that we need to rejoice in. The prophet's Isaiah's question to his own generation, 'Why do you waste your money on that which is not bread, and why do you labour for that which will never satisfy you?' is as apposite today as it was then. In their restlessness, people have always searched for that which will satisfy them, and I believe that the Church has both the resilience and the confidence to point people to God in whom alone is our peace.

In a study such as this it is not possible to formulate neat conclusions. So instead, I end with a saying from the fourth century of one of the Desert Fathers. An old monk was once asked, 'How can I find God?' The old man replied, 'In fasting, in watching, in labours, in devotion, and above all in discernment. I tell you, many have injured their bodies without discernment and have gone away from us disappointed. Our mouths smell bad through fasting, we know all the scriptures by heart, we can recite all the psalms of David, but we have not that which God seeks: charity and humility.'

We too can work and pray and reorganize ourselves, concocting strategies and generally reinventing ourselves. But if God is not at the centre of all that we do, people will go away disappointed. Ultimately what re-shapes the Church is also what re-shapes a human being: charity and humility. God seeks these things in us for then he can make his home in us.

Bibliography

Abrams, M. *et al.* (eds) (1985), *Values and Social Change in Britain*, The European Value Systems Study Group, Basingstoke: Macmillan.

Acock, A. C. and Bengston, V. L. (1978), 'On the relative influence of mothers and fathers: a covariance analysis of political and religious socialization', *Journal of Marriage and the Family*, 40, pp. 519–30.

Albrecht, D. E. (1993), 'The renewal of population loss in the non-metropolitan Great Plains', *Rural Sociology*, 58 (2), pp. 223–46.

Ash, R. T. (1969), 'Jewish adolescents' attitudes towards religion and ethnicity', *Adolescence*, 4, pp. 245–82.

Bailey, E. (1998), *Implicit Religion: An Introduction*, London: Middlesex University Press.

Bailey, E. (2000), *The Secular Faith Controversy: Religion in Three Dimensions*, London: Continuum.

Bailey, E. (ed.)(2002), *The Secular Quest for Meaning in Life*, Lampeter: The Edwin Mellen Press.

Barley, L. (2007a), *Community Value*, London: Church House Publishing.

Barley, L. (2007b), *Christian Root, Contemporary Spirituality*, London: Church House Publishing.

Barley, L. (2007c), *Churchgoing Today*, London: Church House Publishing.

Barratt, D. B. *et al.* (2001a, second edn), *World Christian Encyclopedia: A Comparative Survey of Churches and Religions in the Modern World*, vol. 1, Oxford, Oxford University Press.

Barratt, D. B. *et al.* (2001b, second edn), *World Christian Encyclopedia: A Comparative Survey of Churches and Religions in the Modern World*, vol. 2, Oxford, Oxford University Press.

Barry, J. *et al.* (eds) (1996), *Witchcraft in Early Modern Europe: Studies in Culture and Belief*, Cambridge: Cambridge University Press.

Bayes, P. (2004), *Mission-Shaped Church: Missionary Values, Church Planting and Fresh Expression of Church*, Cambridge: Grove Books.

Bayes, P. and Sledge, T. (2006), *Mission-Shaped Parish*, London: Church House Publishing.

Bending, R. (2002), 'Church buildings: thinking the unthinkable', *Rural Theology*, the Journal of the Rural Theology Association, 58, pp. 12–19.

Bevington, C. (1994), 'Working together', in C. Napier and J. Hamilton-Brown (eds), *A New Workbook on Rural Evangelism*, Blandford Forum: Parish and People, pp. 57–60.

Board of Education of the General Synod (1985), *All Are Called*, London: CIO Publishing.

Board of Education of the General Synod (1987), *Called to Be Adult Disciples*, London: Board of Education.

Board of Education of the General Synod (1999), *Called to New Life: The World of Lay Discipleship*, London: Church House Publishing.

Booker, M. and Ireland, M. (2003), *Evangelism – Which Way Now? An Evaluation of Alpha, Emmaus, Cell Church and Other Contemporary Strategies for Evangelism*, London: Church House Publishing.

Bourdieu, P. (1985), 'The forms of capital', in J. G. Richardson (ed.), *Handbook of Theory and Research for the Sociology of Religion*, New York, Greenwood, pp. 241–58.

Bouyer, L. (1982), 'Bishops in the Church: the Catholic tradition', in P. Moore (ed.), *Bishops: But What Kind?*, London, SPCK, pp. 25–40.

Boyle, P. and Halfacree, K. (1998), *Migration into Rural Areas*, Chichester: Wiley and Sons.

Breaking New Ground: Church Planting in the Church of England (1994), Church of England Working Party on Church Planting, London: Church House Publishing.

Brierley, P. (ed.)(1980), *Prospects for the Eighties*, MARC Europe.

Brierley, P. (1991), *Prospects for the Nineties: Trends and Tables from the English Church Census*, MARC Europe.

Brierley, P. (1999), 'Religious Trends No. 2, 2000/2001', *UK Christian Handbook*, London: Christian Research.

Brierley, P. (ed.) (2006), 'Religious Trends 6: Pulling out of the Nosedive', *UK Christian Handbook*, London: Christian Research.

Brown, C. (2001), *The Death of Christian Britain: Understanding Secularisation 1800–2000*, London: Routledge.

Brown, D. (2003), *The Da Vinci Code*, London: Transworld.

Bruce, F. F. (1951), *The Acts of the Apostles*, Leicester: IVP.

Bruegemann, W. (2002, second edn), *The Land: Place as Gift, Promise, and Challenge in Biblical Faith*, Minneapolis: Fortress Press.

Buller, H. and Hoggart, K. (1994), *International Counterurbanisation*, Aldershot: Avebury.

Bunker, B. B. and Alban, B. T. (1997), *Large Group Interventions: Engaging the Whole System for Rapid Change*, San Francisco: Jossey-Bass Publishers.

Burton, L. (2004), 'Blackshawhead: a local case history in rural church categorisation', *Rural Theology*, the Journal of the Rural Theology Association, 2 (1), pp. 41–51.

Cawley, M. (1994), 'Desertification: measuring population decline in rural Ireland', *Journal of Rural Studies*, 10 (4), pp. 395–407.

Church of England Board of Education (1991), *All God's Children: Children's Evangelism in Crisis*, GS Publications, number 988.

Church of England's Mission and Public Affairs Council (2004), *Mission-Shaped Church: Church Planting and Fresh Expressions of Church in a Changing World*, London: Church House Publishing.

Church of England National Assembly (1945), *Towards the Conversion of England*, London: The Press and Publications Board of the Church Assembly.

Clark, C. A. *et al.* (1988), 'The transmission of religious beliefs and practices from parents to firstborn early adolescent sons', *Journal of Marriage and the Family*, 50, pp. 463–72.

Clinebell, H.O. (1967), *Basic Types of Pastoral Counseling: New Resources for Ministering to the Troubled*, Nashville: Abingdon Press.

Cloke, P. *et al.* (2001), 'Homelessness and rurality: exploring connections in local spaces of rural England', *Sociologia Ruralis*, 41 (4), pp. 438–53.

Cloke, P. and Edwards, G. (1986), 'Rurality in England and Wales 1981: a replication of the 1971 Index', *Regional Studies*, 20, pp. 289–306.

Commission for Rural Communities (2006a), *The State of the Countryside 2006 tackling rural disadvantage*, http://www.ruralcommunities.gov.uk/files/SoTC06_ Complete.pdf.

Commission for Rural Communities (2006b), *Rural Insights: assessing the views, concerns and priorities of rural England*, http://www.ruralcommunities.gov.uk/ publications/ruralinsights.

Cottrell, S. (2006), *From the Abundance of the Heart: Catholic Evangelism for all Christians*, London: Darton, Longman and Todd.

Council of Europe (1980), *Methods to Stop Rural Depopulation and to Involve Citizens in the Development of these Regions*, Strasbourg.

Countryside Agency (2003a), *The State of the Countryside 2020*, Wetherby: Countryside Agency Publications.

Countryside Agency (2003b), *The State of the Countryside 2004*, Wetherby: Countryside Agency Publications.

Cox, J. (1982), *The English Churches in a Secular Society, 1987–1930*, Oxford: Oxford University Press.

Criteria for Selection for Ministry in the Church of England (Ordained and Lay Ministry) (2005), London: Church House Publishing.

Croft, S. (ed.) (2006), *The Future of the Parish System: Shaping the Church of England for the 21st Century*, London: Church House Publishing.

Cundy, I. (2006), 'Reconfiguring a diocese towards mission', in S. Croft (ed.), *The Future of the Parish System: Shaping the Church of England for the 21st Century*, London: Church House Publishing, pp. 152–69.

Currie, R. *et al.* (1977), *Churches and Churchgoers: Patterns of Church Growth in the British Isles since 1700*, Oxford: Clarendon Press.

Davies, D. *et al.* (1991), *Church and Religion in Rural England*, Edinburgh: T and T Clark.

Dawkins, R. (2006), *The God Delusion*, London: Bantam.

De Graaf, N. D. and Need, A. (2000), 'Losing faith: is Britain alone?', in R. Jowell *et al.* (eds), *British Social Attitudes: The 17th Report*, London: Sage Publications, pp. 119–36.

De Hart, J. (1990), 'Impact of religious socialisation in the family', *Journal of Empirical Theology*, 3 (1), pp. 59–78.

De Vaus, D. A. (1983), 'The relative importance of parents and peers for adolescent religious orientation: an Australian study', *Adolescence*, 18, pp. 147–58.

Dingwall, G. and Moody, S. (eds) (1999), *Crime and Conflict in the Countryside*, Cardiff: University of Wales Press.

Drane, J. (1991), *What Is the New Age Saying to the Church?*, London: Marshall Pickering.

Dudley, R. L. (1978), 'Alienation from religion in adolescents from fundamentalist religious homes', *Journal for the Scientific Study of Religion*, 17 (4), pp. 389–98.

Dudley, R. L. and Dudley, M. G. (1986), 'Transmission of religious values from parents to adolescents', *Review of Religious Research*, 28, pp. 2–15.

Duffy, E. (1992), *The Stripping of the Altars: Traditional Religion in England, 1400–1580*, Yale: University of Yale Press.

Dulles, A. (1971), *A History of Apologetics*, London: Hutchinson.

Economist (17 February 2007), 'Giving to charity: bring back the Victorians', London: *Economist* newspaper Ltd, pp. 33–4.

Edson, B. (2006), 'An exploration into the missiology of the emerging church in the UK through the narrative of Sanctus1', *International Journal for the Study of the Christian Church*, 6 (1), pp. 24–37.

Episcopal Ministry: The Report of the Archbishops' Group on the Episcopate (1990), London: Church House Publishing.

Erickson, J. A. (1992), 'Adolescent religious development and commitment: a structural equation model of the role of family, peer group, and educational influences', *Journal for the Scientific Study of Religion*, 31, pp. 131–52.

Faith in the City: A Call to Action by Church and Nation (1985), London: Church House Publishing.

Faith in the Countryside: Report of the Archbishops' Commission on Rural Areas (1990), Worthing: Churchman Publishing.

Falk, I. and Kilpatrick, S. (2000), 'What is social capital? A study of interaction in a rural community', *Sociologia Ruralis*, 40 (1), pp. 87–110.

Fane, R. S. (1999), 'Is self-assigned religious affiliation socially significant?', in L. J. Frances (ed.), *Sociology, Theology and the Curriculum*, London: Cassell, pp. 113–24.

Farnell, R. *et al.* (2006), *Faith in Rural Communities: Contributions of Social Capital to Community Vibrancy*, Stoneleigh Park, Warwickshire: Acora Publishing.

Ferguson, N. (2006), *The War of the World: History's Age of Hatred*, London: Allen Lane, Penguin Books Ltd.

Finney, J. (1992), *Finding Faith Today: How Does It Happen?*, Stonehill Green: British and Foreign Bible Society.

Finney, J. (1996), *Recovering the Past: Celtic and Roman Mission*, London: Darton, Longman and Todd.

Finney, J. (2000), *Fading Splendour: A New Model of Renewal*, London: Darton, Longman and Todd.

Francis, L. J. (1982), *Youth in Transit: A Profile of 16–25-Year-Olds*, Aldershot: Gower.

Francis, L. J. (1985), *Rural Anglicanism: A Future for Young Christians?*, London: Collins.

Francis, L. J. (1986), *Partnership in Rural Education: Church Schools and Teacher Attitudes*, London: Collins.

Francis, L. J. (1989), 'Method and interpretation', in M. Wilson (ed.), *The Rural Church: Towards 2000*, Corby, Rural Theology Association, pp. 69–77.

Francis, L. J. (1990), 'The religious significance of denominational identity among eleven year old children in England', *Journal of Christian Education*, 97, pp. 23–8.

Francis, L. J. (1996), *Church Watch: Christianity in the Countryside*, London: SPCK.

Francis, L. J. and Atkins, P. (2005), *Exploring Matthew's Gospel: A Guide to the Gospel Readings in the Revised Common Lectionary* (Personality Type and Scripture Series), London: Continuum.

Francis, L. J. and Gibson, H. M. (1993), 'Parental influence and adolescent religiosity: a study of church attendance and attitude toward Christianity among adolescents 11 to 12 and 15 to 16 years old', *International Journal for the Psychology of Religion*, 3 (4), pp. 241–53.

Francis, L. J. and Kay, W. K. (1995), *Teenage Religion and Values*, Leominster: Gracewing.

Francis, L. J. and Lankshear, D. W. (1990), 'The impact of church schools on village church life', *Educational Studies*, 16, pp. 117–29.

Francis, L. J. and Lankshear, D. W. (1992a), 'The rural rectory: the impact of a resident priest on local church life', *Journal of Rural Studies*, 8, pp. 97–103.

Francis, L. J. and Lankshear, D. W. (1992b), 'The rural factor: a comparative survey of village churches and the liturgical work of rural clergy', *Modern Churchman*, 34, pp. 1–9.

Francis, L. J. and Martineau, J. (2002), *Rural Mission: A Parish Workbook for Developing the Mission of the Rural Church*, Stoneleigh Park, Warwickshire: Acora Publishing.

Francis, L. J. *et al.* (1991), 'The influence of Protestant Sunday schools on attitudes towards Christianity among 11–15 year olds in Scotland', *British Journal of Religious Education*, 14, pp. 35–42.

Frend, W. H. C. (1984), *The Rise of Christianity*, London: Darton, Longman and Todd.

Frost, M. and Hirsch, A. (2003), *The Shaping of Things to Come: Innovation and Mission for the 21st Century Church*, Massachusetts: Hendrickson Publishers.

Gaze, S. (2006), *Mission-Shaped and Rural: Growing Churches in the Countryside*, London: Church House Publishing.

Geisler, N. L. (1999), *Baker Encyclopedia of Christian Apologetics*, Grand Rapids: Baker Books.

Gill, R. (1989), *Competing Convictions*, London: SCM Press.

Gill, R. (1993), *The Myth of the Empty Church*, London: SPCK.

Gill, R. (1994), *A Vision for Growth: Why Your Church Doesn't Have to be a Pelican in the Wilderness*, London: SPCK.

Gill, R. (1999), *Churchgoing and Christian Ethics*, Cambridge: Cambridge University Press.

Gill, R. (2003), *The 'Empty' Church Revisited*, Aldershot: Ashgate.

Gill, R. and Burke, D. (1996), *Strategic Church Leadership*, London: SPCK.

Glendinning, T. and Brice, S. (2006), 'New ways of believing or belonging: is religion giving way to spirituality?, *British Journal of Sociology*, 57 (3), pp. 399–414.

Green, L. (1990), *Let's Do Theology*, London: Mowbray.

Gunnoe, M. L. and Moore, K. A. (2002), 'Predictors of religiosity among youth aged 17–22: a longitudinal study of the national survey of children', *Journal for the Scientific Study of Religion*, 41 (4), pp. 613–22.

Hall, P. A. (1999), 'Social capital in Britain', *British Journal of Political Science*, 29 (3), pp. 417–61.

Halman, I. (2001), *The European Values Study: A Third Wave*, source book of the 1999/2000 European Values Study Surveys, Tilburg: WORC, Tilburg University.

Halpern, D. (1995), 'Values, morals and modernity: the values, constraints and norms of European youth', in M. Rutter and D. J. Smith (eds), *Psychosocial Disorders in Young People: Time Trends and their Causes*, Chichester: Wiley and Sons, pp. 324–87.

Hardy, A. (1979), *The Spiritual Nature of Man: A Study of Contemporary Religious Experience*, Oxford, Clarendon Press.

Harries, R. (2002), *God Outside the Box: Why Spiritual People Object to Christianity*, London: SPCK.

Hay, D. (1979), 'Reports of religious experience by a group of post-graduate students: a pilot study', *Journal for the Scientific Study of Religion*, 18 (2), pp. 164–82.

Hay, D. (1987), *Exploring Inner Space: Scientists and Religious Experience*, London: Mowbray.

Hay, D. and Morisy, A. (1978), 'Reports of ecstatic, paranormal, or religious experience in Great Britain and United States – a comparison of trends', *Journal for the Scientific Study of Religion*, 17 (3), pp. 255–68.

Heald, G. (2000), 'The Soul of Britain', *The Tablet*, 3 June 2000.

Heelas, P. and Woodhead, L. (2005), *The Spiritual Revolution: Why Religion is Giving Way to Spirituality*, Oxford: Blackwell Publishing.

Hodgkin, R. H. (1952, third edn), *A History of the Anglo-Saxons*, vol. 1, London: Cumberlege.

Hoge, D. R. and Petrillo, G. H. (1978), 'Determinants of church participation and attitudes among high school youth', *Journal for the Scientific Study of Religion*, 17, pp. 359–79.

Hoge, D. R. *et al.* (1982), 'Transmission of religious and social values from parents to teenage children', *Journal of Marriage and the Family*, 44 (3), pp. 569–80.

Hole, C. (1980), *Witchcraft in Britain*, London: Paladin Grafton Books.

Hope, S. (2006), *Mission-Shaped Spirituality*, London: Church House Publishing.

Hopkins, B. (not dated), 'Making sense of emerging church', The Anglican Church Planting Initiatives website, http://www.acpi.org.uk/stories/5%20Making%20 sense%20of%20emerging%20church.htm

House of Bishops of the Church of England (1974), *The Deployment of the Clergy*, The Report of the House of Bishops' Working Party, London: Church Information Office.

House of Bishops of the Church of England (1997), *Eucharistic Presidency: A Theological Statement by the House of Bishops of the General Synod*, London: Church House Publishing.

Howell-Jones, P. and Wills, N. (2005), *Pints of View: Encounter Down the Pub*, Cambridge: Grove Books.

Hull, J. M. (2006), *Mission-Shaped Church: A Theological Response*, London: SCM.

Hunsberger, B. (1976), 'Background religious denomination, parental emphasis and the religious orientation of university students', *Journal for the Scientific Study of Religion*, 15, pp. 251–5.

Hunsberger, B. (1985), 'Parent–university student agreement on religious and non religious issues', *Journal for the Scientific Study of Religion*, 24, pp. 314–20.

Ineson, K. and Burton, L. (2005), 'Social capital generated by two rural churches: the role of individual believers', *Rural Theology*, 3 (2), pp. 85–97.

Inge, J. (2003), *A Christian Theology of Place*, Aldershot: Ashgate.

Jackson, B. (2002), *Hope for the Church: Contemporary Strategies for Growth*, London, Church House Publishing.

Jackson, B. (2005), *The Road to Growth: Towards a Thriving Church*, London: Church House Publishing.

Jackson, B. (2006), *Going for Growth: What Works at Local Church Level*, London: Church House Publishing.

John Paul II (1989), *Christifideles Laici: Apostolic Exhortation, Vocation and Mission of the Lay Faithful*, London: Catholic Truth Society.

Kay, W. K. and Francis, L. J. (1996), *Drift from the Churches: Attitude Toward Christianity during Childhood and Adolescence*, Cardiff: University of Wales Press.

Kieren, D. K. and Munro, B. (1987), 'Following the leaders: parents' influence on adolescent religious activity', *Journal for the Scientific Study of Religion*, 26, pp. 249–55.

Kuhrt, G. (2001), *Ministry Issues*, London: Church House Publishing.

Lewis, C. S. (1973), *God in the Dock*, London: Fount Paperbacks.

Lewis, D. (1975), *Religious Superstition through the Ages*, London: Mowbrays.

Lings, G. (2005), *Encounters on the Edge: No 27 The Village and Fresh Expressions: Is Rural Different?*, Sheffield: The Sheffield Centre, Wilson Carlisle Campus, Cavendish Street, Sheffield S3 7RZ.

Lings, G. (2005), *Encounters on the Edge: No 28 Rural Cell Church: a new way-side flower*, Sheffield: The Sheffield Centre, Wilson Carlisle Campus, Cavendish Street, Sheffield S3 7RZ.

Lings, G. (2006), *Encounters on the Edge: No 30 Discernment in Mission: naviga-tional aids for mission-shaped processes*, Sheffield: The Sheffield Centre, Wilson Carlisle Campus, Cavendish Street, Sheffield S3 7RZ.

Lings, G. (2006), 'Unravelling the DNA of the church: how can we know that what is emerging is "church"?', *International Journal for the Study of the Christian Church*, 6 (1), pp. 104–16.

Lings, G. 'What is Mission-Shaped Church?' http://www.encountersontheedge.co.uk.

Lings, G. and Murray, S. (2005), *Church Planting: Past, Present and Future*, Cambridge: Grove Books.

Littler, K. and Francis, L. J. (2003), 'What rural churches say to non-churchgoers', *Rural Theology*, 1 (1), pp. 57–62.

MacCulloch, D. (2004), *Reformation: Europe's House Divided, 1490–1700*, London: Penguin Books.

Martin, M. (1990), *Atheism: A Philosophical Justification*, Philadelphia: Temple University Press.

Martin, T. *et al.* (2003), 'Religious socialization: a test of the channelling hypothesis of parental influence on adolescent faith maturity', *Journal of Adolescent Research*, 18 (2), pp. 169–87.

Martineau, J. *et al.* (eds) (2004), *Changing Rural Life: A Christian Response to Key Rural Issues*, Norwich: Canterbury Press.

Mayr-Harting, H. (1972), *The Coming of Christianity to Anglo-Saxon England*, London: Batsford.

McGrath, A. (1992), *Bridge-Building: Effective Christian Apologetics*, Leicester: IVP.

Methodist Church (1988), *The Ministry of the Whole People of God*, Peterborough: Methodist Publishing House.

Mission Theological Advisory Group (2002), *Presence and Prophecy: A Heart for Mission in Theological Education*, London: Church House Publishing and Churches Together in Britain and Ireland.

Missionary Diocese of Wakefield (2001), *Statistics Project 2000: An Analysis of Attendance Patterns in the Deanery of Almondbury between October and December 2000 and a Comparison with the Figures Collected over the Same Period in 1997*, Paper circulated to members of the Church of England General Synod.

Moorman, J. R. H. (1982), 'The Anglican bishop', in P. Moore (ed.), *Bishops: But What Kind?* London: SPCK, pp. 116–26.

Morison, F. (1983), *Who Moved the Stone?* Bromley: STL Books.

Morisy, A. (2004), *Journeying Out*, London: Morehouse.

Murray, D. B. (2002), 'Implicit religion: the hospice experience', in E. Bailey (ed.), *The Secular Quest for Meaning in Life*, Lampeter: Edwin Mellen Press, pp. 237–50.

Napier, C. and Hamilton-Brown, J. (eds) (1994), *A New Workbook on Rural Evangelism*, Blandford Forum: Parish and People.

Neill, S. (1986, second edn), *A History of Christian Missions*, London: Penguin Books.

Newby, H. (1990), 'Revitalising the countryside: the opportunities and pitfalls of counter-urban trends', *Journal of the Royal Society of Arts*, 138, pp. 630–6.

Okagaki, L. *et al.* (1999), 'Socialization of religious beliefs', *Journal of Applied Developmental Psychology*, 20 (2), pp. 273–94.

Park, A. (2004), 'Has modern politics disenchanted the young?', in A. Park *et al.* (eds), *British Social Attitudes: The 21ˢᵗ Report*, London: Sage, pp. 23–47.

Paul, L. (1964), *The Deployment and Payment of the Clergy*, London: Church Information Office.

Potter, P. (2001), *The Challenge of the Cell Church: Getting to Grips with Cell Church Values*, Oxford: Bible Reading Fellowship.

Putnam, R. D. (1993), *Making Democracy Work*, Princeton, Princeton University Press.

Putnam, R. D. (1996), 'The strange disappearance of civil America', *American Prospect* (Winter), pp. 34–49.

Putnam, R. D. (2000), *Bowling Alone: The Collapse and Revival of American Community*, New York: Simon & Schuster.

Rees, J. (2006), 'Legal matters – what you need to know', in S. Croft (ed.), *The Future of the Parish System: Shaping the Church of England for the 21ˢᵗ Century*, London: Church House Publishing, pp. 170–7.

Richter, P. and Francis, J. L. (1998), *Gone but Not Forgotten*, London: Darton, Longman and Todd.

Roberts, C. (2003), 'Is the rural Church different? A comparison of historical membership statistics between an urban and a rural diocese in the Church of England', *Rural Theology*, 1 (1), pp. 25–39.

Roberts, C. and Francis, L. J. (2006), 'Church closures and membership statistics: trends in four rural dioceses', *Rural Theology*, 4 (1), pp. 37–56.

Robinson, D. (1980), *Visitations of the Archdeaconry of Stafford 1829–1841*, Royal Commission on Historical Manuscripts, number 25, London: HMSO.

Roper, L. (1994), *Oedipus and the Devil: Witchcraft, Sexuality and Religion in the Early Modern Europe*, London: Routledge.

Roud, S. (2003), *The Penguin Guide to Superstitions of Britain and Ireland*, London: Penguin Books.

Rural Affairs Committee of General Synod and the Mission and Public Affairs Council of the Archbishops' Council of the Church of England (2005), *Seeds in Holy Ground*, Stoneleigh Park, Warwickshire: Acora Publishing.

Russell, A. (1993), *The Country Parson*, London: SPCK.

Rutter, M. *et al.* (1979), *Fifteen Thousand Hours: Secondary Schools and their Effects on Children*, London: Open Books.

Savage, S. *et al.* (2006), *Making Sense of Generation X: The World View of 15–25-year-olds*, London: Church House Publishing.

Saville, J. (1957), *Rural Depopulation in England and Wales 1851–1951*, Dartington Hall Studies in Rural Sociology, London: Routledge and Kegan Paul.

Schlossenberg, H. (2002), *The Silent Revolution and the Making of Victorian England*, Columbus: Ohio State University Press.

Senge, P. M. (1990), *The Fifth Discipline: The Art and Practice of Learning Organizations*, London: Random House.

Senge, P. M. *et al.* (1999), *The Dance of Change: The Challenges of Sustaining Momentum in Learning Organizations*, London: Nicholas Brealey Publishing.

Sherkat, D. E. (1998), 'Counterculture or continuity? Competing influences on baby boomers' religious orientations and participation', *Social Forces*, 76, pp. 1087–1115.

Smith, A. G. C. (2002), 'The nature and significance of religion among adolescents in the metropolitan Borough of Walsall', PhD thesis, University of Wales (Bangor).

Smith, A. G. C. (2004), 'Listening to the people: empirical theology, social capital and the rural church', in J. Martineau *et al.* (eds), *Changing Rural Life: A Christian Response to Key Rural Issues*, Norwich: Canterbury Press, pp. 193–213.

Snelson, B. (2006), 'Faith offers vision and hope: let's celebrate', *The Edge*, the Journal of the Economic and Social Research Council, July.

Springboard (not dated), *Discerning Church Vocations: A Listening Exercise for the Local Church*, Springboard, 4 Station Yard, Abingdon, Oxon OX14 3LD.

Stockdale, A. (2004), 'Rural out-migration: community consequences and individual migrant experiences', *Sociologia Ruralis*, 44 (1), pp. 167–94.

Thomas, K. (1997), *Religion and the Decline of Magic: Studies in Popular Beliefs in Sixteenth and Seventeenth Century England*, London: Weidenfeld and Nicolson.

To a Rebellious House? Report of the Church of England's Partners in Mission Consultation (1981), London: CIO Publishing.

Today's Church and Today's World: With a Special Focus on the Ministry of Bishops (1977), The Lambeth Conference 1978 Preparatory Articles, London: CIO Publishing.

Towards the Conversion of England (1945), Westminster: The Press and Publications Board of the Church Assembly.

Van de Weyer, R. (1991), *The Country Church: A Guide for the Renewal of Rural Christianity*, London: Darton, Longman and Todd.

Voas, D. (2003), 'Intermarriage and the demography of secularisation', *British Journal of Sociology*, 51 (1), pp. 83–108.

Voas, D. and Crockett, A. (2005), 'Religion in Britain: neither believing nor belonging', *Sociology*, 39 (1), pp. 11–28.

Warren, R. (1995), *Building Missionary Congregations: Towards a Post-modern Way of Being Church*, London: Church House Publishing.

Warren, R. (2004), *The Healthy Churches' Handbook: A Process for Revitalizing Your Church*, London: Church House Publishing.

Weigert, A. J. and Thomas, D. L. (1972), 'Parental support, control and adolescent religiosity: an extension of previous research', *Journal for the Scientific Study of Religion*, 11, pp. 389–95.

Wilkinson, H. and Mulgan, G. (1995), *Freedom's Children: Work, Relationships and Politics for the 18–34 Year Olds in Britain Today*, London, Demos.

Williams, R. (2004), 'Theological reflection', in J. Martineau *et al.* (eds), *Changing Rural Life: A Christian Response to Key Rural Issues*, Norwich: Canterbury Press, pp. 251–5.

Wilson, A. N. (2005), *After the Victorians*, London: Hutchinson.

Witherington, B. (1998), *The Acts of the Apostles: A Socio-Rhetorical Commentary*, Grand Rapids, Michigan: Eerdmans.

Yarwood, R. and Gardner, G. (2000), 'Fear of crime, cultural threat and the countryside', *Area*, 32, pp. 403–11.

Index

Affiliation, religious 24–6, 120
All age services 90–1
Apologetics 124–37
  in the New Testament 128–30
  in the early church 130–1
  in the Medieval period 131–2
Apologists 159

Baptisms in the Church of England
  21, 28–9, 74
Belief, religious 32
Bishops 190–4
Book of Common Prayer 20–1,
  28, 89, 105, 163, 181
Broadband 7

Café church 68–9, 91–3
Catechumenate 161
Cell church 94–5
Charismatic renewal 161
Children 21, 74–80
Church 15–29
  affiliation 25–26
  and kingdom 56–8
  as a Learning Organization 164
  attendance 15–7, 26–7
  closures 22
  future of rural 21
  planting xii, 101, 161, 169, 203
  selling church buildings 22–3
Church of England
  Wealth of 23–4

Clergy 17–8, 27–9, 152, 161,
  199–203
Collaborative ministry 185–6
Culture x, 59, 65, 124, 145–7,
  155, 162–3, 193

Dairy farmers, decline in number
  of 5
Deanery Synod 208–9
Decade of Evangelism xi, 66, 114,
  152, 157, 158, 187
Decline in church attendance,
  reasons for 21–2, 158
Diocesan Synod 206–7
Diversification in farming 5

Ecumenical Welcomes 23, 173,
  186–8
Ecumenism 162
Elderly people 104–6
Environmental issues and farming
  5
Experience, religious 33
Evangelism xi, xiii, 47, 59–60, 66,
  135, 152, 157–8, 186–8, 193–4,
  199–200

Family 111–22
Farm workers 4
Farming 4–6
Fishing 7
Folk religion 33–4
Fresh Expressions Website 66–70

Gregory the Great 191–2

Home working 7
Horse riding 7
Hospitals 8–9
Housing 4, 8

Implicit religion 33–4
Incomers to villages 6–7
Isolation in rural areas 99–100

Lambeth Conference xi, 153, 157,
  193, 203
Leadership 161, 190–203
Learning 97, 151–71, 178, 200–1
Learning Organizations 164–71
Leisure 4, 6–7, 146–7
Listening 143–55
  to God 143–4
  to the local community 144–6,
    168, 173–4, 206–7
  to the rural cultures 146–8
  to the church 148–9
  to the Christian tradition 149–50
  to each other 150–2
  parents 75–6
  to the worldwide church 153–5

Mission x–xiv, 50–60, 65, 65–8,
  153–5, 170, 186–8, 196–202,
  206–9
Mission Action Plans 67, 165,
  172–78, 208
Mission-Shaped Church xi–xiii,
  51–2, 126, 145
Mission, theology of 50–60
Music 96–7

New Age 35–48

Organizational approaches to
  evangelism 161

Parents, influence of 75–80,
  116–20
Place 46
Post offices 7, 99
Public houses 7, 99
Public transport 5, 8

Religions affiliation 24–6, 120
Rural
  idyll 4, 9
  spirituality 43–5
  traditions 45

St Benedict 151–2, 192
School 8, 84–7
Shops 7–8
Social Capital 71–2
Spirituality 31–48, 84–5, 160
Statistics, use of 148, 174–5
Suicide, in the farming community
  5
Supernatural 35–42

Teaching the faith to children
  111–22
Teenagers 80–3, 102–3
Team learning 170–1
Toddlers 76, 79, 122

Vacancy in parishes 166
Vision,
  building shared 168–9
  discerning and nurturing 194–9,
    201–3
Visiting, pastoral 162
Visitors 190

Welcome 178–81
Worship 88–98
  times of public 95–6
  music and 96–7
  rethinking rural 181–5